ABOUT THE AUTHORS

HELEN F. COUCH

a mother who is keenly interested in young people, has spent much of her time working with them. She has served as a director of Christian education in El Dorado and Hot Springs, Arkansas; as a member of the YWCA program committee in Nashville, Tennessee, and as board president in Hot Springs. She has also been a counselor and teacher in summer camps and has been a speaker to Y-Teen groups on various occasions.

Author of articles, poems, worship materials, and devotions for all ages, Mrs. Couch is editor of *The Christian Home*, a magazine for parents. Formerly she was editor of *The Church School*.

SAM S. BAREFIELD

an experienced worker with youth, holds the position of associate director, Department of Audio-Visual Resources of the Television, Radio, and Film Commission of The Methodist Church. Previously he was audio-visual editor, Board of Education, The Methodist Church.

Mr. Barefield is a former director of the Wesley Foundation at Mississippi Southern College. He frequently contributes articles for Methodist church school literature and has written devotions for *Twelve/Fifteen*, weekly story paper for junior highs.

WORSHIP SOURCEBOOK FOR YOUTH

WORSHIP SOURCEBOOK FOR YOUTH

HELEN F. COUCH
SAM S. BAREFIELD

ABINGDON PRESS 🕭 NEW YORK • NASHVILLE

WORSHIP SOURCEBOOK FOR YOUTH

Copyright © 1962 by Abingdon Press

All rights in this book are reserved.

Library of Congress Catalog Card Number: 62–8104

Scripture quotations from the Revised Standard Version of the Bible are copyright 1946, 1952 by the Division of Christian Education of the National Council of the Churches of Christ in the U.S.A. Scripture quotations from *The New Testament in Modern English* © J. B. Phillips 1958. Used with permission of The Macmillan Company and Geoffrey Bles, Ltd. Scripture quotations from *The New English Bible* © The Delegates of the Oxford University Press and the Syndics of the Cambridge University Press 1961. Scripture quotations from *The Bible: A New Translation* by James Moffatt, copyright 1950 by James Moffatt. Used by permission of Harper and Brothers.

"I think continually of those" by Stephen Spender, copyright 1934 by The Modern Library, Inc. Reprinted from *Collected Poems 1928-1953*, by Stephen Spender, by permission of Random House, Inc., and Faber and Faber, Ltd.

The John Baillie quotation is reprinted with the permission of Charles Scribner's Sons and Oxford University Press from *A Diary of Private Prayer* by John Baillie. Copyright 1949 Charles Scribner's Sons.

"Stars" by Sara Teasdale from *Collected Poems* by Sara Teasdale. Copyright 1920 by The Macmillan Company, renewed 1948 by Mamie T. Wheless. Used with permission of The Macmillan Company. "Perhaps" by Mary Dixon Thayer from *The Child on His Knees* by Mary Dixon Thayer. Copyright 1926 by The Macmillan Company and used with their permission.

"Morning Worship" by Mark Van Doren is from *Morning Worship and Other Poems*, © 1957 by Mark Van Doren. Reprinted by permission of Harcourt, Brace & World, Inc.

(See Notes section for additional acknowledgments)

SET UP, PRINTED, AND BOUND BY THE PARTHENON PRESS, AT NASHVILLE, TENNESSEE, UNITED STATES OF AMERICA

About This Book...

The book you are holding in your hand can help you.

It can help provide meaningful worship for your group. As soon as you glance through it you will see that it is not just a book of planned worship programs. Rather it is a book of many ideas—some short, others long; some little, others big; some barely mentioned, others worked out in detail. Each of these ideas is included for one reason: to help you guide your group in ways of worship that will lead to a growing faith in Christ.

In order to get acquainted with this sourcebook, take a few minutes to see how it is put together.

There are two main sections:

I. Worship for Group Activities

II. Worship for Special Occasions and Holidays

In each of these sections you will find a number of suggestions about worship and a selection of worship resources. For example, in the second section, take a look at the ideas for worship at Advent and Christmas. You will find ideas to help you plan for worship when your group goes caroling, when you visit shut-ins, when you have a special Christmas program, and when you have a Christmas party. There are also some extra materials given at the end of this section to help you think about and plan for other worship times during the season—and improve upon the suggestions we have made.

That's the way with this book—lots of ideas, and many opportunities for you to do your own thinking and planning, making worship come alive in your group!

Remember that there are many good sources for help when you

5

are planning and leading the experience of worship. The best help of all is found in the regular materials your group receives and uses: the handbooks and study materials provided for you. In them you will find many worship suggestions closely related to your interests and concerns. Begin there. From that solid starting point you can move out and find many other valuable ideas. You will be on the way to real excitement as you help others find new meaning in worship.

We hope this book will help.

—HELEN F. COUCH
SAM S. BAREFIELD

6

About Worship...

The word *worship* does not have the same meaning for everyone. Many persons limit their experience of worship to times of personal prayer, meditation, and Bible reading, and to participation in the formal, traditional services of the church. But many others have discovered that not only can they worship in these usual ways, but that adventures of the spirit are possible in an unlimited variety of experiences in all sorts of settings.

It is with this more inclusive idea of worship in mind that the editors have assembled the material in this *Sourcebook*. They believe that a group of persons of any age can become aware of the presence of God anytime, anywhere, if opportunities are provided and some direction is given. Hymns, meditations, moments of quiet, prayers—all these can help us still our minds and reach out in spiritual ventures wherever we may be. And when the whole group is stilled, reaching out, seeking, waiting, we hear his voice, we feel his touch, and we respond in faith and love.

This *Sourcebook* can help you plan many kinds of worship experiences for your group. As a leader of worship you are helping persons grow in the knowledge and love of God. And as they grow, the insight, the strength, the joy, and the purpose that come in moments of communion with God will carry over into everyday attitudes and actions—for true worship changes lives.

Contents

Contents

I. WORSHIP FOR GROUP ACTIVITIES

CHAPTER 1
Business and Committee Meetings

Much of the work of a church group is done through the "council" or "steering committee," the group that has responsibility for leadership. Since this group is of special importance, they often find it a good idea to spend some time together in worship. Special occasions that arise will suggest special worship needs. In order to help a committee that has the job of providing worship for council or committee meetings, here are some specific suggestions to indicate some possibilities.

SOME WORSHIP SUGGESTIONS

When a New Council Meets

PRELUDE

SCRIPTURE:

> The Lord is my light and my salvation;
> whom shall I fear?
> The Lord is the stronghold of my life;
> of whom shall I be afraid?
> —Ps. 27:1 R.S.V.

11

HYMN: "Spirit of God, Descend Upon My Heart."

STATEMENT BY A LEADER:

We are beginning our work together as a council. Each one of us knows that the months ahead of us are important ones for our group. In these months we will all be growing in our own ways, deeper and deeper in the faith we know. We shall be determining the direction our fellowship will move in. We shall be setting the pace for many persons who will come after us. So it is good for us to pause a few moments as a new council, to remind ourselves of the job we have to do, and to seek God's help as we work together. Quietly now, let's think together about some important matters we will be reminded of.

MEDITATION:

FIRST VOICE: I remember that I stand in a long line of succession. Before we came into our places of responsibility, many others had come before us. Because they knew they had a job to do, and did it well, we can now come to do our share in Christ's church.

Quiet music: "Gratitude," the tune of "Lord, Speak to Me, That I May Speak." (One verse should be played quietly on the piano.)

SECOND VOICE: I know that we have a job to do for those who have asked us to be their leaders. Each one of us is a part of our group. We know we have different abilities and different interests. We want to be faithful both to those who have gone before us and to those whom we serve today in our group.

Quiet music: "Gratitude," the tune of "Lord, Speak to Me, That I May Speak." (One verse played quietly.)

FIRST VOICE: I see coming after us many others who will come this way. They will need to find that strong and loyal people have led the way for them. If we serve our day well, then those who follow can build on what we have done.

Quiet music: "Gratitude," the tune of "Lord, Speak to Me, That I May Speak." (One verse played quietly.)

SECOND VOICE: Paul once wrote his friends: "According to the commission of God given to me, like a skilled master builder I laid a foundation, and another man is building upon it. Let each man

12

take care how he builds upon it. For no other foundation can anyone lay than that which is laid, which is Jesus Christ." (I Cor. 3:10-11 R.S.V.) Paul had also told them, "I planted, Apollos watered, but God gave the growth. So neither he who plants nor he who waters is anything, but only God who gives the growth. He who plants and he who waters are equal, and each shall receive his wages according to his labor. For we are fellow workmen for God; you are God's field, God's building." (I Cor. 3:6-9 R.S.V.)

PRAYER, BY A LEADER: Our Father, please help each one of us to remember the importance of his job, no matter what it may be. Help us learn to work together so that as we work for you the way will be smooth and the goals easier to reach. But when our way is rough, and we cannot seem to reach our goals at all, point us in new directions, forgiving us for losing the way. We want to be your disciples. We want to serve you. We need to hear your voice as we begin our work together. In the name of our Master we pray. Amen.

HYMN: "Lord, Speak to Me, That I May Speak."

BENEDICTION:
> The Lord bless you and keep you:
> The Lord make his face to shine
> upon you, and be gracious to
> you:
> The Lord lift up his countenance
> upon you, and give you peace.
> —Num. 6:24-26 R.S.V.

Brief Worship Before a Meeting

PRELUDE: "Trentham," the tune to "Breathe on Me, Breath of God."

CALL TO WORSHIP:
God is a spirit, and they that worship him must worship him in spirit and in truth.

The Lord is good; his mercy is everlasting, and his truth endureth to all generations.

13

If we confess our sins, he is faithful and just and will fogive our sins and cleanse us from all unrighteousness.

HYMN: "Now Thank We All Our God."

SCRIPTURE:

Hear these words of Jesus, spoken to his disciples:

"You are the earth's salt. But if the salt should become tasteless, what can make it salt again? It is completely useless and can only be thrown out of doors and stamped underfoot.

"You are the world's light—it is impossible to hide a town built on top of a hill. Men do not light a lamp and put it under a bucket. They put it on a lampstand, and it gives light for everybody in the house.

"Let your light shine like that in the sight of men. Let them see the good things you do and praise your Father in Heaven." (Matt. 5:13-16 PHILLIPS.)

PRAYER:

Our Father, as we come together to work in thy name guide us in the way you want us to go. We want to serve you as citizens of your kingdom. Help us to find your will and walk in your way in all we do and say today. In Jesus' name we pray. Amen.

When a Crisis Arises

Sometimes—even in the best of groups—troubles get a head start, and difficult moments interfere with the welfare of the fellowship. As Christians, we recognize the fact that we do not always live and work together in peace. When troubles do come, we seek God's forgiveness for our mistakes and try to find out what we should do next. Sometimes these difficulties center in personal conflicts; sometimes they are the result of immature jealousies; sometimes they come from simple misunderstandings. But no matter what causes them, we are honest in seeing that they endanger our Christian fellowship, and we pray about them. We always seek to look at ourselves and our problems in a way that will not embarrass any member of our group, for we are all—every single one of us—seeking to know God's will and to find

14

his strength. When the council is fully aware of a problem it is facing, here is one way the difficulty might be met through worship.

QUIET MUSIC

CALL TO WORSHIP:

Bless the Lord, O my soul: and all that is within me, bless his
holy name.
Bless the Lord, O my soul, and forget not all his benefits:
who forgiveth all thine iniquities;
who healeth all thy diseases;
who redeemeth thy life from destruction;
who crowneth thee with lovingkindness and tender mercies.
What shall I render unto the Lord for all his benefits toward
me?
I will pay my vows unto the Lord now in the presence of all his
people.
O come, let us worship and bow down:
let us kneel before the Lord our maker.
—Ps. 103:1-4; 116:12-14; 95:6 K.J.V.

HYMN: "Master, Speak, Thy Servant Heareth."

PRAYER, BY A LEADER:

Our Father, we come to worship thee now, confessing our weakness and mistakes. We know that our fellowship needs your help in a special way. Hear us as we beseech you to forgive us and lead us in new and happy ways of service for thee. Amen.

QUIET MOMENTS:

(Let the group spend several minutes in quiet meditation, as the pianist plays "Blairgowrie," the tune to "O Young and Fearless Prophet.")

PRAYER, BY A COUNCIL MEMBER:

O God, hear us as we pray now. We need to let your love come to live in our group. In the problems that face us, we all accept our

15

responsibility, recognizing that none of us is perfect. As we think now about ourselves and our responsibilities, show us happier ways to go and give us courage to walk in them. Amen.

QUIET MOMENTS:

(The pianist plays another verse of "Blairgowrie," the tune to "O Young and Fearless Prophet.")

DIRECTED MEDITATION, LED BY THE WORSHIP LEADER:

Let us now spend some moments thinking about our fellowship. I will suggest some thoughts for meditation, giving us some time to think them over.

Let us think about the jobs we have to do (pause). . . .

Let us think back, considering how we have done our jobs (pause). . . .

Let us remember that God has created a happy Christian fellowship among us (pause) . . . .

Let us seek to discover if there are ways we can help encourage and maintain this fellowship God has given us (pause). . . .

Let us pray for those who need our prayers (pause) . . . .

Let us pray for ourselves and our needs (pause) . . . .

And let us thank God for calling us to be his children, doing his work together with him here in our fellowship (pause) . . . .

Now let us close our meditation by singing a prayer-hymn.

HYMN:

> Jesus, united by thy grace,
>   And each to each endeared,
> With confidence we seek Thy face,
>   And know our prayer is heard.
>
> Help us to help each other, Lord,
>   Each other's cross to bear;
> Let each his friendly aid afford,
>   And feel his brother's care.
>
> Up unto Thee, our living Head,
>   Let us in all things grow,
> Till Thou hast made us free indeed
>   And spotless here below.

16

Touched by the loadstone of Thy love,
Let all our hearts agree;
And ever toward each other move,
And evermore toward Thee. Amen.

—CHARLES WESLEY

PRAYERS BY THE MEMBERS OF THE COUNCIL, INTRODUCED BY RE-
MARKS SUCH AS THESE, MADE BY A LEADER:

If any of us, in this quiet worship time, would like to express
himself to the group in any way, or if anyone would like to pray a
short prayer, we will be glad to share these moments together.
(*Pause for comments or prayer from the group; allow plenty of
time, since some members of the group may be reluctant to speak
out.*)

BENEDICTION, BY A LEADER:

Almighty God, our heavenly Father, who of thy great mercy
hast promised forgiveness of sins to all them that with hearty repentance and true faith turn unto thee; have mercy upon us
(pause). . . . Pardon and deliver us from all our sins (pause) . . . .
Confirm and strengthen us in all goodness (pause) . . . . And bring
us to everlasting life (pause) . . . . Through Christ our Lord. Amen.

When Setting Out on a New Project

This suggested service[1] might be used or adapted when a council
or committee is ready to begin some new and exciting venture that
will demand the very best of the group. At such a time, it will be
good for the group to remember that all of its work is done in the
name of Christ.

PRELUDE: "Laudes Domini," the tune to "When Morning Gilds
the Skies," or "Trinity," the tune of "Come, Thou Almighty
King."

CALL TO WORSHIP:

Come, let us worship.
Let us kneel in spirit before God, our Father.
Let us still our minds and listen for his voice.

17

HYMN (*the first two stanzas only*):
> Jesus calls us, o'er the tumult
> Of our life's wild, restless sea;
> Day by day His sweet voice soundeth,
> Saying, "Christian, follow me!"
>
> Jesus calls us from the worship
> Of the vain world's golden store,
> From each idol that would keep us,
> Saying, "Christian, love me more!"
> —CECIL F. ALEXANDER

SCRIPTURE:

As he walked by the Sea of Galilee, he saw two brothers, Simon who is called Peter and Andrew his brother, casting a net into the sea; for they were fishermen. And he said to them, "Follow me, and I will make you fishers of men." Immediately they left their nets and followed him. (Matt. 4:18-20 PHILLIPS.)

QUIET MUSIC: (*The pianist plays one verse of "Jesus Calls Us."*)

MEDITATION, BY THE SCRIPTURE READER AND THREE OTHERS:

SCRIPTURE READER: "As he walked by the Sea of Galilee. . . ."

FIRST VOICE: They say that the Sea of Galilee is a pretty sea—very small, really more like a large lake. It must have been especially beautiful that morning with the sun shining on the waves and the fishing boats in the distance.

SCRIPTURE READER: "He saw two brothers, Simon who is called Peter and Andrew his brother. . . ."

SECOND VOICE: The brothers Simon and Andrew must have seen Jesus too as he came striding down the beach toward them. Probably they had seen him before and quite likely they had talked about this strange man who went about teaching the people.

Now as they looked up from their nets they were aware of something different about him—something unlike what they saw in other men—something that spoke to them even more than words, that drew their attention to him, and held it.

SCRIPTURE READER: "Simon and Andrew, his brother, casting a net into the sea. . . ."

THIRD VOICE: Maybe they had waded out from the shore. They

18

might have been standing there in the water with the net in their hands when Jesus came toward them.

SCRIPTURE READER: "And he said to them, 'Follow me, and I will make you fishers of men.' "

FIRST VOICE: They couldn't imagine why he was asking them to follow him. Nor did they have any idea of what it would mean to follow.

SCRIPTURE READER: "Immediately they left their nets. . . ."

SECOND VOICE: I can almost see those two strong fishermen, can't you? When they heard him call they hurriedly pulled their net in to the shore, then just left it there on the sand.

SCRIPTURE READER: ". . . and followed him."

THIRD VOICE: Yes, they followed him along the sandy beach, on to the roadway, on into the town—on into a new life filled with adventure such as they had never dreamed of. Wherever he led they had determined they would follow.

QUIET MUSIC: (*The pianist plays one verse of "Jesus Calls Us."*)

SCRIPTURE READER: "Come, follow me. . . ."

FIRST VOICE: He called to Simon and Andrew and the others. But he did not call to them only. He still calls today—

SECOND VOICE: To John, to Mary, to Betty, to Joe. (*Use names of persons present in the group if you like.*)

THIRD VOICE: To each of us.

SCRIPTURE READER: "Come, follow me." (Pause.) "Come, follow me."

POEM, READ BY THE LEADER:

> Jesus' way with people
> Was an individual way.
> He merely stretched forth his hand,
> Gently touched one human life,
> Then walked on, beckoning—
> "Come, follow me."
> And they did.
> They rose up—dreams in their eyes,
> High courage in their hearts—
> To follow him, their Master new . . .

19

On . . . and on . . . and on . . .
Long centuries through.

Jesus' way with people
Has not changed. There is
No strident call, no glittering appeal
For great turnings of the masses.
But there's a touch, a whispered, "Come,"
A vision of new life . . . a beckoning . . .
And as we rise to follow
So will others . . .
Rise to share our dreams,
Join hearts with ours courageously—
To make his way our way
And dreams reality.[2]

HYMN (*the last two stanzas only*):
In our joys and in our sorrows,
   Days of toil and hours of ease,
Still He calls, in cares and pleasures,
   "Christian, love me more than these."

Jesus calls us! By thy mercies,
   Saviour, may we hear Thy call,
Give our hearts to Thine obedience
   Serve and love Thee best of all! Amen.
                    —CECIL F. ALEXANDER

PRAYER:

Our Father, like Simon and Andrew and the others that were
called, we want to follow Jesus. But sometimes we are not certain
what being a follower means. And often when we do understand
we do not have the courage to follow. As we launch out on our
new project, help us understand more fully what it means to be a
disciple of Jesus Christ. Help us give ourselves to the Master. In
his name we pray. Amen.

BENEDICTION (*if this service is used at the end of a council meeting*):

The grace of the Lord Jesus Christ, and the love of the Father,
and the communion of the Holy Spirit, be with you all. Amen.

SOME ADDITIONAL RESOURCES

An Affirmation

We believe in the one God, Maker and Ruler of all things, Father of all men; the source of all goodness and beauty, all truth and love.

We believe in Jesus Christ, God manifest in the flesh, our Teacher, Example, and Redeemer, the Saviour of the world.

We believe in the Holy Spirit, God present with us for guidance, for comfort and for strength.

We believe in the forgiveness of sins, in the life of love and prayer, and in grace equal to every need.

We believe in the Word of God contained in the Old and New Testaments as the sufficient rule both of faith and of practice.

We believe in the Church as the fellowship for worship and for service of all who are united to the living Lord.

We believe in the kingdom of God as the divine rule in human society; and in the brotherhood of man under the Fatherhood of God.

We believe in the final triumph of righteousness, and in the life everlasting. Amen.[3]

Scripture Selections

GOD'S GIFTS

FIRST READER: I therefore, a prisoner for the Lord, beg you to lead a life worthy of the calling to which you have been called,

SECOND READER: With all lowliness and meekness, with patience, forbearing one another in love, eager to maintain the unity of the Spirit in the bond of peace.

FIRST READER: There is one body and one Spirit, just as you were called to the one hope that belongs to your call,

SECOND READER: One Lord, one faith, one baptism, one God and Father of us all, who is above all and through all and in all. But grace was given to each of us according to the measure of Christ's gift.

FIRST READER: Now there are varieties of gifts, but the same Spirit;

SECOND READER: And there are varieties of service, but the same Lord;

21

FIRST READER: And there are varieties of working, but it is the same God who inspires them all in every one.

SECOND READER: To each is given the manifestation of the Spirit for the common good.

FIRST READER: To one is given through the Spirit the utterance of wisdom, and to another the utterance of knowledge according to the same Spirit,

SECOND READER: To another faith by the same Spirit, to another gifts of healing by the one Spirit,

FIRST READER: To another the working of miracles,

SECOND READER: To another prophecy,

FIRST READER: To another the ability to distinguish between spirits,

SECOND READER: To another various kinds of tongues, to another the interpretation of tongues.

FIRST READER: All these are inspired by one and the same Spirit, who apportions to each one individually as he wills.

SECOND READER: For just as the body is one and has many members, and all the members of the body, though many, are one body, so it is with Christ. For by one Spirit we were all baptized into one body—Jews or Greeks, slaves or free—and all were made to drink of one Spirit.

FIRST READER: For the body does not consist of one member but of many.

SECOND READER: If the foot should say, "Because I am not a hand, I do not belong to the body," that would not make it any less a part of the body.

FIRST READER: And if the ear should say, "Because I am not an eye, I do not belong to the body," that would not make it any less a part of the body. If the whole body were an eye, where would be the hearing?

SECOND READER: If the whole body were an ear, where would be the sense of smell?

FIRST READER: But as it is, God arranged the organs in the body, each one of them, as he chose. If all were a single organ, where would the body be?

SECOND READER: As it is, there are many parts, yet one body. The eye cannot say to the hand, "I have not need of you," nor again the head to the feet, "I have no need of you."

FIRST READER: If one member suffers, all suffer together; if one member is honored, all rejoice together.

SECOND READER: Now you are the body of Christ and individually members of it. (Eph. 4:1-7; I Cor. 12:4-21, 26-27 R.S.V.)

THIS IS THE WAY

So the Eternal longs to
    favour you,
    and moves to show you pity;
    for the Eternal is a loyal God;
    happy for all who long for him!
No more tears for you,
    O folk of Sion in Jerusalem!
For he will show you favour
    when you sigh,
    and answer you, soon as he
    hears your cry,
Though scant and scarce may
    be
    your bread and water from
    the Lord,
yet he your Teacher never leaves
    you now;
You see your Teacher for
    yourselves,
and when you swerve to right
    or left,
you hear a Voice behind you
    whispering,
"This is the way, walk here."
    —Isa. 30:18-21 MOFFATT

THE CHRISTIAN'S STRENGTH

Finally, be strong in the Lord and in the strength of his might. Put on the whole armor of God, that you may be able to stand against the wiles of the devil. For we are not contending against flesh and blood, but against the principalities, against the powers, against the world rulers of this present darkness, against the spirit-

23

WORSHIP SOURCEBOOK FOR YOUTH

ual hosts of wickedness in the heavenly places. Therefore take the whole armor of God, that you may be able to withstand in the evil day, and having done all, to stand. Stand therefore, having girded your loins with truth, and having put on the breastplate of righteousness, and having shod your feet with the equipment of the gospel of peace; above all taking the shield of faith, with which you can quench all the flaming darts of the evil one. And take the helmet of salvation, and the sword of the Spirit, which is the word of God. Pray at all times in the Spirit, with all prayer and supplication. To that end keep alert with all perseverance, making supplication for all the saints, and also for me, that utterance may be given me in opening my mouth boldly to proclaim the mystery of the gospel, for which I am an ambassador in chains; that I may declare it boldly, as I ought to speak. (Eph. 6:10-20 R.S.V.)

WE SOW AND WE REAP

Even if anyone is detected in some trespass, my brothers, you are spiritual, you must set the offender right in a spirit of gentleness; each looking to himself, in case he too is tempted. Bear one another's burdens, and so fulfil the law of Christ. Again if anyone imagines he is somebody, he is deceiving himself, for he is nobody; let everyone bring his own work to the test—then he will have something to boast about on his own account, and not in comparison with his fellows. For everyone will have to bear his own load of responsibility.

Those who are taught must share all the blessings of life with those who teach them the Word. Make no mistake—God is not to be mocked—a man will reap just what he sows; he who sows for the Spirit will reap life eternal from the Spirit. Never let us grow tired of doing what is right, for if we do not faint we shall reap our harvest at the opportune season. (Gal. 6:1-9, MOFFATT)

Hymns

"Jesus Shall Reign Where'er the Sun."
"Master, No Offering Costly and Sweet."
"Break Thou the Bread of Life."
"'Mid All the Traffic of the Ways."
"It May Not Be Our Lot to Wield."
"For All the Blessings of the Year."

24

Prayers

THANKS FOR GOD'S HELP

We know that our work is really your work, God. Forgive us when we fumble with it so long and so fretfully that we begin to think that the burden is ours alone, that it must be carried by our strength. Remind us that we always depend on you—that our burdens are lightened only by your guidance and love—and that we can always work in hope, knowing that you are our God. In the name of Christ we seek your forgiveness, and accept your love. Amen.

FOR GUIDANCE IN WORK

As we come to the work of our group, O God, we ask thy guidance. We want to do our tasks well, and do them so that they contribute to thy plan for our lives and for the life of our world. With thy Spirit in our midst, and thy love undergirding us, we will seek to serve thee in all we do and say together in the work that is before us. In Christ's name. Amen.

FOR DIRECTION

When knotty problems tangle us up, and trip up our work, take us, O God, to the trail that can lead us to light and truth. And give us courage to walk in the path you show us. Deliver us from praying for the light and then refusing to walk in it. In his name we pray. Amen.

Litanies

AT THE BEGINNING OF A MEETING

LEADER: For the task thou hast set before us, and for friends who work by our side,

GROUP: We thank thee.

LEADER: For courage that comes when we are weak, and for wisdom that dispels our confusion,

GROUP: We thank thee.

LEADER: For the group that supports us, and looks to us for leadership,

GROUP: We thank thee.

25

LEADER: For the strength that has come out of our weakness, the miracle of thy hand,

GROUP: We thank thee.

LEADER: For the next few moments together when we shall seek to serve and please thee,

GROUP: We thank thee, Lord, we thank thee. Amen.

A LITANY OF PENITENCE

LEADER: When we carelessly perform our tasks, unmindful that it is thy work we do,

GROUP: Have mercy upon us, O God, according to thy loving-kindness.

LEADER: When we pursue our own interests in our group, forgetting to seek the goals thou hast set for us,

GROUP: Blot out our transgressions, according to the multitude of thy tender mercies.

LEADER: When we let selfishness, hatreds, and indifference interfere with our work for thee,

GROUP: Wash us thoroughly from our iniquity, and cleanse us from our sins.

LEADER: Show us the way to go, and we will walk in it:

GROUP: For we acknowledge our transgressions and our sin is ever before us.

LEADER: The sacrifices of God are a broken spirit: a broken and a contrite heart, O God, thou wilt not despise.

GROUP: Create in us a clean heart, O God, and renew a right spirit within us. Cast us not away from thy presence, and take not thy holy spirit from us.

LEADER: O Lord, open thou our lips,

GROUP: And our mouths shall show forth thy praise. Amen.[4]

Poems

PRAYER TO THE MOUNTAIN SPIRIT

Lord of the mountain
Reared within the mountain,
Young man, Chieftain,
Hear a young man's prayer!
Hear a prayer for cleanness.

Keeper of the strong rain,
  Drumming on the mountain;
Lord of the small rain,
  That restores the earth in newness;
Keeper of the clean rain,
  Hear a prayer for wholeness.
Young man, Chieftain,
  Hear a prayer for fleetness.
Keeper of the deer's ways,
  Reared among the eagles,
Clear my feet of slothness.

Keeper of the paths of men,
  Hear a prayer for straightness.
Hear a prayer for courage.
  Lord of the thin peaks,
Reared among the thunders;
  Keeper of the headlands,
Holding up the harvest,
  Keeper of the strong rocks,
Hear a prayer for staunchness.
Young man, Chieftain,
  Spirit of the mountain! [5]

—MARY AUSTIN

WHO JOINS HIS HOST?

God's trumpet wakes the slumbering world;
  Now, each man to his post.
The red-cross banner is unfurled;
  Who joins the glorious host?
He who, in fealty to the truth,
  And counting all the cost,
Doth consecrate his generous youth;
  He joins the noble host.

He who, no anger on his tongue,
  Nor any idle boast,
Bears steadfast witness 'gainst the wrong,
  He joins the sacred host;

27

He who, with calm undaunted will
Never counts the battle lost,
But, though defeated, battles still,
He joins the faithful host.

He who is ready for the cross,
The cause despised loves most,
And shuns not pain or shame or loss,
He joins the martyr host.
God's trumpet wakes the slumbering world;
Now, each man to his post;
The red-cross banner is unfurled;
We join the glorious host.

—SAMUEL LONGFELLOW

THE WORLD'S WORK

Were it a task
Of one, alone,
It were a greater task
Than could be borne
By one—alone.
But from the tired grasp
Of those who pass
Beyond its portals,
The world's work
Falls to all of us.
    (—to build a better
    world for all,
    on each of us depends).
Each moment brings
    To each pair
Of living hands,
Some job unfinished;
Some job badly done;
Some job, as yet a vision.
Dimly glimpsed and vague,
    Still to be begun.

(—to make the world
a better world,
is work that never ends.)[6]

A PRAYER FOR EVERY DAY

O Son of Man, Thou madest known,
Through quiet work in shop and home,
The sacredness of common things,
The chance of life that each day brings.

O Workman true, may we fulfill
In daily life Thy Father's will;
In duty's call, Thy call we hear
To fuller life, through work sincere.

Thou Master Workman, grant us grace
The challenge of our tasks to face;
By loyal scorn of second best,
By effort true to meet each test.

And thus we pray in deed and word,
Thy kingdom come on earth, O Lord;
In work that gives effect to prayer
Thy purpose for thy world we share.[7]

—MILTON S. LITTLEFIELD

THE DESIGN

O God,
Help me take the darker threads
I did not choose,
And with a sure and steady hand
Let me weave each strand
In place.
The brighter ones I loved so well
Were woven with such ecstasy.

O God, help me see
That they will only lovelier be
against those fraught with pain.
And as I watch the sunset
Bless an evening sky
I shall know why.[8]

—FRANCES G. TOWER

29

OTHERS WILL STAND

When we lie down worn out,
  other men will stand young and fresh.
By the steps that we have cut they will climb;
  by the stairs that we have built they will mount.
They will never know the names
  of men who made them.
At the clumsy work they will laugh;
  and when the stones roll they will curse us.
But they will mount, and on our work;
  they will climb, and by our stairs!
No man liveth to himself,
  and no man dieth to himself.[9]

—O. Schreiner

FOR THEM

We shall not travel by the road we make;
  Ere day by day the sound of many feet
Is heard upon the stones that now we break
  We shall come to where the cross-roads meet.
For us the heat by day, the cold by night,
  The inch-slow progress and the heavy load,
And death at last to close the long grim fight
  With man and beast and stone: for them the road;
For them the shade of trees that now we plant,
  The safe, smooth journey and the certain goal—
Yea, birthright in the land of covenant;
  For us day-labor, travail of the soul.
And yet the road is ours as never theirs;
  Is not one gift on us alone bestowed?
For us the joy of joys, O pioneers;
  We shall not travel, but we make the road! [10]

—H. Friedlander

Meditations

THE OLD AND THE NEW

Oldness and newness have always fascinated us. We enjoy new things—new clothes, new cars, new schools, and new styles. We like new movies, new books, new games, and new ideas.

At the same time, however, we hold on to the old. We don't

want to throw away that favorite pair of old loafers or dirty buckskins. We stuff scrapbooks full of letters, newspaper clippings, and pieces of paper. We keep photographs and look at them fondly. Our daily lives are curious mixtures of oldness and newness.

Jesus was aware of this human trait. He always spoke in terms and experiences drawn from daily life. Yet his thoughts about God were startlingly new. His ideas about the purpose of his own life on earth were also new.

The land in which Jesus lived and worked was an old land even two thousand years ago. Jesus' teachings came as a fresh wind across those desert lands. His message was new; it could not be held by an old form. Jesus thus created a new faith.

He did not do it by ignoring the old faith, for he observed the commandments of the Hebrew religion. He said on one occasion, "Think not that I have come to abolish the law and the prophets; I have come not to abolish them but to fulfill them." Jesus created a new faith by breathing new life into the old.[11]

—PEGGY BILLINGS

WE SHARE

There is an ancient Chinese poem.

When the sun comes up, I go to work.
When the sun goes down, I go to rest.
I dig a well and drink from it.
I dig my soil and eat the food it gives.
I share creation.
Does a King do anymore?

"I share creation," the Chinese peasant farmer said. He said it simply because he went about his daily routine.

We too share in creation. We do not perform God's task of creating, of course. He is the Creator of all that is, and we are his creatures. But he has set us about the job of sharing in the creation of the world around us. The simple tasks we do—our regular loyalty to the groups we belong to, our patient working at our own little jobs, our daily friendliness and helpfulness—these tasks bring us into a proper role with God, our Creator. We acknowledge that he is our Maker. We accept his invitation to help make a world in the way he wants it made. We begin to share in creation.

Does a king do anymore?

31

FLASHERS AND PLUGGERS

Some officers approached Napoleon to recommend a young captain for promotion. Napoleon asked them, "Why do you suggest this young man?"

Their answer was that through unusual courage and cleverness he had won an important victory several days before. "Good," said Napoleon, "but what did he do the next day?" That had been the last that was ever heard of that young man.

Our world includes both the flashers and the pluggers. The flashers show an occasional burst of brilliancy and do some amazing things that entitle them to the headlines.

The pluggers grow steadily with perseverance and determination to the goal before them. They can be depended upon to do their best every day in the year.

The backbone of a Christian civilization is its dependable people. These are the ones who can always be counted on for a steady stream of influence and service no matter what happens anywhere.

One father paid this tribute to his son: "If I was going away and there was anything I wanted him to do, I would tell him; but when I returned I never thought of going to see if he had done it—I knew it was done. . . ."

Help me, O God, so to develop my courage and perseverance-power that I may join the fellowship of those dependable people who are continually serving thee and working for thy kingdom. Amen.[12]

—JAMESON JONES

WAITING

Now—we can be quiet awhile and wait.
Here in the quietness we can wait for God.
In him we know there is
    forgiveness for what is past—
    hope for tomorrow—
    and strength for today.
Before us, he sets our tasks.
Within us, he speaks words of courage.
Beyond us, he calls—beckoning and promising, urging,
    demanding all we have.

Will we answer?

Do we want to walk with him? (*Pause.*)
Can we follow where he goes? (*Pause.*)
Can we give what must be given? (*Pause.*)
Will we seek what must be sought? (*Pause.*)
Dare we love what must be loved? (*Pause.*)

Here in the quietness we wait for God.
We wait for the Living God!

Here in our quietness, O God, find us!
Speak! Command!
We wait.

There are many occasions when a brief time of worship will be appropriate for the choir. Possibly before the regular service of worship in which the choir will participate, a moment of quiet and turning to God may be helpful, and the special service of worship in music may be the better for a few preliminary moments of worship by those who are to sing. Again, it may be that a brief worship time is called for at a social gathering of those who minister through music—a party, a banquet, or an outing. Suggestions given in this chapter are possible patterns for such times of worship. However, it will be necessary always to adapt the material given here to fit the needs of your particular group and to make it appropriate for the occasion on which it is to be used.

SOME WORSHIP SUGGESTIONS

Before a Special Program of Music or Service of Worship

CALL TO WORSHIP:

Come, let us worship. Let us still our minds for this brief moment and seek awareness of God's presence.

LITANY:

LEADER: Thou who has created beauty eternal, who has made man a little lower than the angels, endowing him with power akin to thine,

GROUP: May we be workmen who need not be ashamed.

LEADER: Thou who are the sanctuary for the communion of the saints, uniting in thyself all peoples of the earth,

GROUP: Teach us, that we may know the secret of entrance into the eternal fellowship.

LEADER: Thou before whom the generations pass,

GROUP: Permit us to see life in its far purposes; let us justly estimate past failures and achievements; let us give ourselves to no petty and useless endeavors.

LEADER: Thou who are the reservoir of omnipotent knowledge,

GROUP: Gird up our minds, that we may solve intelligently the problems that await us.

LEADER: Thou who has trusted in the power of growth—the grain of corn hidden in the earth, the mustard seed, which is the smallest of all seeds—knowing that if life be in them they will bear fruitage out of all proportion to themselves,

GROUP: Endow us also with faith in the unseen processes of growth. Let us undertake no work that finds no root of conviction within our hearts.

LEADER: Thou who has enlightened the eyes of the blind and strengthened the hands of the weak, thou who has guided the paths of those who searched for new truths, who has set aflame the tongues of prophets,

GROUP: Consider thou our manifold needs.

LEADER: Thou, the infinite source of love and understanding,

GROUP: Grant us to labor in thy spirit.

LEADER: Thou, the worker in stars and planets, in oceans and all mountains, fashioner, Thou, of the vast spaces that lie beyond our finite knowledge,

ALL: Share with us the quality of infinity in every daily task. Establish Thou within our hearts the holiness of beauty, the sacredness of the common need of those who are bound on earth in one humanity. Consecrate Thou every resource which it is within our power to give, to the work which lies ahead of us. Amen.[1]

Choir Dinner or Party

SCRIPTURE READING:
My heart is ready, O God,
my heart is ready!
I will sing, I will sing praises!
—Ps. 108:1a R.S.V.

HYMN: "Joyful, Joyful, We Adore Thee."

TALK (based on the following):

The picture, among the advertisements in a magazine, captures your attention. There is a band of light blue sky. A darker blue of sea. White breakers foam toward the shore. Yellow sands shine in the sun. A lonely figure walks along the beach as if going toward some horizon beyond the picture and known only to himself. He is short, dumpy, not young, and carries an old black umbrella opened to protect him from the sun. In the sand his footprints are deep and firm.

As the son of an organist-composer-pianist, it was natural enough that Pablo wanted to become a musician too. And it was just as natural that his father who was very poor in spite of—perhaps because of—his talents, thought the boy would do better by becoming a carpenter. "No," said Pablo's farsighted mother, "this boy has a gift and it's our duty to help him make the most of it."

She took him to Barcelona where Pablo entered the Municipal School of Music. Word that a remarkable boy cellist was playing in a Barcelona cafe got around to the noted Spanish composers, Granados and Albeniz. Skeptical about his being as good as people said, they went to hear him for themselves. Impressed and excited by his talent, they decided to take him with them to London. But again his wiser mother said no. He must first study much more. So Albeniz gave him a letter of introduction to the secretary to the Queen of Spain and four years later, when Pablo, his mother and two little brothers, went to Madrid, that letter got him a scholarship.

But still it was always the same story: bitter poverty. In Paris, he played in vaudeville for four francs a week. When his health failed, his mother cut off her beautiful hair and sold it.

As Casals loved music and his cello, just so greatly he loved freedom. In 1936 he was in Barcelona conducting a final rehearsal of Beethoven's Ninth Symphony when he was interrupted by an order to get out of the hall because Franco's forces were about to attack the city. Casals turned to the orchestra: "Probably we shall not meet again," he said, "would you like to finish the symphony?" To a man they shouted "Yes."

Pablo Casals is a musician, not a soldier. He takes his stand for

36

his freedom against tyranny as he has it in his power to do. Self-exiled from his native Spain he lived in Prades in the south of France. "Every wrong thing seems possible today and is accepted," he explains, "I don't accept it. That's all."

On the page opposite the picture in the magazine, Puerto Rico announced its 1959 Casals Music Festival with this word from its great leader: "My message is always the same. My wish is for happiness . . . for people to have courage . . . for people to manifest this courage in their love of liberty."

In Spain, across Europe, in the United States, in Puerto Rico, there are now footprints of music, footprints of a great man's love of freedom, which no tyrannies, no "waves of the future" can erode or erase.[2]

SCRIPTURE READING:
My heart is ready, O God,
    my heart is ready!
I will sing, I will sing praises!

HYMN: "All People That on Earth Do Dwell."

Moments of Worship Before Rehearsal

SCRIPTURE SENTENCE:
Make a joyful noise to the Lord . . .
Serve the Lord with gladness!
Come into his presence with singing!
    —Ps. 100:1-2 R.S.V.

PRAYER:
O God, source of all music and light, teach us new lessons in harmony as we work together now. Direct us, God, so that our voices may be attuned to the harmony that sings at the center of our universe, so that ours may truly be a ministry of music when we have disciplined ourselves in preparation. We pray in Jesus' name. Amen.

SCRIPTURE SENTENCE:
Having gifts that differ according to the grace given to us, let us use them. (Rom. 12:6 R.S.V.)

37

Before the Regular Service of Worship

SCRIPTURE READING:

> Praise the Lord.
> Praise the name of the Lord,
>   give praise, O servants of the Lord,
> you that stand in the house of the Lord,
>   in the courts of the house of our God!
> Praise the Lord, for the Lord is good;
>   sing to his name, for he is gracious!
>   —Ps. 135:1-3 R.S.V.

PRAYER:

Our Father, we would truly sing to thy name this day. We would praise thee with the music that we have prepared for this service. As we sing, may we forget ourselves and remember only that we are serving thee—that we are ministering to persons who come to this hour of worship searching for thee. Help us now to make the best use of our gifts from thee, our voices, in serving thee today and always. We pray in Jesus' name. Amen.

Worship Moments for a Business Meeting

Perhaps at the beginning or close of the business meeting of the choir you might want just a moment of worship. Why not start by singing:

> All things shall perish
> From under the sky;
> Music alone shall live
> Never to die.[3]

Then the leader might say something like this:

Hearing this song for the first time, a non-Christian youth listened in surprise and said, "You mean this is what you Christians really believe, that music alone shall live? What about your Christ —your God?"

And what does this mean? Does it mean that . . . the "rock 'n' roll" generation's music shall live?

Or does it mean the "long-hair" classics of Bach, Beethoven or Handel?

38

Or does it mean the great hymns of the church—the hymns of Watts, Wesley, or Whittier?

Or could it have a much broader meaning of eternal melody—the harmony of all the universe—the master perfection of The Great Composer?

The music of man, like walls, will crumble in time. But that greater music of God will never die.[4]

Worship moments could be brought to a close with this or a similar prayer:

Almighty God, our Creator, who knowest us better than we know ourselves, and whose will for us far surpasses in splendor and joy anything that we devise or imagine for ourselves, inspire us to surrender our restlessness to thy peace, our futile self-will to thy creative purpose, and our foolish independence to thy sustaining and directing love. Lift us out of our petty concerns and give new depth and dignity to our lives by enlisting us again for thy kingdom . . . And this we ask in his name. Amen.[5]

SOME ADDITIONAL RESOURCES

Scripture Selections

I WILL SING

I will sing of thy steadfast
  love, O Lord, for ever;
with my mouth I will proclaim
  thy faithfulness to all generations.
For thy steadfast love was established for ever,
  thy faithfulness is firm as the heavens.
Let the word of Christ dwell in you richly, as you . . .
sing psalms and hymns . . . with thankfulness in your
hearts to God. (Ps. 89:1-3; Col. 3:16 R.S.V.)

OTHER APPROPRIATE SCRIPTURE REFERENCES

Psalms 135:1-3   A hymn of praise
Psalms 117   Praise for God's steadfast love
I Cor. 14:15   Sing with understanding

39

Prayers

PRAYER FOR MUSICIANS

O Thou, who art the God of David the psalmist, in whose worship and adoration music has ever been a servant: Help us to keep our noble art always a means of inspiration and enlightenment, that it may cheer and uplift the human soul and lead us on to higher endeavor. Guard it from the onslaught of degrading tendencies. Bless the fellowship of those who seek to perpetuate and spread abroad the beautiful, aspiring ideals of music. This we ask in the name of Him who, on the eve of His supreme sacrifice for humanity, sang a hymn in company with His disciples and retired to the stillness of the garden to feel His Father's presence.[6]

—EDGAR L. PENNINGTON

THANKS FOR OUR VOICES

O God, we thank thee that thou hast given us minds to know thee, hearts to love thee, and voices to sing thy praise. Help us to sing hymns to thee with loving hearts and understanding minds. In the name of Jesus. Amen.[7]

—ELIZABETH PATTON MOSS

A PRAYER OF DEDICATION

Heavenly Father, we give unto thee the utmost we can render of power and riches, and might and honor, and glory and blessing. We thank thee that thou hast so made us that by music our hearts can be lifted up to thee. As thou has called us to service in this church, grant that we may so love thee that thy glory may fill this house. Send thy spirit upon us that we may sing with the spirit and with the understanding also, and that we may become partakers of the inheritance of the saints in light, who sing the new song about thy throne. Through Jesus Christ our Lord. Amen.[8]

Poems

A HARMONY

O there are times when I can hear
The music of our little world
A-singing with all other worlds!
Unlike any singing I have known,

40

Its harmony is strangely sweet,
Yet there's a strong, exultant beat
That swells into a mighty hymn of praise.

Sometimes
It comes echoing through the arches
Of the church, and marches
With the tramp of ages down the aisle
To throb 'round me at the altar
Where I kneel, listening . . .
And sometimes
It's but a whisper
As I gaze into the sunset's flame
Or look close enough to see His name
Upon a perfect rose . . .

But most of all do I rejoice
When that harmony breaks through
The humdrum tasks and drab routine,
Singing out that life is good
And, according to His way,
Even these have meaning
In His plan for every day.[9]

—HELEN F. COUCH

BRAHMS AMONG THE METHODISTS

Listen! The music of the spheres,
Sung by our choir of volunteers!
As thirty people, so sincere,
Clamor in voices brassy-clear,
In tinny tenor, thundrous bass,
"How Lovely Is Thy Dwelling Place"!

Have mercy, Lord, on such as these
Who sing for love, not salaries;
And also, Lord, upon the rest
Who, listening, are humbly blest.
Who, unaware of pitch and form,

Feel suddenly and strangely warm.
Who may, through undeserved grace,
Catch glimpses of Thy dwelling place.

But send a deeper mercy, Lord,
On those whose creeds are unrestored.
On sadder souls who stand aside,
Judge, and remain unsatisfied.
Unquiet souls, who, comfortless,
From church to church, from year to year,
Weep for a song they will not hear.[10]

—BARBARA HARR OVERMYER

MORNING MEDITATION

"He has put a new song into my mouth" . . .
A song that speaks of trust, of love, of surety
In this desperate and uncertain age—
A new song that swells from the depths within
A song of exultation—
I am one with the infinite!
I can walk in confidence with Him
Knowing that my work this day
Is not for today alone—nor yet tomorrow—
But for eternity.
Yea, truly, "He has put a new song into my mouth!" [11]

—HELEN F. COUCH

KEEP US SINGING

Dear Father, with a touch divine,
Give to our voices tones like Thine.
And keep us singing as we go—
Thy love to tell: Thy praise to show.[12]

—ELIZABETH STINSON

Meditations

GOD AND MUSIC

Listen! It is a symphony concert. Far below, the soloist with
his violin stands a little apart from the great orchestra. From his
frail instrument pours forth a flood of notes that seem to be the

42

very music of life itself. Weary people forget the workaday grayness of their lives, and faces light up with new hope, while eyes grow luminous under the spell of beauty.

And God who said, "Let there be light," said also, "Let there be music." And musicians who catch in their listening spirits the caroling of birds, the singing of winds in the tree tops, the melody of brooks, the lilt in the voices of little children, the singing of the spheres in space, and put them down in black marks on white paper, that others may read and bring forth again on piano or violin or 'cello, are in very truth co-workers with God. And any musician who brings in through the walls of a hot, crowded city building the beauty of brooks and waterfalls, mountains and great distances, winds and soaring birds, setting free the spirits of weary people "that they may have life more abundantly," is, consciously or unconsciously, a co-worker with God.[13]

MUSIC IN THE BIBLE

It is no mere chance that the Bible is full of music, from Jubal, the father of art, to the vision in Revelation with which the record ends. It was heard in the Hebrew nation's feasts and festivals. It formed a large part of the temple worship. So marked was its effect, according to the picture of the Chronicler, when the great chorus "lifted up their voice with the trumpets and cymbals and instruments of music, and praised the Lord, saying, For he is good; for his mercy endureth forever: that then the house was filled with a cloud, even the house of the Lord, so that the priests could not stand to minister by reason of the cloud: for the glory of the Lord filled the house of God." The Psalms, those most wonderful of hymns, have been the voice of the Church in all ages. Jesus went from the last Supper to Gethsemane singing. Paul counseled his converts, "Let the word of Christ dwell in you richly in all wisdom; teaching and admonishing one another with psalms and hymns and spiritual songs, singing with grace in your hearts unto God." The great symbolic pictures of heaven have ever been filled with music, which is not merely a means of jubilant worship but the incarnation of that harmonious living, that spiritual oneness with Jesus, which makes melody with its heart to the Lord. Such is the ideal and aim of worship in music and song, the making of heaven through the reincarnation of Jesus in our lives.[14]

43

CHAPTER 3

Camping

Camping days are happy days, and among the highest happy moments at camp sites are the times of worship. Children and youth and adults—campers of all ages, and of every age—gladly offer their thanks to God for the loving care they rediscover and accept anew in the informal days of outdoor living. Today, churches provide camping experiences not only for the younger members of their fellowship, but also for entire families and for those in their "golden years." The suggestions offered in this section will enable these groups to find meaningful ways to worship God in the midst of camp life. Many similar opportunities arise in every camping experience, and the good camp leader is aware of the fact that campers do not worship best simply by being put on schedule. There may be "morning watch" and "sunset time" in the camp schedule—but there will also be holy moments, unplanned and unexpected. These too are worship, and every camper thanks God for them, for the experience of worship—whether it be planned or spontaneous—comes as His gift to us.

Additional material can be found in the next chapter.

SOME WORSHIP SUGGESTIONS

Beginning the Day

Many camps set aside the first few moments of the day for an informal and brief worship time. This time is called by varying titles, some of them original and a part of the tradition of each camp. Whether it is "morning watch" or "quiet time" or "getting ready," the intent is the same: to come together in the fresh day, ask God's blessing on the day's plans, and offer him the hours that lie before us.

If these moments precede breakfast, they will need to be very brief! But their brevity need not limit their effectiveness. Consider this possible procedure, for example:

OPENING PRAYER:

Open wide the window of our spirits, and fill us full of light;
Open wide the door of our hearts, that we may receive and entertain thee with all our powers of adoration and love.[1] Amen.

HYMN (*sung as the group gathers*):
"When Morning Gilds the Skies."

SCRIPTURE:

The heavens are telling the glory of God;
    and the firmament proclaims his handiwork.
Day to day pours forth speech,
    and night to night declares knowledge.
There is no speech, nor are there words;
    their voice is not heard;
yet their voice goes out through all the earth,
    and their words to the end of the world.

In them he has set a tent for the sun,
which comes forth like a bridegroom leaving his chamber,
    and like a strong man runs its course with joy.
Its rising is from the end of the heavens,
    and its circuit to the end of them;
    and there is nothing hid from its heat.
                                    —Ps. 19:1-6 R.S.V.

PRAYER (*a few moments of silence, followed by this prayer*):
O God, our father, into whose world we come anew at every dawning, hear our prayer this new day. We have sung thy praise, and have heard the psalmists witness to thy steadfast love. We offer to thee our lives this day, that as the sunshine hours pass and the night comes to us, we shall have lived as your children, loving one another, and honoring thy will for us. Help us to remember

that you are with us throughout his day, to keep us and help us. In the name of Jesus Christ we pray. Amen.

At Mealtime

The tradition of "grace at meals" fits naturally into life at camp. If this moment at every meal is not made to appear routine and lifeless it can add immeasurably to the worship life of the camp community. It deserves to be well planned, even though it consumes only a few minutes a day. The unplanned grace that is snickered through by half the group and merely tolerated by the others can hardly be expected to bear its share of enriching the worship life of the camp. Nor can the grace period be usurped for the purposes of preaching—not even by some visiting dignitary. It must stand simply in its own right as the group's remembrance of the source of the food that is to be eaten. By strictly avoiding these three temptations—to look on grace as routine, to consider it too brief and transitory to need serious planning, and to use it for a disguise for sermonizing—the "thank-you" time can serve its purpose, and campers will find that this brief pause of recognition is important in their day.

The planning that must be done need not be complicated. Many natural approaches will suggest themselves—each table might be asked to have a turn, or each cabin, or each camper. And always there will be help from a leader for anyone who needs it. Since the purpose of camping and the role of worship will have already been considered by the leaders before the camp opens, a general orientation in worship should not be necessary before the camp can get to the business of planning how it will express its gratitude at mealtime.

By way of suggestion, here are several graces, scripture selections, and hymns that can appropriately be used:

GRACES

We thank you, God, our Father, for this meal that we are about to eat. Remind us to be grateful in all our ways. In Christ's name. Amen.

Bless this food, God, and bless us so that we can become the persons you want us to be. In Christ's name we pray. Amen.

We thank you for the many gifts you have given us, our Father. When we forget that you have taken care of us all our lives, remind us to remember your love, and to give you thanks, as we are doing now. We pray in Christ's name. Amen.

For the food before us—for the fellowship around us—for the joy within us—we thank you. Amen.

SCRIPTURE SELECTIONS

Bless the Lord, O my soul;
   and all that is within me, bless his holy name!
Bless the Lord, O my soul,
   and forget not all his benefits,
who forgives all your iniquity,
   who heals all your diseases,
who redeems your life from the Pit,
   who crowns you with steadfast love and mercy,
who satisfies you with good as long as you live
   so that your youth is renewed like the eagle's.
      —Ps. 103:1-5 R.S.V.

Give thanks to the Lord,
   call upon his name;
make known his deeds among the nations,
   proclaim that his name is exalted.
Sing praises to the Lord, for he has done gloriously;
   let this be known in all the earth.
      —Isa. 12:4b-5 R.S.V.

HYMNS

THE DOXOLOGY
(Tune: Old 100th)

Praise God for whom all blessings flow;
Praise Him, all creatures here below;
Praise Him above, ye heavenly host;
Praise Father, Son, and Holy Ghost. Amen.

A WESLEY GRACE
(Tune: Uxbridge)

Be present at our table, Lord;
Be here and everywhere adored;
Thy creatures bless; and grant that we
May feast in paradise with Thee. Amen.

Personal Meditation

Many a person has had his first experience with regular personal devotions at camp. With the leisurely pace that is set at camp, and with the overwhelming closeness of beauty and fellowship, it is easy to turn to God in a few quiet moments of prayer and thoughtful meditation. The churches provide camp leaders with many suggestions concerning the possible approaches to this aspect of the camper's worship. Some camps provide printed or mimeographed "thoughts for the day" and each camper goes to his own preferred spot for his time apart. Other groups come together briefly, then separate for a time of prayer. Others come together and remain together, allowing a period for personal prayer, and ending with a hymn or litany together. Whatever the system chosen, the camp leaders will want to plan for it long before the camp opens.

Vespers

For a group of persons not used to living in the outdoor world, the sunset hour holds a special attraction. In many camps, the main planned worship experience coincides with that special time, and vespers is a moment of special value to the life of the camp. Vespers can be as formal or as informal as the group wants it to be. One camp will celebrate this evening prayer with a regular, traditional order of worship, bringing a bit of their ongoing church life to the camp setting—but another group will proceed with complete informality, beginning with a series of informal songs, moving into several favorite spirituals, and then into a dignified but unpretentious time of meditation and prayer.

The group that desires a more formal service for this time of day will have its own ideas about the order it wants to use, and material that will be of help in such a service will be found in the latter part of this chapter. Of special value will be the list of suggested Scripture readings. An order of service similar to this one will combine the desire for an orderly and dignified service with the recognition that the group is worshiping in a special, outdoor setting.

CALL TO WORSHIP:

O give thanks to the Lord, call on his name,
  make known his deeds among the peoples!
Sing to him, sing praises to him,
  tell of all his wonderful works!
Glory in his holy name;
  let the hearts of those who seek the Lord rejoice!
                    —Ps. 105:1-3 R.S.V.

HYMN: "Day Is Dying in the West."

SCRIPTURE:

And he said to his disciples, "Therefore I tell you, do not be anxious about your life, what you shall eat, nor about your body, what you shall put on. For life is more than food, and the body more than clothing. Consider the ravens: they neither sow nor reap, they have neither storehouse nor barn, and yet God feeds them. Of how much more value are you than the birds! And which of you by being anxious can add a cubit to his span of life? If then you are not able to do as small a thing as that, why are you anxious about the rest? Consider the lilies, how they grow; they neither toil nor spin; yet I tell you, even Solomon in all his glory was not arrayed like one of these. But if God so clothes the grass which is alive in the field today and tomorrow is thrown into the oven, how much more will he clothe you, O men of little faith? And do not seek what you are to eat and what you are to drink, nor be of anxious mind. For all the nations of the world seek these things; and your Father knows that you need them. Instead, seek his kingdom, and these things shall be yours as well.

(Luke 12:22-31 R.S.V.)

MEDITATION (followed by a period of silence):

At the close of this glad day, we come to thank thee, God—
  for the ever-arching sky, unending . . .

49

for the ever-reaching trees, above us . . .
for the heart of life deep with the earth . . .
for beauty all around us, everywhere.
We remember now, in the quietness of our worship—
thy love that keeps us forever . . .
thy call that keeps us moving toward thee . . .
thy children whom thou hast made our neighbors . . .
The world around us thou hast clothed in brightness and wonder,
and thou hast surrounded us with challenge and hope.
We thank thee, and praise thy name.
Thou art our father; we are thy children.
Show us the way to walk.

SOLO: "Now on Land and Sea Descending" or "At Even, Ere the Sun Was Set."

BENEDICTION:
May the loveliness of this place and the kindly remembrance of God's love for us in all our ways keep us in his love as the night comes with its shadows and its peace. Amen.

Around the Campfire

Campfire moments are magic moments for all campers, whatever age. Around the twisting, struggling flames, stories are told, songs sung, quietness enjoyed—friendships are made—and the love of God in Christ is remembered. The warmth of these glowing moments never ends. No wonder so many camp traditions center around the campfire and its bright attraction.

Consider several possibilities for worship around the campfire, remembering that some of these moments cannot be planned, but realizing that they can be meaningful when the time is right, and the opportunity present.

Fire-lighting time.

A brief time is spent in some camps at the moment when each evening's campfire is lit, and the group remembers to thank God for the gift of light and warmth—and fellowship. This time of worship

50

should be very short, and preferably not a routine matter. The right song, and a plain prayer by one of the group, will suffice to bring the group to this moment. Following the quiet moment when the flame leaps up, the group can sing joyfully one of its favorite hymns —perhaps "Immortal, Invisible, God Only Wise."

The first fire-lighting can be made a very special occasion, if the group desires. The following meditation and suggestions will set the stage for moments of worship that will never be forgotten:

In the darkness of this circle we cannot see one another, and we are practically strangers. When we light this fire, even the small light of the match (or the first flame of the flint and steel fire) gives us some idea of those around us. As the fire grows we can see each other more and more clearly, until we can even make out the faces of those across the circle from us.

The lighting of this fire is a symbol of what Christ can mean to us in this camp. We have come to camp as strangers to one another. Many of our lives are in darkness, just as we were in darkness before lighting this fire. During this week of camping we have the opportunity of learning what Christ meant when He said, "I am the light of the world: he that followeth me shall not walk in darkness, but shall have the light of life." If Christ does come into the center of our living here, he will bring new light and love into all our friendships and our activities. If we do not bring him to the center of our lives, we will be in darkness. So, just as we have lit this fire to start our camping together, let us pray that we can learn to live in the light of his life and teaching in the days ahead.

A simple prayer and a few appropriate hymns—"Fairest Lord Jesus," "This Is My Father's World," "Lord, I Want to Be a Christian"—may follow. The director may wish to speak briefly about the larger company of campers of which these campers are a part; those who have preceded them in the use and enjoyment of this camp, who have left a part of themselves in the improvements they made as Christian stewards of God in the Christian community that is camp. He may wish to challenge them to grow "in wisdom and in stature, and in favor with God and man." A brief prayer and another hymn could follow before the groups leave the circle to go back to their shelters.[2]

51

On a special day.

When a day has brought some special or unexpected turn, it will be natural at campfire for the group to turn together in worship —brief and pointed—to the issue. A misunderstanding that ruffled feelings and burst out into the open, or a serious accident, or bad news for one of the campers—these and similar events may call for a few moments of serious quietness, and a short prayer. Do not prolong the period—and close with a note of hope.

On the last night.

Some groups will want to make special plans for the closing campfire period. One possible development is the one below, designed to be used as the campfire is extinguished on the last night of camp.

Following the usual campfire fun, the group can make the transition to this time of worship by singing a few quiet songs and hymns. Or, if it seems better, the leader can simply announce that the group will now close the evening with a short worship time, beginning with a few moments of silence.

SPECIAL MUSIC (*by a small group of singers, seated together, but as a part of the campfire circle*):

The day Thou gavest, Lord, is ended,
The darkness falls at Thy behest;
To Thee our morning hymns ascended,
Thy praise shall hallow now our rest.

We thank Thee that Thy Church unsleeping,
While earth rolls onward into light,
Through all the world her watch is keeping,
And rests not now by day or night.

As o'er each continent and island
The dawn leads on another day,
The voice of prayer is never silent,
Nor die the strains of praise away.

So be it, Lord; Thy throne shall never,
Like earth's proud empires, pass away;

Thy kingdom stands, and grows forever,
Till all Thy creatures own Thy sway.
Amen.
—JOHN ELLERTON

LEADER:

We have come to our last night together. Seated around our fire, we remember many moments that have come and gone this week. We know that tomorrow we shall all turn to our own ways, and our circle of fellowship will break so that we can no more see it. Let us pause now in this late evening to remember our time together, and to think of days ahead.

HYMN. (Choose a hymn that is familiar so that hymnbooks will not be needed—for example, "Now the Day Is Over.")

PRAYER:

We thank you, God, for the time we have had together. Here we have made friends who will be with us always in our hearts. Here we have found a new vision of you, and as we prepare to leave we know that we know a little bit more about your will for us. As we dedicate ourselves to you again tonight, accept our sincere offering of ourselves, forgiving us for the many ways we have disappointed you in the past. We want to learn to serve you, and tonight we will promise again to follow in your way. In Christ's name we pray. Amen.

LEADER:

Look at the campfire, with its sprightly flames. We have looked at it often this week. We have seen it leap high, and burn low. We have left it smoldering when we went to our rest, and we have slept with its happy dancing flames in our memory. It has warmed us while we have been together. In a way, it has helped to make us one, to pull us together, as around it we have found new fellowship that sprung to life in our hearts.

To help us recall its brightness and warmth, one of our group (who has been named in advance) will build up its flames so that they will leap before us, reaching toward the high heavens above. (Pause while the fire gains new brightness.)

53

See it reach—up—up—up—carrying our thoughts toward the One who has kept our fellowship growing and reaching for him while we have been together? As we have come to know each other, we have also come to know our Master better. The light of the fire has given us light, even as he has. It has called us beyound ourselves to think of higher things, even as he has. It has warmed and cheered us, even as he has. Do you remember his words about himself?

"I am the light of the world; he who follows me will not walk in darkness, but will have the light of life." (John 8:12 R.S.V.)

When our fellowship around this fire ends, so will the brightness of our fellowship in him dim. Here we have sat in dazzling light as we were together reminding each other of God's love for us. But now the dazzling fire that has burned for us on this mountain-top experience must burn dim as each of us prepares to go in his own way, to his own life and responsibility. (*Note: Let a person named in advance steadily toss sand upon the fire until the flames are extinguished and only glowing coals remain.*)

But the light is not extinguished, is it? It is no longer dazzling —that is true—but see the afterglow! And when we leave here, we know the glow from Christ's light is not gone either. The brilliant light that we witnessed as we were together here is scattered into many sparkling, glowing bits of light—and we remember some words Jesus said about us:

"You are the light of the world. A city set on a hill cannot be hid. Nor do men light a lamp and put it under a bushel, but on a stand, and it gives light to all the house. Let your light so shine before men, that they may see your good works and give glory to your Father who is in heaven." (Matt. 5:14-16 R.S.V.)

POEM (*or the words may be sung to the tune "Salve Domine"*):
Light of the world, we hail Thee,
  Flushing the eastern skies;
Never shall darkness veil Thee
  Again from human eyes;
Too long, alas, withholden,
  Now spread from shore to shore;
Thy light, so glad and golden,
  Shall set on earth no more.

Light of the world, Thy beauty
   Steals into every heart,
And glorifies with duty
   Life's poorest, humblest part;
Thou robest in Thy splendor
   The simplest ways of men,
And helpest them to render
   Light back to Thee again.

Light of the world, illumine
   This darkened earth of Thine,
Till everything that's human
   Be filled with the divine;
Till every tongue and nation,
   From sin's dominion free,
Rise in the new creation
   Which springs from love and Thee. Amen.
                         —JOHN S. B. MONSELL

PRAYER. (*The leader will invite every person who wants to do so to offer a brief prayer, either in gratitude for the moments that have been spent together or in dedication for days ahead. The benediction should follow the last prayer.*)

BENEDICTION:

May the kinship of new friends, the strength of a new purpose, and the loving care of our Lord Christ go with us and keep us all aglow. Amen.

Some Other Ideas

As you can see from the suggestions above, the opportunities for worship experiences at camp are limitless. Your own imagination, and the wonderful moments of insight that come from God's spirit will lead your camp group into many other experiences. A few that we have not mentioned are listed here—and you will think of many others.

A *Hymn Sing.* When the time is appropriate, the group will find real Christian joy in a time of hymn singing. The wise camp leader will have on hand a sufficient number of copies of a well-planned

55

hymnal—if not the official hymnal of your church, then a smaller camp songbook that contains excellent, challenging hymns. If they are not too bulky, they will be welcome on a hike if someone thinks to tuck them in a spare corner of a knapsack.

Sunrise Service. The group might enjoy the experience of anticipating and planning for a sunrise service one morning. Whether it is held in the regular worship spot—or in a very special and secluded spot sought out by the campers—such a service will be a high point in the campers' memory.

Sunday Service. Would the campers like to plan a special— maybe a more formal—service of worship for Sunday morning? Some groups prefer to follow the usual order of service they would follow at home in their own churches, including in it some special elements that recognize their outdoor setting and interests. But other groups seek for an entirely different type of service so that Sunday morning at camp will be unique.

Dedication Ceremony. Out of the life at camp there may arise the possibility of giving the campers opportunity to express themselves together in a service of worship—dedicating themselves to some new course or new project they have accepted. With proper leadership—and some materials that should be on hand—this service can evolve into a significant part of the time together.

SOME ADDITIONAL RESOURCES

Scripture Selections

PRAISE TO THE LORD

Praise the Lord!
> For it is good to sing praises to our God;
>> for he is gracious, and a song of praise is seemly.
> The Lord builds up Jerusalem;
>> he gathers the outcasts of Israel.
> He heals the brokenhearted,
>> and binds up their wounds.
> He determines the number of the stars,
>> he gives to all of them their names.
> Great is our Lord, and abundant in power;
>> his understanding is beyond measure.

56

The Lord lifts up the downtrodden,
 he casts the wicked to the ground.
Sing to the Lord with thanksgiving;
 make melody to our God upon the lyre!
He covers the heavens with clouds,
 he prepares rain for the earth,
 he makes grass grow upon the hills.
He gives to the beasts their food,
 and to the young ravens which cry.
His delight is not in the strength of the horse,
 nor his pleasure in the legs of man;
but the Lord takes pleasure in those who fear him,
 in those who hope in his steadfast love.
Praise the Lord, O Jerusalem!
 Praise your God, O Zion!
For he strengthens the bars of your gates;
 he blesses your sons within you.
He makes peace in your borders;
 he fills you with the finest of the wheat.
He sends forth his command to the earth;
 his word runs swiftly.
He gives snow like wool;
 he scatters hoarfrost like ashes.
He casts forth his ice like morsels;
 who can stand before his cold?
He sends forth his word, and melts them;
 he makes his wind blow, and the waters flow.
He declares his word to Jacob,
 his statutes and ordinances to Israel.
He has not dealt thus with any other nation;
 they do not know his ordinances.
Praise the Lord!

—Ps. 147 R.S.V.

THE KINGDOM OF GOD

And he said, "The kingdom of God is as if a man should scatter
seed upon the ground, and should sleep and rise night and day,
and the seed should sprout and grow, he knows not how. The
earth produces of itself, first the blade, then the ear, then the full

57

grain in the ear. But when the grain is ripe, at once he puts in the sickle, because the harvest has come." (Mark 4:26-29 R.S.V.)

CONSIDER THE LILIES

Consider the lilies, how they grow; they neither toil nor spin; yet I tell you, even Solomon in all his glory was not arrayed like one of these. But if God so clothes the grass which is alive in the field today and tomorrow is thrown into the oven, how much more will he clothe you, O men of little faith? (Luke 12:27-28 R.S.V.)

OTHER APPROPRIATE SCRIPTURE SELECTIONS

Gen. 8:16-22. God blesses the earth after the flood.
Ps. 96. The creation praises the Maker.
Matt. 5–7. The Sermon on the Mount.
Gen. 1:1 through 2:3. God creates the world.

Hymns

"For the Beauty of the Earth."
"Day Is Dying in the West."
"Now, on Land and Sea Descending."
"All Creatures of Our God and King."
"This is My Father's World."
"The Shadows of the Evening Hours."
"All Things Bright and Beautiful."
"My God, I Thank Thee."
"When Morning Gilds the Skies."
"The Harp at Nature's Advent Strung."
"Now Doth the Sun Ascend the Sky."

Prayers
FOR STRENGTH OF PURPOSE

O God, so often we start out in the morning meaning to be good. We want to be clean and joyous and helpful all day. Then something happens, and first thing we know, we've spoken an unkind word and made a shadow come across somebody's face. Or we've done something we're ashamed of. What makes us like that, God? We're sorry and ashamed.

Somehow we feel You understand; You know what's weak inside us—make us strong. Forgive us, and help us to be understanding

58

and forgiving toward others that may hurt us. Help us learn to love, from the bigness of Your love. Amen.[3]

FOR STORMY DAYS

We thank Thee, O Lord, for the stormy days! When the rain falls and the wind blows, and the clouds move in regiments across the sky, they somehow seem to say the thing that cries in us for utterance and cannot be expressed! The glittering lights of a rainy night shine so weird and wonderful that we leave the dusty day and narrow earth and find a world of flash and gleam and shadow! The fresh and cool air of the storm soothes to rest our troubled spirits! The shock of thunder breaks the tension of tired spirits and jars us free again! The patter of the raindrops on the roof lulls us to a sleep both strong and sweet! The home seems more filled with comfort and content because the storm beats without! And when the clouds break and the King of the heavens comes forth in splendor to drive his frowning foes from the sky, he paints a gorgeous glory in the west and bids us take our rapturous glimpses through Heaven's gate while we catch our breath and think of glories unrevealed! Amen.[4]

—*Services for the Open*

FOR CAMP LEADERS

We thank you, God, for the men and women who have been our leaders here at camp. They have helped us have lots of fun, but they have also helped us remember that life is not all fun. As they have pointed us to new ways and higher trails, we heard you speaking through them. For them—and for your love for them and us—we thank you. In Jesus' name. Amen.

A CALL TO PRAYER

O Great Spirit: whose voice I hear in the winds, and whose breath gives life to all the world, hear me. I come before you, one of your many children—I am small and weak. I need your strength and wisdom.

Let me walk in beauty and make my eyes ever behold the red and purple sunset. Make my hands respect the things you have made, my ears sharp to hear your voice. Make me wise, so that

59

I may know the things you have taught my people, the lesson you have hidden in every leaf and rock.

I seek strength not to be superior to my brothers, but to be able to fight my greatest enemy—myself. Make me ever ready to come to you with clean hands and straight eyes, so when life fades as a fading sunset, my spirit may come to you without shame.[5]

—Chief Yellow Lark

PRAYER OF A CAMPER

God of the hills, grant us thy strength to go back into the cities without faltering, strength to do our daily task without tiring and with enthusiasm, strength to help our neighbors who have no hills to remember.

God of the lake, grant us thy peace and thy restfulness, peace to bring into a world of hurry and confusion, restfulness to carry to the tired whom we shall meet every day, content to do small things with a freedom from littleness, self-control for the unexpected emergency and patience for the wearisome task, with deep depths within our souls to bear us through the crowded places. Grant us the hush of the nighttime when the pine trees are dark against the sky line, the humbleness of the hills who in their mightiness know it not, and the laughter of the sunny waves to brighten the cheerless spots of a long winter. . . .

God of the wilderness, with thy pure winds from the northland blow away our pettiness; with the harsher winds of winter drive away our selfishness and hypocrisy; fill us with the breadth and the depth and the height of thy wilderness. May we live out the truths which thou hast taught us, in every thought and word and deed. Amen.[6]

—The New Hymnal for American Youth

FOR THE EVENING

O Lord, we lift our souls to Thee in the awe of the eventide. Above the tree-tops hang the heavens in their glory, but above the stars art Thou and the eternal silence. We rejoice that in the quiet of Thy day of rest our spirits have been attuned to the melodies of Thy beauty. We bless Thee for every word of solemn truth which has entered our hearts—for every touch of loving hand that has comforted us, for every opportunity we have had . . . Forgive us if any hours have been wasted on profitless things that have brought us no satisfaction, or if we have dragged our dusty cares into Thy sacred day and made the holy common. We pray for Thy blessing on all who have brought us strength, on all who are sad and hungry for Thee, on all Thy great humanity in its sin and beauty. May our last waking thought be a benediction for our fellows and in our sleep may we still be with Thee. Amen.[7]

—*Services for the Open*

GOOD NIGHT

Good night, God. We have said goodnight to our friends. The day you gave us is over. We need the rest that your nighttime promises, and so we go to our sleep. Thank you for the day, and for this night—and for our rest. Amen.

WHEN IT'S TIME TO SAY GOOD-BYE

Our Father, it is time for us to say good-bye to each other and to our camping days. We pause to thank you for the gifts you have given us here:

For friends who have come into our lives bringing new laughter and higher purpose. . . .

For leaders who have shared with us the dreams and goals of their lives. . . .

For quietness and rest, and a long, long look at our world. . . .

For a new glimpse of you, and of your Son, our Lord. . . .

For new directions, new challenges, new courage. . . .

Be with us as we leave this happy place. Remind us that the fellowship we have known here never ends, but that it carries us in your purpose into all the rest of our days, and gives us strength to live in your Spirit.

In Jesus' name we pray. Amen.

Litanies

FOR LIFE AT CAMP

LEADER: For the beauty of the world around us,
GROUP: We give thee thanks, O Lord.
LEADER: For new friendship, in which we find thy love,
GROUP: We give thee thanks, O Lord.

LEADER: For leaders who show us thy way,
GROUP: We give thee thanks, O Lord.
LEADER: For times of quiet thought, and prayer, and study,
GROUP: We give thee thanks, O Lord.
LEADER: For food, and health, and courage.
GROUP: We give thee thanks, O Lord. We give thee thanks. Amen.

A LITANY OF PRAISE

LEADER: O sing to the Lord a new song;
sing to the Lord, all the earth!
GROUP: Sing to the Lord, bless his name;
tell of his salvation from day to day.
LEADER: Declare his glory among the nations,
his marvelous works among all the peoples!
GROUP: For great is the Lord, and greatly to be praised;
he is to be feared above all gods.
LEADER: For all the gods of the peoples are idols;
but the Lord made the heavens.
GROUP: Honor and majesty are before him;
strength and beauty are in his sanctuary.
Say among the nations, "The Lord reigns!
LEADER: Yea, the world is established, it shall never be moved;
he will judge the peoples with equity."
GROUP: Let the heavens be glad, and let the earth rejoice;
LEADER: let the sea roar, and all that fills it;
GROUP: let the field exult, and everything in it!
LEADER: Then shall all the trees of the wood sing for joy before
the Lord, for he comes,
for he comes to judge the earth.
GROUP: He will judge the world with righteousness,
and the peoples with his truth.

—Based on Ps. 96:1-6, 10-13 R.S.V.

Poems

MORNING WORSHIP

I wake and hear it raining.
Were I dead, what would I give

Lazily to lie here,
Like this, and live?. . .

How shall I praise them:
All the sweet beings
Eternally that outlive
Me and my dying?

Mountains, I mean; wind, water, air;
Grass, and huge trees; clouds, flowers,
And thunder, and night.

Turtles, I mean, and toads; hawks, herons, owls;
Graveyards, and towns, and trout; roads, gardens,
Red berries, and deer.

Lightning, I mean, and eagles; fences; snow;
Sunrise, and ferns; waterfalls, serpents,
Green islands, and sleep.
Horses, I mean; butterflies; whales;
Mosses, and stars; and gravelly
Rivers, and fruit. . .

Maidens, I mean, and apples; needles; leaves;
Worms, and planets, and clover; whirlwinds, dew;
Bulls, geese—

Stop. Lie still.
You will never be done.
Leave them all there,
Old lover. Live on.[8]

—MARK VAN DOREN

EARTH IS WAKING

Earth is waking, day is breaking!
Darkness from the hills has flown;
Pale with terror, trembling error
Flies forever from her throne.
Up, to labor, friend and neighbor;
Hope and work with all thy might:
Heaven is near thee, God will see thee,
He does ever bless the right.

Earth is waking, day is breaking!
Fellow toiler, bend thine ear;
Hear ye not the angels speaking
Words of love and words of cheer?
Then to labor, friend and neighbor;
With thy soul's resistless might;
Never fear thee, God is near thee,
He doth ever bless the right.

—ANONYMOUS

THANK YOU, GOD

I love to see a tree
I love to feel the bark so firm,
From such a seed to grow so tall!
For this great mystery,
Thank you, God.

I love an open field
With dandelions—this is a weed?
Yellow against the green or fluffy white of seed,
Within my soul is the urge to kneel and say:
Thank you, God!

I love to watch the clouds,
Slow and lazy drifting by.
In each one lies the hand of God,
Patting, shaping as I would shape a pie.
Thank you, God!

I love to read a book,
Thoughts deep, profound; thoughts gay and light,
For eyes that see and know to look,
For ideas instilled so man must write,
Thank you, God!

Music! to sing with, to think and dream with,
To be fired with zeal with,
A feeling so sublime—each note through me doth
    roll—
This mortal body can barely contain my joyous soul.
Thank you, God!

Birds and beast, sea and fish,
My heart does yearn and ever wish
That some day in your dazzling sight
I can truly
Thank you, God.[9]

—Jo Searcy

A SONG IN PRAISE OF THE LORD OF HEAVEN AND EARTH

O come, let us worship and fall down,
And kneel before the Lord, our Maker.

O sing unto the Lord a new song;
Sing unto the Lord, all the earth.
Sing unto the Lord, bless his name;
Show forth his salvation from day to day.

O worship the Lord in the beauty of holiness;
Fear before Him, all the earth.
Sky so bright,
Blue and light,
Stars how many hast thou?
Countless stars.
Countless times
Shall our God be praised now.

O sing unto the Lord a new song,
For he hath done marvelous things;
Sing unto the Lord with the harp,
With the harp and the voice of a psalm.
With trumpets and sound of cornet
Make a joyful noise before the Lord, the King.
Let the sea roar, and the fulness thereof.
Deepest sea,
Wide and free,
Waves how many hast thou?
Countless waves.
Countless times
Shall our God be praised now.

Make a joyful noise unto the Lord,
All ye lands.

65

Serve the Lord with gladness;
Come before his presence with singing.
Know ye that the Lord, He is God;
It is He that hath made us, and not we ourselves;
We are his people,
And the sheep of his pasture.
Enter into his gates with thanksgiving,
And into his courts with praise.
Be thankful unto Him,
And bless his name.
For the Lord is good, his mercy is everlasting;
And his truth endureth to all generations.

Eternity,
Hours how many hast thou?
Countless hours.
Countless times
Shall our God be praised now.[10]
—HELEN A. DICKINSON

WHY SHOULD I?

Dear God, I cannot pray as others do.
I cannot say long, ponderous phrases
About thy "word," thy "coming," and thy "king-
    dom."
Nor can I always keep eyes closed
And head contritely bowed
While others drone out endlessly
The sermon preached as a prayer to thee.

But God, surely you understand
What I cannot find words to say
When I see you in a tree's perfection
Or feel your strength in purple hills.
Surely you understand me
When I lift to you in thought
Children with hunger burning in their eyes,
Or the aged bent in suffering hopelessness—
The lonely, the anguished, those grief-stricken. . . .

66

How foolish I have been!
Why should I try to pray as others do?
Dear God, I know you hear and understand
Or your love could not come surging through
My heart, and give me strength each day
To try to do thy will
As I serve thee in my humble way.[11]

—HELEN F. COUCH

A SILENT TE DEUM

We thank Thee, Lord,
For all Thy Golden Silences,—
For every Sabbath from the world's turmoil;
For every respite from the stress of life;—
Silence of moorlands rolling to the skies,
Heath-purpled, bracken-clad, aflame with gorse;
Silence of gray tors crouching in the mist;
Silence of deep woods' mystic, cloistered calm;
Silence of wide seas basking in the sun;
Silence of white peaks soaring to the blue;
Silence of dawnings, when, their matins sung,
The little birds do fall asleep again;
For the deep silence of high golden noons;
Silence of gloamings and the setting sun;
Silence of moonlit nights and patterned glades;
Silence of stars, magnificently still,
Yet ever chanting their Creator's skill;
For that high silence of Thine Open House,
Dim-branching roof and lofty-pillared aisle,
Where burdened hearts find rest in Thee awhile;
Silence of friendship, telling more than words;
Silence of hearts, close-knitting heart to heart;
Silence of joys too wonderful for words;
Silence of sorrows, when Thou drawest near;
Silence of soul, wherein we come to Thee,
And find ourselves in Thine Immensity;
For that great silence where Thou dwell'st alone—
—Father, Spirit, Son, in One,
Keeping watch above Thine Own,—

67

Deep unto deep, within us sound sweet chords
Of praise beyond the reach of human words;
In our souls' silence, feeling only Thee,—
We thank Thee, thank Thee,
Thank Thee, Lord! [12]

—JOHN OXENHAM

SKY CREATURES

Thank you, God, for taking care
Of things with wings that use the air
To dip and hover, dart and fly,
Or glide with ease across the sky.
Flower-bright butterflies, and bees,
Songbirds nesting in shade trees,
Shimmering green dragon flies,
And V-shaped flocks of ducks whose cries
Make us want to be in flight
Across the star-bright skies of night.
Thank you, too, for watching over
Hummingbirds who sip at clover,
Weed-seeds hooked to parachutes
And night-moths lured by ripening fruits,
Silver planes which carry men
Away from home and back again,
No matter when they fly, nor where,
None go beyond your loving care.[13]

—MERIAL B. OLSSON

FOR ALL VACATION DAYS

Thy blessing, Lord, on all vacation days!
For weary ones who seek the quiet ways,
Fare forth beyond the thunder of the street,
The marvel of Emmaus Road repeat;
Thy comradeship so graciously bestow
Their hearts shall burn within them as they go.
Grant those who turn for healing to the sea
May find the faith that once by Galilee
Flamed brighter than the glowing fire of coals.

And when thou hast refreshed their hungry souls,
Speak the old words again, beside the deep,
Bid all who love thee, Master, Feed thy sheep!

Be thou with those who bide where mountains rise,
Where yearning earth draws nearest to the skies!
Give them the peace, the courage that they ask:
New strength to face the waiting valley task,
New light to lead through shrouding valley haze!
Thy blessing, Lord, on all vacation days! Amen.[14]

—MOLLY ANDERSON HALEY

GOD OF THE EARTH, THE SKY, THE SEA

God of the earth, the sky, the sea,
Maker of all above, below,
Creation lives and moves in thee,
Thy present life through all doth flow.

Thy love is in the sunshine's glow,
Thy life is in the quick'ning air;
When lightnings flash and storm-winds blow,
There is thy power; thy law is there.

We feel thy calm at ev'ning's hour,
Thy grandeur in the march of night;
And, when the morning breaks in power,
We hear thy word, "Let there be light."

We give thee thanks, thy name we sing,
Almighty Father, heav'nly King. Amen.

—SAMUEL LONGFELLOW

GOOD COMPANY

Today I have grown taller from walking with the trees,
  The seven-sister-poplars who go softly in a line;
And I think my heart is whiter for its parley with a star
  That trembled out at nightfall and hung above the pine.

The call-note of a redbird from the cedars in the dusk
  Woke his happy mate within me to answer free and fine;

And a sudden angel beckoned from a column of blue smoke;
Lord, who am I that they should stoop—these holy folk of
thine? [15]

—KARLE WILSON BAKER

UP! UP! MY FRIEND

Up! up! my Friend, and quit your books;
Or surely you'll grow double:
Up! up! my Friend, and clear your looks;
Why all this toil and trouble?

. . . .

And hark! how blithe the throstle sings!
He, too, is no mean preacher:
Come forth into the light of things,
Let Nature be your teacher.

She has a world of ready wealth,
Our minds and hearts to bless—
Spontaneous wisdom breathed by health,
Truth breathed by cheerfulness.

. . . .

Enough of Science and of Art;
Close up those barren leaves;
Come forth, and bring with you a heart
That watches and receives.

—WILLIAM WORDSWORTH

GOD'S BOUNDLESS GRACE

There's not a bird with a lonely nest,
In pathless wood or mountain crest,
Nor meaner thing, which does not share,
O God, in thy paternal care.
Each barren crag, each desert rude,
Holds thee within its solitude;
And thou dost bless the wand'rer there,
Who makes his solitary prayer.

In busy mart and crowded street,
No less than in the still retreat,

70

Thou, Lord, art near, our souls to bless
With all a parent's tenderness.

And we, where'er our lot is cast,
While life, and tho't, and feeling last,
Thro' all the years, in every place,
Will bless thee for thy boundless grace.
—BAPTIST W. NOEL

LIKE A TREE AGAINST THE SKY

Let me stand upon the hilltop
Like a tree against the sky.
Let me mark the way for travelers—
Rooted deep, and pointing high.

Here surveyors chart their courses,
Climbers, lost, regain the trail,
Kneel, with new and clearer vision
Of the long-sought Holy Grail.

Keep me pure O Breath of God,
Worthy of this crest so high!
Help me stand upon the hilltop
Like a tree against the sky.[16]
—J. LESTER HANKINS

I WILL BRING PEACE

I will bring peace and love and silence.
There is no way to bring peace
unless I can be that peace.
There is no way to give love
unless I can be that love.
There is no way to bring silence
unless I can be that silence.[17]
—LOIS LENSKI

GOING TO SCHOOL TO GOD

I like to go to school to God!
I hear such strange revealing things;

71

He talks to me where rivers run
And where a skylark soars and sings.

He teaches me his love and care
Through every tree and blade of grass
Here on the hill, where I may sit
And listen while the wild winds pass.

He writes with glaciers on the rocks
And with the stars that blaze on high;
With fossil shells and ferns that fall
And leave their imprint as they die.

His books are beds of slate and coal;
His manuscripts sequoia trees;
While earthquakes punctuate the tale
And turn the pages of the seas.

His blackboard is a canyon wall
Whereon he writes of ages past.
In even lines the strata tell
Of things that shall forever last.

He writes with rivers, and they carve
The crevices he leaves, to tell
The story of his living love
In temple, tower and pinnacle.

I like to go to school to God!
Because it always seems to me
He talks in every breeze that blows;
Through every bud and bird and tree.[18]
—WILLIAM L. STIDGER

LOVELY IS THY UNIVERSE

How infinitely tall are Thy skies, O Lord!
The wings of men's minds grow weary; still rise
In vastness beyond them Thy skies.

The night winds blow and the stars wheel
In the enormity of Thy space;

[18] Copyright 1934 by William L. Stidger in "I Saw God Wash The World."
Used by permission.

The great sun sets and the shadows steal
Across the smallness of the earth's face.
Night grows and the darkness around us.
Yet we are not afraid while the earth runs
Its course, for we know Thou hast found us
And comforted us and called us Thy sons.

Lovely is Thy universe, O Lord;
Teach us to be unafraid of the vastness that lies
About us, and above us as in Thy skies.[19]
—KEITH THOMAS

WE DO NOT SEE THE WIND
We do not see the wind,
    We only hear it sigh;
It makes the grasses bend
    Whenever it goes by.
We do not see God's love,
    But in our hearts we know
He watches over us
    Wherever we may go.[20]
—ELIZABETH C. TAYLOR

RAIN IN SUMMER
It has been dry, dry, dry.
The berries hang thin and shriveling on the canes,
The farmers watch their pastures, brown, the grass
No higher than a month ago,
The rust deeper and more deep in the shrunken earth.

Now I lift my head to a long absent sound.
I lift unbelieving eyes to the apple tree
Outside my window.
There is a whisper of rain among the parched branches,
The leaves move lightly with the growing weight
Of water upon them!

Thanks be to God for rain!
Let the earth lift up its head and rejoice!
Let every living thing give thanks and sing! [21]
—GRACE W. McGAVRAN

TWENTY-THIRD PSALM

(As interpreted by the Crow Indians)

The Great Maker up in heaven is. I belong to Him.
When I am with Him, I want not.
He throws out to me a rope and the name of the rope is love.
He draws me gently to a place where the grass is green and the
water is not dangerous. I eat and lie down satisfied.
Some days I get very weak and fall down, but afterwards
He lifts me up again and leads me into a good trail.

He always keeps His word, it may be a long time, a long, long
time,
I do not know when.
He draws me into a deep place between mountains.
It is dark there, but I will go back not and I will be afraid not
For it is there that the great Shepherd Chief will meet me
And then the hunger I felt in my heart will satisfied be.
Sometimes He makes the love rope into a whip, but afterwards
He gives me a good stick to lean on.

For me He sets a table with every thing good to eat on it.
He puts His hand on my head and all the tired is gone.
He fills my cup till it runs over.
What I tell you is straight, I speak with one tongue, I talk two
ways not.
All along the trail ahead I will have good things,
And afterwards I will move to the big tepee
And live with the great Shepherd Chief.

GOD'S DRUM

The circle of the Earth is the head of a great drum;
With the day, it moves upward—booming;
With the night, it moves downward—booming;
The day and the night are its song.

I am very small, as I dance upon the drum-head;
I am like a particle of dust, as I dance upon the
drum-head;
Above me in the sky is the shining ball of the drum-
stick.

74

I dance upward with the day;
I dance downward with the night;
Someday I shall dance afar into space like a particle of
    dust.[22]

                 —HARTLEY BURR ALEXANDER

THE SACRAMENT OF FIRE

Kneel always when you light a fire!
Kneel reverently, and thankful be
For God's unfailing charity,
And on the ascending flame inspire
A little prayer, that shall upbear
The incense of your thankfulness
For this sweet grace
Of warmth and light!
For here again is sacrifice
For your delight.[23]

                 —JOHN OXENHAM

THE FIREMAKER'S DESIRE

As fuel is brought to the fire
So I purpose to bring
My strength,
My ambition,
My heart's desire,
My joy and
My sorrow
To the fire of humankind:
For I will tend
As my fathers have tended
And my fathers' fathers
Since time began
That fire which is called
The love of man for man,
The love of man for God.[24]

                 —JOHN COLLIER

THE PASSING OF DAY

Day has such a lovely way of going;
The moon and the stars wait quietly, and then

75

They steal across the silent sky. The glen
Is Calm—does it have a way of knowing,
Of feeling, that He above is sowing
On the earth seeds that govern fearing men?

Off in the lonely shadows pipes a wren,
Joyous song that sets the heart a-glowing.
Such sounds and sights of wonder stir the heart;
Often I search my mind for just one word
To help describe these wonders of God's art.

The trees a vigil through the night will keep;
The stir of leaves may now and then be heard
But once again, the world is lost in sleep.[25]
—RUTH SCHUCHART

STARS

Alone in the night
On a dark hill
With pines around me
Spicy and still,

And a heaven full of stars
Over my head,
White and topaz
And misty red;

Myriads with beating
Hearts of fire
That aeons
Cannot vex or tire;

Up the dome of heaven
Like a great hill,
I watch them marching
Stately and still,

And I know that I
Am honored to be
Witness
Of so much majesty.[26]
—SARA TEASDALE

THE VESPER HOUR

The deepening shadows in the east
  Slowly change from blue to gray.
The golden sun, low in the west,
  Is ready now to ease the day.

All nature seems to pause awhile
  In silence before an Unseen Power,
Suggesting to the heart of man
  To worship at the Vesper Hour.
                    —AUTHOR UNKNOWN

I WALK THE SILENT NIGHT

When problems seem too big for me
I seek the heaven's majesty.
I walk the silent starlit night
And watch the vault of ancient light
Begun how many years ago?
I am not sure, but this I know:
These stars have shone on other's tears
And watched while others fought their fears.
Stars relight faith, and so shall I,
Made small, yet tall, by God's great sky.[27]
                    —NANCY GIBBONS ZOOK

HE GIVETH HIS BELOVED SLEEP
(Psalm 127)
Around green earth, the heavier wings
Of night are curved; the dusk is deep;
No bird from flowering orchard sings;
Across the wall vague shadows creep.
But there are steadfast stars that keep
Vigil; and through the dark hours run
Words softly sweet as benison:
He giveth His beloved sleep! [28]
                    —KATHERINE EDELMAN

EVENTIDE

The Sun is gone: Those glorious chariot wheels
Have sunk their broadening spokes of flame, and left

77

Their rosy films wimpled across the West,
Whose last faint tints melt slowly in the blue
As the last trembling cadence of a song
Fades into silence sweeter than all sound.

Now the first stars begin to tremble forth
Like the first instruments of an orchestra
Touched softly, one by one.—There in the East
Kindles the glory of moonrise: how its waves
Break in a surf of silver on the clouds!—
White, motionless clouds, like soft and snowy wings
Which the great Earth spreads sailing round the Sun.[29]
—EDWARD ROWLAND SILL

A BENEDICTION

May the silence of the hills,
The joy of the winds,
The peace of the fields,
The music of the birds,
The fire of the sun,
The strength of the trees,
And the faith of youth
In all of which is God
Be in your hearts.
—AUTHOR UNKNOWN

Meditations

AN OASIS FOR THE SOUL

Be alert to enter unexpected openings for the soul, paths that
lead into quietness and communion with God. Always there is
some door opening into an oasis if we will but use our eyes.

There are the few minutes we must spend waiting for a bus
on some crowded corner. Instead of chafing or sitting numb like
a potato, we can invite God's presence and even there in those
moments walk with him into green pastures, beside still waters.

There is that moment at night when we pull down the garage
door and stand under the stars, or walk toward the house when
the last chores are done. Instead of trudging into our home like
a drone, we can look up and let the winds of heaven sweep pettiness out of our soul.

There is opportunity to attend a retreat with fellow Christians. We can say, "Oh, I'm too busy. It's inconvenient. This camping is for the birds. Give me my favorite television programs, my soft bed, breakfast the next morning just the way I like it." Or, we can go and find a deepening with our fellows and with God that nurtures and strengthens the inner man.

There is the blessing received from long-tired and proven religious disciplines: a reflective and devout reading of the Bible, regular church attendance, family worship, daily private devotions, the observance of one day each week as a Holy Day, reserved for attendance upon God and nurture of the soul. These practices, long revered, each of itself is an oasis for the soul in the sun-blistered journey of life.[30]

—EVERETT W. PALMER

AT BREAK OF DAY

What do we today, who no longer have any fear or awe of night, know of the great joy that our forefathers and the early Christians felt every morning at the return of light? If we were to learn again something of the praise and adoration that is due the triune God at break of day, God the Father and Creator, who has preserved our life through the dark night and wakened us to a new day, God the Son and Saviour, who conquered death and hell for us and dwells in our midst as Victor, God the Holy Spirit, who pours the bright gleam of God's Word into our hearts at the dawn of day, driving away all darkness and sin and teaching us to pray aright—then we would also begin to sense something of the joy that comes when night is past and brethren who dwell together in unity come together early in the morning for common praise of their God, common hearing of the Word, and common prayer. Morning does not belong to the individual, it belongs to the Church of the triune God, to the Christian family, to the brotherhood. Innumerable are the ancient hymns that call the congregation to common praise of God in the early morning. So the Bohemian Brethren sing at break of day:

The day does now dark night dispel;
Dear Christians, wake and rouse you well,
Give glory to God our Lord.

79

. . . .

Once more the daylight shines abroad,
O brethren let us praise the Lord,
Whose grace and mercy thus have kept
The nightly watch while we have slept.

We offer up ourselves to Thee,
That heart and word and deed may be
In all things guided by Thy mind,
And in Thine eyes acceptance find.[31]

—DIETRICH BONHOEFFER

THE DEPENDABILITY OF GOD'S PROMISES AND HIS LAWS

In the beginning, the only records that were kept, were kept by God. He wrote his history in rock and soil, with coal and oil, with skeletons and fossils, and later—much later—in the mind of man.

God promised man that, "While the earth remains, seedtime and harvest, cold and heat, summer and winter, day and night, shall not cease" (Gen. 8:22).

By observing that day always follows night; that spring always follows winter; that the tide always flows in after it has reached its ebb; that the North Star always indicates north; that anything that is thrown into the air will return to the earth, we are reminded that there are laws of the universe which God will not, and man cannot, change.

God worked out a perfect balance in nature. These laws man can and has upset on many counts.

There are men who put too many head of cattle to an acre of land. The grass is eaten too low; the rains come and wash the soil away, because there is no grass to protect it. Gullies carry the precious topsoil away, so grass will no longer grow; and the winds blow and finish the job. Not only the livestock must leave, but the rabbits, mice, hawks, eagles, fox, deer and others—and also man—because man out of his foolishness, and perhaps greed, upset the balance in nature.

There are men who clear the forests from their hillsides in order to put the plow into the rich earth. The rains come and wash the soil away because there are no leaves to break the fall of the rain drops; and the roots that once held the soil in place are gone. So the forest, that would have brought some income if selective cutting and planting had been practiced, is gone; rapidly the topsoil is washed away; all wildlife must leave—and also man—because man upset the balance in nature.

The grass and trees that once held the soil made it possible for the soil to hold the water. Now the water flows to the sea, and the land is becoming exceedingly thirsty—and so may man.

It is beyond our ability to imagine how even God could plan so well in every detail. The world of man might become very selfish, and come near to bringing about its own destruction, but eventually man will learn—because God gave him a mind and a soul—that he cannot survive without love for one another and God. When we learn this, we will learn how to "tend the garden." We will love the land and the creatures of the land, the sky and the sea—and one another. We will do all we can to preserve the balance in nature, to cooperate with God's laws.[32]

—LYNN AND CAMPBELL LOUGHMILLER

THE STRENGTH OF THE TREE

The tree is tremendously alive.

How implacable it stands. How marvelous is its growth. How deep the great roots burrow into the soil, there carefully to select the elements which shall nourish it and bring the whole tree to a splendid assertion of life. The great tree draws strength from the Lord God, from his rich soil and clear air and warm sunlight. In quiet and serene wisdom it grows strong by taking from God the nourishment which he has provided.

The psalmist found the tree to be a parable of the possibilities of human life (Ps. 1). Meditate upon these thoughts: Do not I need to live quietly and serenely like the tree . . . to put my hands into the good earth . . . to look up at the clear sky . . . to live by the law of God and to meditate upon it day and night? . . . Then may I achieve the natural strength and beauty and usefulness of the tree. Meditate upon those experiences which give you strength and beauty, and those experiences which sap your vital energy. . . .

Now pray . . . finishing your prayer in these words:

Almighty God, in whom I live and move and have my being, grant me the wisdom to depend more fully upon thee. Prompt me to put forth my hands to take the nourishment which thou hast provided for my welfare. Help me carefully to select, among all the varied experiences which are open to me, only those that are in harmony with thy will. Help me to become as certain in this wisdom as the tree. So shall I grow and prosper like the tree as I rest my life upon thy never-failing strength. Amen.[33]

—C. L. SEIDENSPINNER

THINK OF THE WIND

Think of the wind, fresh and strong, carrying the leaves so lightly. We cannot see the wind; yet it touches us.

Jesus said:

"The wind blows where it wills; you hear its voice; but you cannot tell from whence it comes or where it goes. So is God's spirit."

God is Spirit.

We cannot see the wind; but the wind is here.

We cannot see God.

But He is here.[34]

—N. SIMPSON AND L. E. COX

MAKE A JOYFUL NOISE

Make a joyful noise to the Lord . . . serve the Lord with gladness, come into his presence with singing . . . give thanks to him . . . for the Lord is good. (Ps. 100:1, 2, 4b, 5a.)

Yes, the Lord is good! He has given me so many wonderful things to be thankful for, that I often find it hard to comprehend how wonderful He really is!

He has given me: the Church . . . a Christian home and friends . . . an opportunity for education . . . food and shelter; health and strength . . . my talents and opportunities for service . . . the beauty of His world and nature, and the senses with which to appreciate this beauty . . . forgiveness for my sins and an opportunity to become a better Christian . . . and best of all, He has given me His love.

I wonder if God ever gets tired of my selfish complaining prayers and wishes I would "make a joyful noise" unto Him, and put more praises and thanksgiving into my prayers. Today I will live a joyful, thankful life, thanking God for my many blessings and striving to "serve the Lord with gladness!" [35]

—RUTH ANN TENNANT

LOOKING FOR GOD IN LITTLE THINGS

Look for God in little things—

—in the mottled reflections of a rain-glazed street; in a tree's stark lines, cutting into a winter sky; in the smooth warmth of a baby's skin; which express a beauty of divine perfection.

—in the simple childhood Bible verses, which, long forgotten, suddenly grip us with new dimensions of God's truth.

—in the little words of advice and assurance from friends genuinely interested in lives other than their own, whose love comes from a greater love.

—in the seldom listened-to hymns and rushed-through responses of a worship service, which may have, hidden in their intricate gothic phrases, a balm of strength for battered and confused minds.

—and in the quiet obscure fleeting moments when suddenly the boundaries of human experience are transcended, and we find ourselves strangely aware that we are in the presence of the One who said "Be still, and know that I am God."

For it is in the little things in life that we know God—in simple beauty, the quiet words, the forgotten kindnesses. And we must first look for God in the little everyday things, before we can find Him in the fullness of life.[36]

—MARK JUERGENSMEYER

THE STRONGEST WOOD

I remember going up a mountain path one day when I met a mountaineer with an ax in his hand. We were so high that there were few large trees above us; only rocks, a sparse growth of craggy and gnarled bushes and stunted trees, and the immensity of the blue sky above. As we were going the same way I walked with him, and eventually asked him what he was going to cut.

"I need a piece of timber to fix my timber wagon," he said. "You know that does the heaviest and most rackingest kind of work, and the tree that grows on the top, where the storms hit it hardest, is the tree that has the toughest wood. If ever you want to get a piece of timber to stand all the jolts and strains, cut it from a place where all its life it has been obliged to stand the same kind of roughness. A tree that ain't shielded," he said, "is the last one to

83

fall. It has stood so much in the way of storms, little by little, that when the big gale comes, it can weather it." [37]

—ARCHIBALD RUTLEDGE

THE ELEVENTH COMMANDMENT

Thou shalt inherit the holy earth as a faithful steward, conserving its resources and productivity from generation to generation. Thou shalt safeguard thy fields from soil erosion, thy living waters from drying up, thy forests from desolation, and protect thy hills from overgrazing by the herds, that thy descendants may have abundance forever. If any shall fail in this stewardship of the land thy fruitful fields shall become sterile stony ground and wasting gullies, and thy descendants shall decrease and live in poverty or perish from off the face of the earth. [38]

—WALTER LOWDERMILK

PRAISE GOD FOR PLANTS AROUND YOUR FEET

And God said, Let the earth put forth grass, the herbs yielding seed (Gen. 1:11a).

Look at the plants around your feet. There is the grass, soft and green. It makes a carpet for the foot of the man who walks carefully over it. It shelters thousands of tiny living things, bugs and crickets. It acts as a reservoir to hold the water falling from the sky. The roots of the grass hold the soil in place, and yet keep it loose and mellow. Grass, is food for the deer, the sheep, and the cattle, who, in turn, provide food for man. Quietly thank God for grass.

Perhaps you see a beautiful mushroom. It is like a fairy's umbrella. Why is it white, while some other mushroom is red, or another orange? Never mind, just now, it is enough that God had made it that way in all its beauty. Let the wonder of it fill your heart. Praise God for the beauty of a lowly mushroom!

Over there is a beautiful vine. Its five leaves spell friendliness. Its graceful beauty enchants you. Nearby is the Virginia creeper covering the earth with its creeping beauty. Thank God for vines!

But wait, yonder is a vine with three leaves. That is poison ivy! It is not friendly; it poisons those who touch it, and others who only come near. Why did God make it so? We do not know—perhaps to keep man from pulling it, and thus leaving the soil bare

84

for the rains to wash away. Perhaps we should thank God for the poison ivy, too.

Have you ever come upon a wild strawberry patch when the berries were ripe? How the small red berries beckoned to you as they peeped out from under the green leaves! How delicious they were as you popped them into your hungry mouth! As the summer progresses, wild raspberries, blackberries, huckleberries, even the sour gooseberries add their delicious flavors to our world of taste and beauty. In the autumn the wild grape and the chokecherry invite you to stop and gather their fruits so they may come forth in the winter as delicious jams and jellies on your tables. Praise God for fruit-yielding plants about your feet!

And the flowers around you! How dull life would be without their beauty! There are the violet and the laurel in the springtime; the liverwort, the wild rose, the sunflower in the summer. And what wonders man has wrought with flowers in his garden! Think of the giant dahlias, the gladioli, the myrtle, and the roses. Quietly, but joyously, thank God for flowers.

The wild flowers spoke their message to Jesus, too. He interpreted this message to men when he said:

"Consider the lilies, how they grow; they neither toil nor spin; yet I tell you, even Solomon in all his glory was not arrayed like one of these. But if God so clothes the grass which is alive in the field today and tomorrow is thrown into the oven, how much more will he clothe you, O men of little faith?" (Luke 12:27, 28 k.j.v.)

The plants around your feet speak to you of God. They say, "If God cares for me, clothes me with beauty, and makes me useful to those around me, how much more he must care for you! You can walk and run and talk and laugh and love. So surely God loves and cares for you. After God created me he put me in your care. I am in your hands. You can protect me and use me for the best good of yourself and others or you can trample me under foot, destroy me, or use me to harm other men. God has put me in your care. So I speak to you of God." [39]

—MAE SIGLER

MEET YOURSELF IN QUIETNESS

Invite your soul to quietness. Each of us needs a time and place where we shut the door against the world's loud roar and bid all our striving cease.

Here we meet ourselves face to face. We look upon what we are and what we are meant to be. Here we come to know ourselves as we are.

We may conceal our real self from others, hiding under many a mask, fleeing behind walls of pretense. But when we enter into stillness the masquerade ends, each trusted covert fails.

We may avoid confrontation with our real self by rushing madly about from this to that to something else, keeping too busy to think, losing ourselves in the service of trivia, or pursuit of status and security; slipping down the back alleys of illicit sex, or taking refuge in a bottle. But in quietness we cannot escape what we are. We look ourselves full in the face.

In our quietness our soul stands inspection. Everything that is the property of our soul is summoned for judgment: every motive, goal, hope, and ambition. Everything that is potential within us knocks at the door of our awareness: every dark depth and shining height, all that is "the grandeur and misery of man."

Nothing good could begin for the Prodigal Son, our Lord reminds us, until "he came to himself." That observation, we have reason to believe, includes us.

There is given in quietness that stark encounter, that moment of truth by which we come to ourselves.[40]

—EVERETT W. PALMER

Some Thoughts on Silence

The real silence . . . surrounds us on every side; in it is the source of the undercurrents of our life. . . . Some there are that have no silence . . . that still the silence around them . . . these are the only creatures that pass through life unperceived.

—MAETERLINCK

They that pluck the feathers from the wings of silence are ungodly.

—MUKERJI

86

As gold and silver are weighed in pure water, so does the soul test its weight in silence, and the words that we let fall have no meaning apart from the silence that wraps them round.

—MAETERLINCK

Silence is the element in which great things fashion themselves together, that at length they may emerge, full-formed and majestic, into the daylight of life, which they are henceforth to rule.

—CARLYLE

Audio-Visuals

In a camp setting, audio-visuals as we usually think of them—films and filmstrips—will be used sparingly in worship. The more unusual "visuals" will take their place: the snake skin found along a path, a freshly dropped blue bird's feather, a passion-flower in bloom. But there are worship occasions when a good film or filmstrip will enrich the campers' experience. For those times, the following titles are possibilities.

The High Room. For young people, this twenty-minute animated film, in color, will prove to be a source of inspiration. The story tells of "Cotton," who becomes a member of a youth prayer fellowship. The story is told reverently, but with realistic language and situation; campers will respond to its message if it is seen in a well-planned worship context. A guide is available and may be ordered ahead of time. Available from denominational film libraries and from Cathedral Films, 2921 West Alameda Avenue, Burbank, California.

This Sustaining Bread. A group of campers accustomed to the techniques of modern art will find this resource a rich worship experience. The entire filmstrip and its accompanying record are designed to be used as a worship service. Bread is used here as the symbol of brotherhood and of the body of Christ. Through blank verse readings, orchestra background, and unison readings from the screen, this material catches its viewers up to a high devotional level. It will prove difficult if not chaotic to the group that is not used to a rather sophisticated and modern artistic expression, however, and must by all means be previewed by the leader planning to use it. Available from denominational film libraries and from Friendship Press, 475 Riverside Drive, New York 27, New York.

Each With His Own Brush. This color filmstrip offers a breathtaking portrayal of the life of Christ as seen in the paintings of Chinese, Japanese and Indian artists. The recording presents two possible uses of the filmstrip, one for art appreciation, the other for worship. Campers will respond readily to the beauty of the pictures and the reverent narration of the life of Christ. Available from denominational film libraries and Friendship Press, 475 Riverside Drive, New York 27, New York.

CHAPTER 4

Out-of-doors

The out-of-doors often becomes the setting for group worship. You will sometimes want to plan services of a somewhat formal nature for use out-of-doors—an evening meeting beside a stream, or lake, or seashore—a sunrise service, or a morning service in the "green cathedral" of the woods. On other occasions, say after a picnic, or swimming party, or cook-out, you may want to pause only briefly for a moment of worship—just long enough to sing a hymn, or read a poem, or pray a prayer.

You will find here suggestions for several types of outdoor worship, both the informal worship moments and the more formal service of worship. It will be necessary, of course, to adapt any of the suggestions given here to the needs of your particular group. You will find some additional resources which may be helpful in Chapter III, Camping.

SOME WORSHIP SUGGESTIONS

When You Worship Among the Trees[1]

Often the group will be worshiping out-of-doors among the trees, or in the shade of one great tree. Here is a service of worship which may be adapted to your needs on such occasions.

The group is seated in a circle. Readers and speakers do not rise, but speak informally from various points in the circle where they are seated. Words of the hymn may be duplicated in advance and hymns started by two or three persons in the circle.

SCRIPTURE SENTENCES:

The earth is the Lord's and the fulness thereof,
the world and those who dwell therein:

89

for he has founded it upon the seas,
and established it upon the rivers.

· · · · · · · · ·

—Ps. 24:1-2 R.S.V.

Sing to the Lord, bless his name;
tell of his salvation from day to day.
Declare his glory among the nations,
his marvelous works among all the peoples!
For great is the Lord, and greatly to be praised.
—Ps. 96:2-4 R.S.V.

HYMN: "For the Beauty of the Earth."

SCRIPTURE READING:
Blessed is the man
who walks not in the counsel of the wicked,
nor stands in the way of sinners
nor sits in the seat of scoffers;
but his delight is in the law of the Lord,
and on his law he meditates day and night.
He is like a tree planted by streams of water . . .
—Ps. 1:1-3 R.S.V.

LEADER:
"Like a tree planted by streams of water. . . ." Trees have always been an important part of man's folklore and his religion. From ancient times poets have written about trees; storytellers have woven story magic about the trees; and the artist has painted the image of trees on untold numbers of canvasses. Through the ages people have loved the trees and appreciated them for many reasons. Seated here today amidst the trees, let us think of some of these reasons.

FIRST SPEAKER (seated in group, speaking informally):
People in the desert and the open plains love the trees because of the shade they give. Trees mean rest and coolness, relief from the heat and glare of the sun. I like to compare the shade of a tree to a brief period of prayer. It means a quiet withdrawal from the

90

heated struggles going on around us, a place from which we can go forth, comforted, strengthened, and refreshed.

(*Pause*)

SECOND SPEAKER:

Trees seem important to me because they supply so many of our daily needs—our houses, furniture, many of our foods, drugs, paper, perfumes, dyes, rubber—so many useful things. If we could serve our world as well as the tree serves us, we would certainly be living in accord with God's plan.

(*Pause*)

THIRD SPEAKER:

The great strength of trees has always impressed me. They sway and bend beneath the lashing of the winds, but when the storm is over they still stand—a symbol of courage and strength. Their strength comes from roots far underground. Some people are like trees, strong, deep-rooted in a faith that feeds and gives strength and meaning to the visible part of their living.

(*Pause*)

LEADER:

To me, one of the most interesting things about trees is that they continue growing for so many years. In our spiritual growth many of us are not at all like trees. We stop growing too soon. If we, as Christians, will follow the example of the tree and let ourselves grow as long as we live, we too may become like a tree—tall, beautiful, useful in service, a source of strength to all who need and depend upon us. We shall be like trees—planted by streams of water.

HYMN: "This Is My Father's World."

PRAYER:

"Create in me a clean heart, O God, and renew a right spirit within me." Help me to grow tall and straight like the trees about me. Raise my eyes to the heavens and keep me seeking, growing. For I would be like a tree—planted by streams of water—deep-rooted, standing firm against whatever difficulties the days ahead my bring. In Jesus' name. Amen.

Worship Out-of-doors in the Evening

Sometimes the group may be seated informally in a lovely outdoor setting. Perhaps this is a hillside overlooking a valley, or it may be a cliffside where you can look across a deep gorge to other cliffs or to a beautiful waterfall. Again, it may be a valley where you can look up at the mountains, or out in the open where the mountains or hills can be seen in the distance. Whatever the setting, yours can be a beautiful evening service of worship, but you must make adequate preparation so that the service moves easily and with seeming spontaneity. In the service given here, speakers are seated in the group; they do not rise to speak. Hymns are sung without accompaniment either by the entire group or by a few persons selected in advance.

HYMN (first stanza):

> Now the day is over,
> Night is drawing nigh,
> Shadows of the evening
> Steal across the sky.[2]

FIRST SPEAKER:

The day is nearly over . . . nighttime will soon cover the earth. . . .

READER:

> The heavens are telling the glory of God;
> and the firmament proclaims his handiwork.
> Day to day pours forth speech,
> and night to night declares knowledge.
> —Ps. 19:1-2 R.S.V.

SECOND SPEAKER:

In these moments now—between the bright gold of the day and the purple darkness of night—let us seek God's presence.

READER:

> O come, let us worship and bow down,
> let us kneel before the Lord, our Maker!
> For he is our God,

92

and we are the people of his pasture,
and the sheep of his hand.
—Ps. 95:6-7 R.S.V.

PRAYER:

O God of peace, who hast taught us that in returning and rest
we shall be saved; in quietness and confidence shall be our strength;
lift us we pray thee by the might of thy Spirit, into thy presence,
where we may be still, and know that thou art God. Amen.[3]

FIRST SPEAKER:

In the quiet of this hour . . . in the knowledge of his presence,
we can look back upon the day that is slowly passing here before
our eyes. We can look back and ask his forgiveness for our mistakes and failures. (*Pause.*) We can look back and rejoice in our
successes, our friendships, our dreams. (*Pause.*) And we can give
thanks for all that this day has meant in so many ways to each of
us. (*Pause.*)

HYMN: "Day Is Dying in the West."

FIRST SPEAKER:

Yes, night is drawing nigh. Soon the sky will darken. One by one
we will see the stars come out—we can identify some of them. We
can point out the constellations and remark about the Milky Way
. . . once again the wonder of it all will flood over us. . . .

READER:

Praise the Lord!
Praise the Lord from the heavens,
    praise him in the heights!
Praise him, all his angels,
    praise him, all his host!

Praise him, sun and moon,
    praise him, all you shining stars!
Praise him, you highest heavens,
    and you waters above the heavens!

Let them praise the name of the Lord!
For he commanded and they were created.

93

And he established them for ever and ever;
he fixed their bounds which cannot be passed.

. . . .

Mountains and all hills,
fruit trees and all cedars!
Beasts and all cattle,
creeping things and flying birds!

Kings of the earth and all peoples,
princes and rulers of the earth!
Young men and maidens together,
old men and children!

Let them praise the name of the Lord,
for his name alone is exalted;
his glory is above earth and heaven.
Praise the Lord!

—Ps. 148 r.s.v.

MOMENTS OF SILENCE

SECOND SPEAKER:
The day is gone . . . the night comes once again. . . .

May the peace— The peace of still waters,
Of mighty mountain tops,
Of green valleys,
And the love— Of a little child,
Of a mother,
Of a good shepherd,
Of God the Father
Guide us and keep us safe in the way of truth. Amen.[4]

Worship Moments at a Picnic or Outing

Often the picnic or all-day outing calls for moments of worship.
You've had a fine day in the out-of-doors, plenty of good food, lots
of fun and laughter. Now you're ready to go home. Somehow it
seems that the day is not quite complete without a few quiet moments—a time of thanksgiving for everything good.

94

SCRIPTURE SENTENCES:

The Lord reigns; let the earth rejoice . . .
The heavens proclaim his righteousness;
and the peoples behold his glory;
—Ps. 97:1, 6 R.S.V.

I lift up my eyes to the hills

. . . .

My help comes from the Lord,
who made heaven and earth.
—Ps. 121:1, 2 R.S.V.

PRAYER HYMN: "God Who Touchest Earth With Beauty." (Sung prayerfully or read as a prayer).

Worship at an Outdoor Breakfast

HYMN: "When Morning Gilds the Skies."

POEM:

Look to this day!
For it is life, the very life of life.

In its brief course lie all the verities
and realities of your existence:
The bliss of growth;
The glory of action;
The splendor of beauty;
For yesterday is already a dream and
tomorrow is only a vision;

But today, well lived, makes every
yesterday
A dream of happiness, and every
tomorrow a vision of hope.
Look well, therefore, to this day!
Such is the salutation of the dawn.[5]

HYMN: "Awake, Awake to Love and Work."

95

PRAYER:

For the healing of the dark, the refreshment of sleep, and the unfailing round of day and night, I bring thee, O God, this my morning prayer of petition and of praise.

Let me leave the evil of my heart behind me with the days that are forever gone.

Cover my sin and weakness with the dark night of thy forgiving forgetfulness.

Stir thou my heart with the eternal hope of a new day.

Broaden my vision with the widening sweep of sunlight across the earth.

Deepen the purposes of my life because I am a day older in the learning of thy will.

Thus enlarge and empower me for the holy summons of this new day.

In the name of One who before the day had dawned sought thy face. Amen.[6]

Worship Moments for Nighttime Hikes or Stargazing Groups

SCRIPTURE READING:

(May be read by flashlight, or better, spoken when the moment is right by someone who has memorized the passage and is sensitive to the group's mood.)

When I look at thy heavens, the work of thy fingers,
 the moon and the stars which thou hast established;
what is man that thou art mindful of him,
 and the son of man that thou dost care for him?
 (Moments of silence)

. . . .

O Lord, our Lord,
 how majestic is thy name in all the earth!
 —Ps. 8:3-4, 9 R.S.V.

POEM:

I looked long at a star,
Deeply, and long,
And the star looked at me,

Till suddenly I looked beyond the star
For one precarious instant, and caught a glimpse
Of God.

And now I go with astonishment in my heart
And sorrow,
Knowing that the earth is too narrow
And the sky too low,
And the souls of men too small
To contain such vastness
Of love.
God,
Help us grow.[7]

HYMN (*started by one or two in the group who sing well and know the words from memory*): "Fairest Lord Jesus, Ruler of All Nature."

SOME ADDITIONAL RESOURCES

Scripture Selections

CONSIDER THE LILIES

No servant can be slave to two masters; for either he will hate the first and love the second, or he will be devoted to the first and think nothing of the second. You cannot serve God and Money.

'Therefore I bid you put away anxious thoughts about food and drink to keep you alive, and clothes to cover your body. Surely life is more than food, the body more than clothes. Look at the birds of the air; they do not sow and reap and store in barns, yet your heavenly Father feeds them. You are worth more than the birds! Is there a man of you who by anxious thought can add a foot to his height? And why be anxious about clothes? Consider how the lilies grow in the fields; they do not work, they do not spin, and yet, I tell you, even Solomon in all his splendour was not attired like one of these. But if that is how God clothes the grass in the fields, which is there today, and tomorrow is thrown on the stove, will he not all the more clothe you? How little faith you have! No, do not ask anxiously, "What are we to eat? What are we to

97

drink? What shall we wear?" All these are things for the heathen to run after, not for you, because your heavenly Father knows that you need them all. Set your mind on God's kingdom and his justice before everything else, and all the rest will come to you as well. So do not be anxious about tomorrow; tomorrow will look after itself. Each day has troubles enough of its own.

(Matt. 6:24-34 NEW ENGLISH BIBLE)

LIKE A SEED

Then he said:

"The kingdom of God is like a man scattering seed on the ground and then going to bed each night and getting up every morning, while the seed sprouts and grows up, though he has no idea how it happens. The earth produces a crop without any help from anyone: first a blade, then the ear of corn, then the full-grown grain in the ear. And as soon as the crop is ready, he sends his reapers in without delay, for the harvest-time has come."

Then he continued:

"What can we say the kingdom of God is like? How shall we put it in a parable: It is like a tiny grain of mustard seed which, when it is sown, is smaller than any seed that is ever sown. But after it is sown in the earth, it grows up and becomes bigger than any other plant. It shoots out great branches so that birds can come and nest in its shelter."

So he taught him his message with many parables such as their minds would take in. He did not speak to them at all without using parables, although in private he explained everything to his disciples.

(Mark 4:26-35 PHILLIPS)

OTHER APPROPRIATE SCRIPTURE REFERENCES

Is. 40:28	God, Our Creator
Ps. 8	Praise for God's Wonders
Ps. 19	All the World Is His
Ps. 136:1-9, 26	Give Thanks to God
Ps. 95:1-7a	A Call to Worship
Jer. 17:7-8	Men Like Trees

98

Hymns

"All Things Bright and Beautiful"
"Beauty Around Us"
"The Day Thou Gavest, Lord, Is Ended"
"Joyful, Joyful, We Adore Thee"
"My God, I Thank Thee"
"Praise the Lord! Ye Heavens Adore Him"
"The Spacious Firmament on High"

Prayers

A PRAYER FOR OUR WORLD

O God, Maker of us all, in whose mighty hand the planets swing, in whose mighty ways our destinies reside, touch us to newer, deeper sensitivities, that wherever there are hurts or wistful aspirations we may be made responsive—until from our hands may come deeds of kindly, wise, up-building love, and from our hearts the warmth of thine own concern. Bless in thy special ways the suffering everywhere, the hungry, the hurt yet hopeful peoples. Yes, O our God, may we truly pray this, even though it may mean that such blessing may have to come through what we say and do and give. In his name, whose daily life calls us to love. Amen.[8]

—CLARICE M. BOWMAN

CANTICLE OF THE SUN

O most high, Almighty, good Lord God, to thee belong praise, glory, honor, and all blessing!

Praised be my Lord God for all his creatures, especially for our brother the sun, who brings us the day and who brings us the light; fair is he and shines with a very great splendor: O Lord, he signifies to us thee!

Praised be my Lord for our sister the moon, and for the stars, the which he has set clear and lovely in heaven.

Praised be my Lord for our brother the wind, and for air and cloud, calms and all weather, by the which thou upholdest life in all creatures.

Praised be my Lord for our sister water, who is very serviceable unto us and humble and precious and clean.

Praised be my Lord for our brother fire, through whom thou

99

givest us light in the darkness; and he is bright and pleasant and very mighty and strong.

Praised be my Lord for all those who pardon one another for his love's sake, and who endure weakness and tribulation: blessed are they who peaceably shall endure, for thou, O most Highest, shalt give them a crown.

Praised be my Lord for our sister, the death of the body, from which no man escapeth. Woe to him who dieth in mortal sin!

Blessed are they who are found walking by thy most holy will, for the second death shall have no power to do them harm.

Praise ye and bless the Lord, and give thanks unto him, and serve him with great humility.[9]

Litanies

LITANY OF PRAISE

LEADER: For earth and skies,
        Sunset and sunrise,
GROUP: We thank you, God.
LEADER: For the rhythms of your world,
        For night and day,
        For rest and play;
        For sun and rain, and sun again,
GROUP: We thank you, God.
LEADER: For food, and health,
        For life itself,
GROUP: We thank you, God.
GROUP: For people all around the world,
        For friends, and love and marriage,
        For homes and little babies,
LEADER: We thank you, God.
LEADER: For you, yourself, God, and the ways
        We have of knowing you,
GROUP: We thank you, God. Amen.[10]

—JOHN AND BETTY JOHANNABUR

AWARENESS

LEADER: The beauty of the world with flowers, grass, and trees,
GROUP: O God, our Father, comes from thee.

LEADER: Creatures of the world, beast and fish, bird and bee
GROUP: O God, our Father, comes from thee.
LEADER: The plain and desert, mountain and sea
GROUP: O God, our Father, comes from thee.
LEADER: The sun and moon and stars shining brightly
GROUP: O God, our Father, comes from thee.
LEADER: Man and woman, child and baby
GROUP: O God, our Father, comes from thee.
LEADER: Christ's love for man in all its glory
GROUP: O God, our Father, comes from thee.
LEADER: All that is and is to be
GROUP: O God, our Father, comes from thee.[11]

Poems

LOOK TO THE MOUNTAINS

How wonderful they are! How staunch they stand!
These timeless temples molded by God's hand:
A rosy glory crowns their peaks at dawn,
Changing color—as the day wears on—
To blue and purple and translucent gray;
Reflects below—where golden sunbeams play—
In crystal mirrors, gemlike lakes and streams
All framed in mystic borders of rich greens.

Enchanted, I survey from head to feet
This majesty and beauty so complete;
I think God made such noble grandeur here
That man—when tossed about by nameless fear,
Confusion, grief, and doubt—might lift his eyes
Behold the Maker's hand and strengthened rise.[12]
—SELMA JOHNSON BAKER

THESE QUIET HILLS

When peace of God is on these quiet hills;
When morning mists lie soft beneath the sun
It shines with gleaming splendor till it fills
My hungry heart, and stays till day is done.
It nestles where the blue of heaven blends
With wooded slopes. It's in the scented loam.

Its incense rises where blue smoke ascends
From chimney-altars of each mountain home.
And I, who once knew walls that shut me in
With all its cares—the sorrows men inherit,
Find in these hills new faith to live again,
Discarding worthless foil for things of merit.
Like king of old, I need but lift my eyes
To find God's peace is here—beneath the skies.[13]

—JESSIE BROWN THOMAS

NATURE PSALM

I will worship Thee, O Lord, my God, all the days of my
life.
I will sing thy praises, O loving Father, with my heart
and with my lips.
Never will I cease!
Thou has replenished my soul with good things as the rain
refreshes the earth.
Everywhere I see thee through the symphony of thy universe.
I see thee in the teasing swish of the wind—in its
lamenting groan—in its madness and discord.
I see thee in the fairyland of the forests—
In the danger of its folds.
I see thee above, in the kingdom of the clouds.
I see thee beneath, in the mystery of the sea. Thou art
in the turmoil of its depth.
I see thee, O Father, in the majesty of the white-tipped
mountains—in the contented slopes of friendly hills.
I see thee in the shy colors of dawn—in their
reflections through the crystal dew-drops.
I see thee in the still arms of the night.
I see thee in the perfection of each flower from which
the bee sips honey.
Thou art present, O God, every place my eye doth fall.
All praises be to Thee, O Maker and Ruler of the universe.[14]

—NELL RANDOLPH HARRISON

RECOMMENDATION

Let there be time enough in
   every day
For noticing how purely and
   entirely
Blue the great sky can be,
   and time to stay
Silent a moment when a star
   is early
About its shining in a sunset
   glow,
And time for courteous ac-
   knowledgment
When some sky-traverler drops
   a note or two
About the sky's attractions
   down to you.
Though roofs may be insist-
   ent, and the doing
Of necessary things requires
   intent
And skillful care, occasional
   sky-reviewing
Assists with every down-to-
   earth event.
However duties crowd, and
   moments fly,
Let every day have space
   enough for sky.[15]
                    —JANE MERCHANT

IN TIME OF INDECISION

Lord of the universe, Lord of my heart,
I would obey thee as the stars obey;
Answer to an invisible guiding rein
As tides and seasons turn; as night and day
Rise and wane, clocked to the pulse of creation's plan.
Lord, rouse in me an awareness of thy lead;
Sharpen my spirit's sensitiveness; make distinct

103

The voice of conscience; grant that nothing impede
The flow of thy directive power—accord
Me certainly of thy plan for me, O Lord.[16]

—EDITH DUNN BOLAR

THOU ART IN SOFT WINDS

. . . Thou art in soft winds
That run along the summit of these trees
In music; Thou art in the cooler breath
That from the inmost darkness of the place
Comes scarcely felt; the barky trunks, the ground,
The fresh moist ground, are all instinct with Thee.

. . . .

My heart is awed within me when I think
Of the great miracle which still goes on,
In silence, round me—the perpetual work
Of thy creation, finished, yet renewed
Forever. Written on thy works I read
The lesson of thy own eternity.[17]

—WILLIAM CULLEN BRYANT

Meditations

WE BELONG TO THE EARTH

We belong to the earth. When we are healthy in body and spirit, we feel at home with her. We know that the soil beneath our feet, the moving air about us, the bright stars above us are all our friends. They were made for us. We were made for them.

To those of us who are aware of this kinship, the earth seems good, and pleasant and companionable. There is nothing in her sunny days or in her dark nights to make us afraid. Her moods, like our own, are calm today and stormy tomorrow, but she is always bountiful in her friendship and we can lean upon her trustfully. . . .[18]

—FRED D. WENTZEL

I MET THE MASTER

I went walking and I met the Master.
"I am glad we have met," said I.
"Have we met?" said he.

104

I brushed the golden poppies with my foot. "You are as real to me as that."

"Is that all?" he said.

Then I looked at him afresh because of this tone of his, and hesitated, unsure what else to say.

"I have wished very much to meet you, good Master."

"When they wished to share my 'throne' I asked them if they were able to share my 'baptism' and my 'cup'. Very lightly they declared that they were able! And you have wished to meet me. Are you able?"

I glanced upward. The sky's blue eyes were watching. The wind shook a tree and waited. All seemed very still . . . except that my heart within me gave one strong throb. I did not know if it were of expectation, defiance, or defence.

"I do not understand," I said. "Here you are, Master, and we have met."

"Then you have met fire. Are you burned?

"Master?"

"You have met pain. Do you suffer?"

"Master, what—?

"You have met the lightning, the earthquake, the whirlwind. You are shaken, riven, if you have met me."

So he turned his back and went.

And the golden poppies were about my feet. I saw them, for my eyes were downward. . . .[19]

—OSWALD McCALL

THE WHOLE EARTH SINGS

"The whole earth sings. Her voices are many and various. The stream that runs through a peaceful valley . . . the tree that lifts its arms to the sun . . . the bird that pours out his heart in wild, sweet melody . . . the wheat field that moves in waves before the wind . . . the rain that falls into the welcoming hands of the dry ground . . . the snow that swirls and dances gayly under gray clouds . . . the constellations that trace their eternal patterns of light against the dark sky,—all these are the voices of the earth, singing of peace and order, beauty and brotherhood; she keeps singing to man, "We belong together; we are made for each other; let us rejoice and be glad." [20]

—FRED D. WENTZEL

CHAPTER 5

Dinners and Banquets

Throughout the year there are many occasions when special dinners or banquets are planned by various groups. Usually the theme is a seasonal one or it is related to some specific community or church interest.

After the good food and lighthearted fellowship, we feel the need to pause for a brief moment—to turn our minds to worship for a little while before starting for home or going on to some other activity. As in the other sections of this book, the suggestions given are suggestions only. They will need to be adapted to your need for the particular occasion. You will also find that worship suggestions in other sections may be adapted in preparing for seasonal dinners and banquets.

SOME WORSHIP SUGGESTIONS

For a Dinner Honoring Leaders

The suggestions here can easily be adapted to fit any occasion when leaders of the group are being recognized or honored. The worship outlined here would be especially appropriate just following an installation or just before new leaders are to take office.

OPENING SENTENCES:
Praise the Lord!

. . . .

Blessed be the name of the Lord
from this time forth and for evermore!
From the rising of the sun to its setting
the name of the Lord is to be praised!
—Ps. 113:1, 2-3 R.S.V.

HYMN: "Praise to the Lord, the Almighty, the King of Creation!"

TALK:

Tonight we have gathered to honor those who have been chosen as our leaders. We congratulate them on attaining their various offices of leadership and we rejoice in their willingness to assume responsibility and to serve others. Some of them have expressed misgivings as they start their new work. They wonder if they are really adequate for the demands made upon them. We who pledge to follow their guidance have some misgivings about ourselves. Are we really disciples of the Master, we ask ourselves? In our various places either as leaders or followers are we adequate for the tasks that speak our Christian convictions? Can we work together to make the teachings of Jesus become real in our own lives, in the life of this fellowship, and on beyond to the life of the community? When we begin to doubt ourselves, let us remember this:

"The twelve disciples were not chosen because they were perfect men. Simon Peter was impetuous throughout the entire relationship with Jesus. Thomas expressed doubt constantly. Judas Iscariot's faith was shallow; he was finally driven to despair and suicide. There was John and his brother James, rightly named the "Sons of Thunder" because of their impatience. There was Andrew, the weak director of the public relations department; and there was Philip, one of the fishermen, who had little imagination when Jesus sought to feed the multitude. Bartholomew was a skeptic and cynic. Matthew, the tax collector of Capernaum, was a collaborator with the Roman government. There were James the Less and Jude, two men who remained obscure. To complete the list of twelve, there was Simon the Zealot, a member of a bloodthirsty underground movement.

"To many, these men appeared weak in faith throughout the ministry of Jesus. And yet it was from these followers that the church sprang forth. Is it not remarkable that God is able to create such greatness out of such ordinary creatures?

"The problem of every age is man's failure to allow God to take hold of him so that man's faith may be enlarged to do the job of building God's kingdom on earth. May our prayers be that our faith may be expanded to encompass the needs of our world. Discipleship is not restricted to one's present capabilities but,

107

rather, to the degree to which he is dedicated in surrender to God's will." [1]

PRAYER (sung or read):

> O Master, let me walk with Thee
> In lowly paths of service free;
> Tell me Thy secret; help me bear
> The strain of toil, the fret of care.
>
> Help me the slow of heart to move
> By some clear, winning word of love;
> Teach me the wayward feet to stay,
> And guide them in the homeward way.
>
> Teach me Thy patience; still with Thee
> In closer, dearer company,
> In work that keeps faith sweet and strong,
> In trust that triumphs over wrong;
>
> In hope that sends a shining ray
> Far down the future's broadening way;
> In peace that only Thou canst give,
> With Thee, O Master, let me live. [2]

SCRIPTURE SENTENCES:

God is utterly dependable, and it is he who has called you into fellowship with his Son Jesus Christ, our Lord. (I Cor 1:4 PHILLIPS)

In this work, we work with God, and that means that you are a field under God's cultivation, or, if you like, a house being built to his plan. (I Cor. 3:9 PHILLIPS)

And so . . . stand firm! Let nothing move you as you busy yourselves in the Lord's work. Be sure that nothing you do for him is ever lost or wasted. (I Cor. 15:51 PHILLIPS)

Worship for a Birthday Banquet

The birthday banquet can be celebrated on the day on which the group was organized, or it may be a collective celebration of birthdays of group members.

TALK (based on the following):

Every life has two birthdays.

The first one you had no choice about. Your physical body was born and every day since that birth your body has had one less day to live. Anybody who puts his money and attention on the body is betting on a horse that is bound to lose. Nobody with intelligence even tries to argue that the human body won't go back to the elements.

The second birth is one that only you can choose. In fact, you have to choose . . . nobody else can choose the second birth for you. This birthday is of the spirit. . . .

The first birth sets you up for the second. No amount of religious talk or church activity can make up for the basic mistake at the center of life. When the hub of the wheel is off center, the spokes and the rim . . . cannot stand the stress of being out of line.[3]

This is what Jesus was talking about when Nicodemus came to him with questions.

READ FROM THE BIBLE:

Now there was a man of the Pharisees, named Nicodemus, a ruler of the Jews. This man came to Jesus by night and said to him, "Rabbi, we know that you are a teacher come from God; for no one can do these signs that you do, unless God is with him." Jesus answered him, "Truly, truly, I say to you, unless one is born anew, he cannot see the kingdom of God." Nicodemus said to him, "How can a man be born when he is old? Can he enter a second time into his mother's womb and be born?" Jesus answered, "Truly, truly, I say to you, unless one is born of water and the Spirit, he cannot enter the kingdom of God. That which is born of the flesh is flesh, and that which is born of the Spirit is spirit. Do not marvel that I said to you, 'You must be born anew.' The wind blows where it wills, and you hear the sound of it, but you do not know whence it comes or whither it goes; so it is with every one who is born of the Spirit." (John 3:1-8 R.S.V.)

This gives us pause for thought. Have we really had our second birthday, or are we only celebrating the anniversary of our first birthday?

PRAYER HYMN (sung or read):

Spirit of God, descend upon my heart;
Wean it from earth; through all its pulses move;
Stoop to my weakness, mighty as Thou art,
And make me love Thee as I ought to love.

· · · · · · · · · · ·

Hast Thou not bid me love Thee, God and King?
All, all Thine own—soul, heart, and strength, and mind.
I see Thy cross—there teach my heart to cling:
O let me seek Thee, and O let me find! [4]

Worship for a Valentine Banquet or Dinner

The Valentine Banquet or Dinner is a perennial social occasion
for many church groups. It's easy to plan attractive decorations and
to work out a clever program around the theme. But when it comes
to worship, that isn't as easy. Here is some material that might
be used in any form that you consider best for those few moments
of worship at the close of the program.

A TALK: [5]

You have probably seen a lot of odd valentines—sweet ones,
mean ones, comic ones, gooey ones. But have you ever seen one
like this:

VALENTINE FOR EARTH

Oh, it will be fine
to rocket through space
and see the dark side
of the man's shadowed face,

to travel to Saturn
or Venus or Mars,
or maybe discover
some uncharted stars.

But do they have anything
better than we
possess on the earth?
Do they have a blue sea

for sailing or swimming?
Do they have hills
with raspberry thickets
where song sparrows fill

the summer with music?
And do they have snow
to silver the roads
where schoolbuses go?

Oh, I'm all for rockets
and worlds cold or hot,
but I'm still in love
with the planet we've got! [6]

This may be a strange Valentine, but it says something important to us. Right here at our feet is an adventurous and exciting world. We may thrill when we hear about the wonders of space and feel funny inside when we read about the men who are pioneers in space travel. But right here, right now, God gives us adventure. All our daydreaming of "somewhere else" and "another day" simply keeps us from the fun of finding out what today holds for us.

Today—is God's gift—a day full of surprises, waiting for us to tear them open and enjoy them.

Right here, wherever we are—a whirling, flaming, stirring back yard of your own, with friends to meet, ideas to explore, tasks to do, a world to be served.

And here you are now.

SCRIPTURE READING:

The earth is the Lord's and the fulness thereof,
  the world and those who dwell therein;

· · · · · · · · ·

O magnify the Lord with me,
  and let us exalt his name together!

· · · · · · · · ·

Look to him, and be radiant . . .
      —Ps. 24:1; 34:3, 5 R.S.V.

111

HYMN (*sung or read as a poem*):
> Jesus, united by Thy grace,
> And each to each endeared,
> With confidence we seek Thy face,
> And know our prayer is heard.

> .   .   .   .

> Touched by the lodestone of Thy love,
> Let all our hearts agree;
> And ever toward each other move,
> And ever more toward Thee. Amen.[7]

Worship for a Family Dinner

The following are suggestions for bringing to a close the program of fun and fellowship when families come together for a dinner or banquet.

HYMN: "All Creatures of Our God and King" (first stanza).

A LITANY:

LEADER: The earth is the Lord's and the fulness thereof, the world and those who dwell therein. . . . (Ps. 24:1 R.S.V.)
(*Pause*)
Seeds flying in the wind, sailing on the water, sticking to animals and people, carried by the birds, to find new homes.
Seeds lying safe from the cold under the blanket of snow.
Plants sprouting and growing when the sun warms, the showers water and the soil feeds them.
Flowers attracting bees with bright colors and sweet smells.
Bees coming for honey and leaving pollen to make new seeds.
GROUP: Great and wonderful are thy works, O Lord God!
LEADER: The earth is the Lord's and the fulness thereof. . . .
(*Pause*)
Foxes growing thick coats of fur to keep them warm.
Bears crawling into caves and sleeping through the cold weather.
Birds starting on their long journey south.
Dogs working with men to draw sleds, tend sheep, lead blind people.
GROUP: Great and wonderful are thy works, O Lord God!

112

LEADER: The earth is the Lord's . . . the world and those who dwell therein.

(Pause)

The farmer raising corn, wheat, vegetables for food.
Cows giving milk, sheep growing wool, horses carrying loads.
Miners digging coal to keep people warm.
Children having fun in the snow.
People painting pictures, playing music, writing poems.
People everywhere thinking and working with other people to make the world better and happier.

GROUP: Great and wonderful are thy works, O Lord God!

ALL: Our Father, help us grow in understanding your great love to us, your children. May our thoughts, our words, and our actions every day express this love in our homes or wherever we may be. We pray in Jesus' name. Amen.[8]

SOME ADDITIONAL RESOURCES

Prayers

A PRAYER

Teach me to look with glad expectancy
For each new day that comes; to see
In everyone I meet a friend and know
That wisdom, infinite, has planned it so.
Teach me to own a sure unshaken calm
To know Thy love a healing balm.
Teach me to humbly bow my head and pray.
To learn new ways of service every day
And teach me how I may unfearing go
Along whatever paths I need to know.[9]

—KATHRYN S. GIBSON

Benedictions

The Lord be with us as each day
His blessings we receive;
His gift of peace on all we pray,
Before His courts we leave.

113

The Lord be with us as we walk
Along our homeward road;
In silent thought or friendly talk,
Our hearts be near to God.

The Lord be with us till the night
Enfold our day of rest;
Be He of every heart the light,
Of every home the guest.

The Lord be with us through the hours
Of slumber calm and deep,
Protect our homes, renew our powers
And guard His people's sleep. Amen
—JOHN ELLERTON

Now may the Lord of peace himself give you peace at all times
in all ways. The Lord be with you all.

(II Thess. 3:16 R.S.V.)

Grace to you and peace from God our Father and the Lord Jesus
Christ.

(Rom. 1:7b R.S.V.)

Litany

WE ARE DISCIPLES

LEADER: We are disciples of Christ and called by his name.
Let us draw near unto him, who is the living way.
GROUP: Help us, O Master, to walk in thy way.
LEADER: Stir us to go forth and serve thee, who art one with all
sufferers, the perplexed, and all who need.
GROUP: Help us, O Master, to walk in thy Way.
LEADER: In thy house and at thine altar, in fellowship with thy
people, grant us, through worship, new power to do thy will.
GROUP: Help us, O Master, to walk in thy Way.
LEADER: By thy gift on the cross, by thine eternal self-giving,
make us ready to share with all who will receive.
GROUP: Help us, O Master, to walk in thy Way. Amen.[10]
—J. K. WETZEL

Poems

FOR COURAGE

Give me courage, Lord
As I walk from day to day
To never be afraid
To walk the narrow way.
Guide my feet e'er onward
to tread the holy ground.
May the guiding of thy spirit
Ever more abound.
May I tread the paths of service,
The roads of thy design,
Walking e'er with thee
My hand placed in thine.
Like saints of days gone by
Give me strength to stand
Supported by thy love,
Upheld by thy right hand.[11]
—James L. Wiggins

KINSHIP

I am aware,
As I go commonly sweeping the stair,
Doing my part of the everyday care—
Humbly simple my lot and my share.
I am aware of a marvelous thing:
Voices that murmur and ethers that ring
In the far stellar spaces where cherubim sing.

I am aware of the passion that pours
Down the channels of fire through infinity's doors,
Forces terrific with melody shod,
Music that mates with the pulses of God;
I am aware of the glory that runs
From the core of myself to the core of the suns.

Bound to the earth by invisible chains,
Blaze of eternity now in my veins,
Seeing the rush of ethereal rains,

Here in the midst of this everyday air—
I am aware.

I am aware,
As I sit quietly here in my chair—
Human and simple my lot and my share.
I am aware of the systems that swing
Through the isles of creation on heavenly wing.
I am aware of a marvelous thing:
Trail of the comets in furious flight,
Thunders of beauty that shatter the night,
Terrible triumph of pageants that march
To the trumpets of time through eternity's arch.

I am aware of the splendor that ties
All the things of the Earth with the things
    of the Skies;
Here in my body the heavenly heat—
Here in my flesh the melodious beat
Of the planets that circle Divinity's feet—
As I sit quietly here in my chair
I am aware.[12]

—ANGELA MORGAN

LETTER TO DREAMERS

As earth had need of Newton and his great
Principia, of Handel and his dreaming,
Of blind and singing Milton to create
Immortal epics, of the patient scheming
Of poor Columbus, pushing past derision,
Of Faraday, and Lincoln, and the brow
That sheltered Edison's gigantic vision—
Still has she urgent need of dreamers now.
For it is but by vision earth advances,
Swiftly or falteringly. All dreaming sons,
Encourage well the vital spark that dances
Brightly across the consciousness and runs,
Beckoning, on into the strange unknown.
Run up to it, and claim it for your own! [13]

—ELAINE V. EMANS

116

A MAN MAY CHOOSE

A man must light his way up hill
And make toe holds of jagged
rocks.
He has hill sides of stepping stones
Or mountains set with stumbling
blocks.[14]

—DAWN FLANERY PARKER

Ideas for Brief Talks

SEEING WHEN YOU LOOK

The most valuable contributions to the world have not always been made by men with the best educations. More often they have been made by the keenest observers. There is nothing in this world too small to deserve attention.

Dunbar once said, "Some people learn more in a walk around the block than others do in a month's tour of Europe."

That's because most people look without seeing, without thinking, without remembering. How close an observer are you?

An airplane engineer saw a seed pod floating through the air. He observed closely its balance and speed and what he saw gave him the idea for a new airplane body.

Sir Samuel Brown observed a spider web, heavy with dew. strung across his garden path and what he saw became the basic idea for suspension bridges.

The art of printing was suggested by a man cutting letters in the bark of a tree.

Sir Isaac Newton gave credit to a child's soap bubble for his important optical discoveries.

Charles Goodyear, getting ready to cook fish over a camp fire, neglected his skillet until it became red hot. Through his close inspection of this he was guided to the manufacture of vulcanized rubber.

The telescope was the outcome of a boy's innocent amusement with two water glasses in his father's shop.

An explorer, one day, was faced with mutiny. The terrified crew threatened his life unless he turned back. Just then he saw some sea weed floating on the water near the ship.

117

"Sea weed," he shouted with great excitement. "Sea weed means land cannot be far away."

The sailors agreed that this was true and decided to go on a little longer. The next morning Columbus discovered America. Small things can indeed become great things if we only look at them with seeing eyes.

Daniel Webster, as a boy, used to walk along the main street of his town and stop before a shop window with many articles in it. He would take a good, square look in the window, then walk on and see how many articles he could name in the window. When he first started he could remember only a few things. But he kept at it until he could remember a dozen or more. After much practice, with a quick glance at the window of the shop he could name every single article that had been placed there.

Keen observation has been the only schooling of many men who have attained great success. Every one can develop this. You can if you practice like Daniel Webster. Start today by going into a room and looking hurriedly around. Then shut your eyes and name over as many things as you can remember seeing. If you keep doing this practice observing, who knows what great things you may give to the world because you learned to really see when you looked? [15]

FROM ANOTHER ANGLE

The great French painter Monet painted a picture of a haystack thirty-two times—each time in a different degree of light. No two pictures were the same. Each portrayed the same haystack but the angle from which it was painted and the way the light fell gave it a different appearance in each one.

Sometimes when we are trying to grow as Christians it is good to remember Monet's haystack. Today we think we can tell pretty surely what being a Christian means. We try to do what we think we should and we try to keep from doing the things we believe are unchristian. Then tomorrow we read a book, we listen to a speech, we see some person giving himself away to help another, and we realize that we were seeing only a small part of the truth. Another day as we read our Bibles and spend some time in prayer and meditation we catch another glimmer of what it means to be a disciple of Jesus.

As long as we are sincerely trying to grow as Christians we will

118

see our actions, our beliefs, or relationships with others and with God from a different angle each day. Today we get a bit more light here, tomorrow a bit more there. Sometimes it may seem that there is no change at all and we may become discouraged. On those days when it seems you are farther than ever from your goal as a Christian, you can remember the haystack and the great painter who was always alert to the changing light.[16]

Audio-Visuals

Overture: This mood film will provide an exciting and profound after-dinner worship experience if a leader is willing to preview it and put it into a setting of Christian responsibility toward the world today. Without a single spoken word, the film presents a powerful portrayal of the distress and need in the world, and ends on a note of hope as it suggests the promise of cooperation in the United Nations. The background music is Beethoven's *Egmont*. In black and white only, it is nine minutes long.

This Sustaining Bread. See the listing of audio-visuals at the end of the chapter on camping.

Often audio-visuals can be the center around which the worship time can be planned. Here are two suggestions. Consult listings in your denominational periodicals and check local film libraries for others.

CHAPTER 6

Parties

The party is just about over. Everyone has had a good time. The games were lots of fun, and the refreshments were just right. And now it is almost time to say good night. It is a shame just to stop, simply to call it quits after the last rollicking game. We can end our evening on a happy note by coming together for a few moments to thank God for the exciting fun we've had together. Here are some ideas about ways we might worship together after the party is over.

SOME WORSHIP SUGGESTIONS

Brief, Informal Worship Where We Are

Without having the group move into a formal setting, let the leader gradually direct the group into a worshipful mood. If the group has been playing active games, perhaps the best way to change the mood is to have a session of informal singing. After a few merry fun songs, the group can begin to sing spirituals or hymns and within a few minutes will be ready for a few moments of worship together.

STATEMENT BY A LEADER:

We have been having a good time together tonight. Now that we are about ready to say goodnight and head for our homes, let's be quiet together so that we can remember who we are and why we are here. Let's pray.

Our Father, we are pausing now to thank you for the happy time we are having tonight. We have come together here just to have fun, for we know that you want us to enjoy life.

Because you have given us the gift of laughter and painted our faces with smiles, we thank you (pause). . . . Because you have brought us together and helped us become friends, we thank you (pause). . . . Because you help us remember that we belong to you and that we are your children, we thank you (pause). . . . Remind us now that all of life comes from you—both the serious and the happy moments (pause). . . . And lead us as we go our ways toward our homes (pause). . . . In Jesus' name we pray. Amen.

HYMN (the first verse):
Saviour, like a shepherd lead us,
Much we need Thy tender care;
In Thy pleasant pastures feed us,
For our use Thy folds prepare:
Blessèd Jesus!
Thou hast bought us, Thine we are.[1]

BENEDICTION: May God's love go with us and keep us always. Amen.

Brief Worship in a Circle

Many young people enjoy the tradition of closing their fellowship times with a friendship or fellowship circle, a tradition that commends itself to other ages as well. Everyone present forms a circle, hands joined together, keeping the circle well-rounded so that each person can see every other person. The forming of the friendship circle is in itself a symbolic act of worship—the group brings itself together, united in one round ring before God. As a group begins to enjoy the tradition of the circle, and as it becomes an important part of group life, tiny but significant rituals gradually become important. Thus each friendship circle is unique, for each group makes the circle its very own.

Where the circle has become meaningful, it usually ends not merely on a note of fellowship but also of worship.

Here is one way it can happen:

When closing time comes, the circle is formed, several jolly fun songs are sung, and then the leader (whoever the evening's leader happens to be) seeks in an informal way to encourage the group to share its feelings. "We've had a good time tonight, haven't we?"

121

"Wasn't it good to have our visitors with us!" "We surely do miss Melissa—wonder how long before she'll be well and back with us?" Everyone joins in these moments of sharing until the leader, sensing the right time, suggests that the group sing a quiet worship song—perhaps "Into My Heart."

LEADER:

Let us pray. Our Father, we thank you for good times together. We thank you for our friends and for opportunities to show our love to them. Help us show our love to thee in all we do. In Jesus' name we pray. Amen.

Then the leader might give everyone in the circle a chance to join in the prayer, and those who want to can offer short prayers.

LEADER:

It's time to go now. Let's sing "Blest Be the Tie that Binds," and then say goodnight.

And so they do.

A Longer, More Formal Service

For this more formal service, the group will probably want to arrange itself facing a worship center, already prepared in a room apart from the recreation area.

PRELUDE: Tune of "Fairest Lord Jesus."

CALL TO WORSHIP:

In our going out and our coming in, in our pleasant moments as well as in those that are sad, we remember the Lord our Maker and give thanks.

The Lord is in his holy temple; let all the earth keep silence before him. Amen.

HYMN: "Joyful, Joyful, We Adore Thee."

MEDITATION, WITH THREE VOICES:

FIRST VOICE: Here are some words from the Bible: "Remember now thy Creator in the days of thy youth." (Eccl. 12:1 K.J.V.)

Tonight let us remember God our Creator (pause). . . .

122

Let us remember that we are his children (pause). . . .

He has made us; the joy and happiness that are ours tonight are gifts from him (pause). . . .

All of life around us, he has made:

The beauty of our world, every season clothed in its own array (pause). . . .

The people of our world—both those we know, and those whom we shall never know (pause). . . .

These days of youth we are living now (pause). . . .

Tonight we remember that God is our creator, the giver of all the gifts of life.

SECOND VOICE: Here are some more words from the Bible: "For the Lord is good; his mercy is everlasting; and his truth endureth to all generations." (Ps. 100:5 K.J.V.) And now these words remind us that we are not alone in remembering that God is our Father and creator. Throughout many ages, and in many lands, God has made himself known (pause). . . .

To boys and girls, men and women who lived generations before us, he was God, and he was love (pause). . . .

To thousands of boys and girls, men and women in our own day, people we shall never know, he is God and he is love (pause). . . .

Together all of us are one, for all of us, as Christians, know that "the Lord is good; his mercy is everlasting; and his truth endureth to all generations" (pause). . . .

Tonight we remember our oneness.

THIRD VOICE: Hear a few more words from the Bible: "What doth the Lord require of thee but to do justly, to love mercy, and to walk humbly with thy God?" (Mic. 6:8 K.J.V.) Yes, God has created us. And his love and mercy are known to many. And he is a God who wants us to serve him in ways that are good and purposeful:

God asks us to "do justly"—to be fair and right in our day-by-day dealings with each other (pause). . . .

God asks us to "love mercy"—to remember the failings and mistakes all of us make, and thus be forgiving (pause). . . .

He asks us to "walk humbly" with him—seeking to know what he wants us to do, but always remembering that he is the leader and not we ourselves (pause). . . .

Tonight we remember many things in these moments. We have

123

had lots of fun together. We have known the warmth of human friendship. We have remembered that God's love is even greater than that. Now we want to offer ourselves to our Father, asking him to lead us through all of life and to use us in the ways he needs us.

Let us pray. Our Father, we thank you for the warmth of friends and for the good times we have together. In all our moments remind us that we are your children, and help us follow you. In Jesus' name we pray. Amen.

SOLO: "Fairest Lord Jesus" or "Lord, Make Me More Holy."

BENEDICTION, BY THE LEADER:

May God's grace and peace and love keep our hearts and minds in Christ Jesus. Amen.

SOME ADDITIONAL RESOURCES

Scripture Selections

OUT OF GOD'S ABUNDANCE

Thy steadfast love, O Lord, extends to the heavens,
    thy faithfulness to the clouds.
Thy righteousness is like the mountains of God,
    thy judgments are like the great deep;
    man and beast thou savest, O Lord.

How precious is thy steadfast love, O God!
    The children of men take refuge in the shadow of thy wings.
They feast on the abundance of thy house,
    and thou givest them drink from the river of thy delights.
For with thee is the fountain of life;
    in thy light do we see light.

—Ps. 36:5-9 R.S.V.

"YOUR HEAVENLY FATHER KNOWS"

Do not be anxious about your life, what you shall eat or what you shall drink, nor about your body, what you shall put on. Is not life more than food, and the body more than clothing? Look at the birds of the air: they neither sow nor reap nor gather into

124

barns, and yet your heavenly Father feeds them. Are you not of more value than they? And which of you by being anxious can add one cubit to his span of life? And why are you anxious about clothing? Consider the lilies of the field, how they grow; they neither toil nor spin; yet I tell you, even Solomon in all his glory was not arrayed like one of these. But if God so clothes the grass of the field, which today is alive and tomorrow is thrown into the oven, will he not much more clothe you, O men of little faith? Therefore, do not be anxious, saying, "What shall we eat?" or "What shall we drink?" or "What shall we wear?" for the Gentiles seek all these things; and your heavenly Father knows that you need them all. But seek first his kingdom and his righteousness, and all these things shall be yours as well. (Matt. 7:25-33 r.s.v.)

PRAISE TO GOD
Praise the Lord.
I will give thanks to the Lord with my whole heart,
    in the company of the upright, in the congregation.
Great are the works of the Lord,
    studied by all who have pleasure in them.
Full of honor and majesty is his work,
    and his righteousness endures for ever.
                                    —Ps. 111:1-3 r.s.v.

Hymns

"Blest Be the Dear Uniting Love."
"Walk in the Light."

Prayers

FOR LEADERS AND PLANNERS
We thank thee, our Father, for those who have planned the good time we have had together. Help us, in turn, to learn to serve those who have need of us. We want to do the tasks thou hast for us, and so we ask thee to lead us into ways that will help us find thy will for our lives. In Jesus' name. Amen.

THANKS FOR A GOOD TIME
Our Father, we have had a good time together here. The warm fellowship that we have known has brought us closer together, and

125

we know that we have been undergirded by thy love. We thank thee for the friends who show thy love to us, and for the undying love of our greatest friend, thy Son, whose joy fills our hearts and gives true happiness to all our days. In his name we pray. Amen.

FOR PURPOSE IN OUR RECREATION

When our time for pleasure is over, our Father, we pause to thank you for happy, jolly moments together. All through our lives we move from work to play and back to work. The joy that comes from both these parts of our lives comes from thee, and we thank thee that thou hast interlaced fun and frolic into the fury and intensity of our workaday world.

We hope you will show us ways to turn our new energies into useful channels. The rest that comes from our play together has prepared us for your use. Refreshed, renewed we come, offering ourselves. What will you have us do?

(Pause)

Thank you, God, for speaking to us, for showing us the way to go. Please give us strength and commitment also, that we can walk in your way forever. In Jesus' name we pray. Amen.

Poems

A SOLITARY WAY

There is a mystery in human hearts,
And though we be encircled by a host
Of those who love us well, and are beloved,
To every one of us, from time to time,
There comes a sense of utter loneliness.
Our dearest friend is "stranger" to our joy,
And cannot realize our bitterness.
"There is not one who really understands,
Not one to enter into all I feel";
Such is the cry of each of us in turn.
We wander in a "solitary way,"
No matter what or where our lot may be;
Each heart, mysterious even to itself,
Must live its inner life in solitude.
And would you know the reason why this is?
It is because the Lord desires our love.

(In every heart He wishes to be first.)
He therefore keeps the secret key Himself,
To open *all* its chambers, and to bless
With *perfect* sympathy, and holy peace,
Each solitary soul which comes to Him.
So when we feel this loneliness, it is
The voice of Jesus saying, "Come to me";
And every time we are "not understood,"
It is a call to us to come *again*;
For Christ alone can satisfy the soul,
And those who walk with Him from day to day
Can never have a "solitary way."

—ANONYMOUS

THE GREATEST

When Jesus walked upon the earth
    He didn't talk with kings,
He talked with simple people
    Of doing friendly things.

He didn't praise the conquerors
    And all their hero host,
He said the very greatest
    Were those who love the most.

He didn't speak of mighty deeds
    And victories. He spoke
Of feeding hungry people
    And cheering lonely folk.

I'm glad his words were simple words
    Just meant for me and you,
The things he asked were simple things
    That even I can do! [2]

—MARION BROWN SHELTON

GOD, TOUCH MY LIFE

God, touch my ears that I may hear,
Above earth's din, Thy voice ring clear;
God touch my eyes that I may see

127

The tasks thou'd have me do for Thee;
God touch my lips that I might say
Words that reveal the Narrow Way;
God touch my hands that I might do
Deeds that inspire men to be true;
God touch my feet that I might go
To do Thine errands here below;
God touch my life that I might be
A flame that ever glows for Thee. Amen.

—ANONYMOUS

TEACH ME

O Lord, teach me how to pray.
Teach me to know thee as a friend . . .
    to talk with thee,
        sharing my sorrow and my joy—
            gaining strength through thy companionship.

Give me a thankful heart
    for all good things from thee.
        I share my burdens with thee,
            but first, let me be thankful.
I pray for health of mind and body.
    Thou hast given me a temple
        to live in and to do with.
            Let me keep it pure and holy.
I pray for good works in thy name—
    missions, schools, hospitals, and many more.
        Give me strength and a will to share.
When I fail to toe the mark of Christian service—
    when I drift into unclean ways—
        when my example is not thy example,
            Father, forgive me, for I know not what I do.
Am I selfish in my prayer, Lord?
    Do I pray for vain, personal gains?
        If I do, please answer, "No."
            Lord, teach me humility.[3]

—DONALD MARSH

ENKINDLE!

Touch us, O God,
With the Flame of the Spirit!
Touch us
With burning consciousness of Thee!
Create in us
An urgent need for giving!
Sear out the roots of our complacency!
Touch us, O God,
That we may truly live!
Bring to us all,
Should such need be,
Our own dark hour of Gethsemane,
Where in its crucible of pain
Alone we falter. . . .
Reach out . . . and gloriously find
That we were never lone, but blind!
Where in its crucible of pain
Shall our petty hates
And discords . . . fused
Into one great, burning ache. . . .
One burning ache for all humanity. . . .
An ache which thou dost bless
To ecstasy when it is laid
With all of life and love
Which we possess
Upon thy altar!
Touch us, O God,
With the flame of the Spirit. . . .
The flame
Were it but kindled
In each heart, the whole world
In one quick tomorrow might
Forever be illumined by its light! [4]
—Pearl Carling Campbell

UNDERSTANDING

If I knew you and you knew me,
If both of us could clearly see,

129

And with an inner sight divine
The meaning of your heart and mine,
I'm sure that we would differ less,
And clasp our hands in friendliness;
Our thoughts would pleasantly agree
If I knew you and you knew me.[5]

—NIXON WATERMAN

Meditations

TRY TO HAVE JOY

"Rejoice in the Lord always, again I will say, Rejoice." (Phil. 4:4 R.S.V.)

Christians are expected to be happy!

Unhappy and disgruntled and grumpy people can hardly be considered much of a recommendation for the followers of Jesus Christ, who believed that life is joyful when men know that God loves them. But look at so many of us! Down in the mouth—very easily angered—gloomy without much cause. Not much of a picture we present to those who see us!

But, you say, sometimes there really are things to get unhappy about? You are right. It is silly to ignore that fact. But we still have to remember that even when we are really troubled, we are still being seen, and our grumpiness has a way of causing troubles in the people around us.

Once St. Francis saw that one of his companions was wearing a very sad frown. "Why are you showing off your sorrow and sadness?" he asked him. "Keep your deep sadness between yourself and God. Pray to him to help you find his gladness once again. But before me and your other friends and all those who will see you, always try to have joy. It is not very good for one of God's men to show his sadness and troubles to his brother or to anyone else!"

Happy times together remind us that our happy countenance can speak to those who never hear our words. Can we try to learn to rejoice in God all the time, so that our joy can show others what real happiness is?

DIGGING IN

In their search for buried cities and ancient roads archaeologists are making good use of aerial photography. From photographs

130

taken in the air they can often trace the old roadways and distinguish mounds that tell of buried cities.

The entire terrain can be photographed from above and the archaeologists can then spot the signs that tell him where to dig—signs that are unrecognizable to men working on the ground where they cannot see beyond the great masses of rock or the vastness of the desert.

Have you ever felt that you had so much to do that you couldn't see where to begin digging? There is an English theme due tomorrow, a special report overdue for science class. Maybe there's a program or party you are responsible for in you church group—to say nothing of the regular tasks to be done at home and at school. And all those hours that have to be given to special practicing—music, sports, drama! And the matter of dates and keeping up with friendships too!

It's overwhelming. You feel as if you're on a fast spinning merry-go-round and that at any minute you may lose your grip on that galloping horse.

Sometimes when things crowd in on us like this our worship can become more meaningful. Whether in a daily time of private worship or the regular worship service at the church, here is our opportunity to draw aside, to rise above all these pressures. With minds and bodies quiet we can become aware of God's presence. And in his presence things that loomed so large just ahead seem to recede and grow smaller. It is as though we were looking at them from a distance.

Then we can begin to see our tasks more clearly in relation to one another. And, like the aerial photographer, we can see them in relation to the total landscape of our lives, that is, in relation to our long-range plans, our deepest purposes and dreams. The tasks that are really important stand out like the mounds in his pictures and we can trace the dim road that winds to the future. Turning our minds to God and yielding to his guidance, we can see more clearly where to "dig."

"Be still and know. . . . My help comes from the Lord, who made heaven and earth." (Ps. 46:10; 121:2.)

O God, help me learn to quiet my busy mind. Show me the way to still my restless body so that I may know your presence and hear you speak. Amen.[6]

131

YOU CAN MEET GOD

Do you know God? Some of us feel that we actually do not know Him.

God is love—in nature, friendship with others, honesty, square dealings, thankfulness, kindness, thoughtfulness, meditation and silence. In every happening throughout this day, you can find Him.

God is not white, He is not black, brown, yellow, or red. He is not American, English, Japanese, French, or any of the many nationalities. Not any of these—God is a combination of all.

When we congratulate someone on doing a good piece of work, we meet God. When we hear gossip and then forget it, stop it from spreading, we have met God. When we have done any one of the many little good things that we have a chance to do each day, we have met God.

When I feel a need for God, I first talk my problem over with Him. Then I go out and take special care to do the specific little things for others that help them and me feel closer to Him.

You can meet God today in all of life. That's the way Jesus knew Him.[7]

—LAURIE NEILL

"YE SHALL HAVE TRIBULATION, BUT . . ."

Is there a duty to be happy? Can one speak of anything such as happiness, which demands by its very nature spontaneity and naturalness, as a duty? A cartoonist of a previous generation, Phil May, once illustrated this contradiction in a famous cartoon. It showed a working mother on a notorious fairground on a bank holiday holding her two small boys each by the scruff of the neck and banging their heads together. She is saying to them, as she does so, "Be 'appy! carn't yer! Be 'appy! carn't yer!" There is certainly some difficulty in creating happiness as a duty!

Yet life is larger than the finest logic and I am sure we all have known times when, if we had not deliberately aroused a happier state of mind in ourselves, we should have failed miserably in our duty to others.

Also, many of us have known what it was to be grateful beyond words, in some crisis of life, to have as a leader a man who did not know what it was to be daunted, who could make light even of grave disasters, who could be cheerful in any adversity—the sort

132

of person who, finding happiness denied by gross circumstances, could be happy still as part of his sacred duty.

What an example Christ gives us of this determined looking upon the bright side of events. When confronted by the little dead daughter of Jairus he insists she is "only sleeping," and lo! she wakes! When faced by his own cross he insists on talking to his disciples of joy. "These things have I said unto you that my joy might remain in you, and your joy be complete."

Even when the disciples are discouraged by their own failure and disobedience he will not let them despair. "In the world" he says, "ye shall have tribulation, but be of good cheer, I have overcome the world." [8]

—ALBERT D. BELDEN

WITNESSING JOY

It was charged that Paul and Silas were causing trouble in the city. "They advocate customs which it is not lawful for us Romans to accept or practice." Because of that they were cast in the inner prison, and what is more, their feet were put in stocks. There in that dismal place, unable to move, seemingly they had little to be happy about.

"But about midnight Paul and Silas were praying and singing hymns to God." As the result of the prayers and songs of praise they were released; the prisoners heard, the prison keeper came and was converted. Why? All because they were joyous.

There is something about a Christian that would make him noticed wherever he goes; his joyousness is a vital part of the picture. Christ said, "Rejoice always" and "Be of good cheer." We should have a song in our hearts and an expression of hope on our faces always. The Christian note is genuine and abiding joy:

Let your light so shine before men, that they may see your good works and give glory to your Father who is in heaven. (Matt. 5:16) [9]

—WALTER J. CARTWRIGHT

II. WORSHIP FOR SPECIAL OCCASIONS AND HOLIDAYS

CHAPTER 7

The New Year

The New Year offers numerous occasions for worship. Many people will celebrate New Year's Eve with gay dinners and parties, but as the old year slips out, will want to pause for a moment to turn their thoughts to God. Many others will plan special Watchnight services of worship, and still others will plan worship for New Year's Day itself. The suggestions that follow are adaptable for use in various types of situations and along with additional resources may be used in creating worship to meet the needs of your particular group.

SOME WORSHIP SUGGESTIONS

A Watchnight Service of Prayer and Meditation

Often a group wants a rather formal service of worship at the church on New Year's Eve. They may wish to time the service so that as the old year passes and the New Year becomes reality they will be at worship. The service that is given here might be used as a pattern for developing such a Watchnight service.

135

This service calls for participation by the entire group in singing hymns, in prayer and meditation. Preferably each section of the service should be led by a different leader to avoid the monotony of one voice. If there are two or three leaders, however, alternate the reading. Leaders may stand at a lectern before the group, or all reading might come from the rear of the room or from a balcony behind the worshipers. If leaders are to stand before the group, they should be seated where they can quietly take their places at the lectern as each preceding speaker is seated. Musical interludes are instrumental. It will add much to the Watchnight service of worship if the church or chapel is decorated with a profusion of greenery and white candles—the greenery symbolizing growth and eternal life, and the white candles symbolizing the newness of life that can be ours in Christ.[1]

PRELUDE: "Take Time to Be Holy"

CALL TO WORSHIP:

"And I said to the man who stood at the gate of the year: 'Give me a light that I may tread safely into the unknown.' And he replied:
'Go out into the darkness and put your hand into the hand of God;
That shall be to you better than light and safer than a known way.' " [2]

HYMN: "O Worship The King, All Glorious Above."

LEADER:
Tonight we have gathered here to bid welcome to a new year. We have put behind us the brightness of the Christmas season. The tinsel has been taken from the tree, the cards have been answered, the tiny figures of the crèche have been packed away. We stand at the gate opening on a new year. Now for one brief hour we can look both ways—backward to the old year as it slips into a dim memory, and forward to the brave new year before us. Let us seek his presence as we stand thus:

Great Spirit
Who art the life of all our living,
The light of all our seeing,
The strength of all our striving,
And the love of all our loving,
Yet round about us and within us each,
We would open our hearts and minds,
Every door and window of our being.
We would open to the intaking and the outgiving
of the breath of life,
Until it shall seem that each one of us is born anew,
And that this place is filled with thy mysterious and
mighty presence.[3]

PERIOD OF SILENCE (followed by musical interlude): "We May
Not Climb the Heavenly Steeps."

LEADER:

It is a joy to give thanks to the Eternal,
to sing thy praise, O Thou Most High,
to proclaim thy goodness in the morning
and thy faithfulness at night,
to the sound of a ten-stringed lute,
to the sweet music of the lyre;
thy doings have made me glad, O thou Eternal,
I sing for joy at all that thou hast done.
How great thy deeds are, O Eternal,
how deep are thy designs!
—Ps. 92:1-5 MOFFATT

In this hour when the year is turning, let us lift up our hearts
in thankfulness for God's boundless love, and recount the many
blessings that have been ours in the year that is passing. Let us be
thankful for the blessing of life itself, life from God, returning to
God, infinitely rich in possibilities for service to him. Let us be
thankful for life in a nation where our value as persons is placed
above that of state, as Jesus taught. And let us not be unmindful
of the blessing of supply for our basic needs—food, shelter, clothing, a share of the world's good—the joy and comfort of love in

137

our homes—friends—the warm fellowship with others seeking Christ's way—opportunity for gaining new knowledge, new skills —for beauty about us, speaking constantly of the goodness at the heart of the universe—the deep, sustaining knowledge that we can reach out and touch that goodness in times of trial and stress. For all these, and countless other blessings, we give thee thanks, O God.

Out of the abundance of our material blessings, let us now give for the building of the Kingdom.

OFFERTORY

LEADER:

During these remaining moments of the year let us look deep within ourselves. Let us look at our real selves, and lay bare our secret hearts before the Master.

Have we placed limitations on the power of God by our unbelief? (*Pause.*)

Have we failed to reveal the spirit of Christ? (*Pause.*)

Have our hearts been cold, lacking in love, sympathy, and overflowing kindness? (*Pause.*)

Have we exhausted ourselves in purposeless activity? (*Pause.*)

Have we been constant in prayer? (*Pause.*)

Have we given ourselves to sinful pride—religious? social? racial? (*Pause.*)

"When ye stand praying forgive,"—so spoke the Lord of life. This is not a suggestion, or a bit of advice, but a command. It cannot be suspended or changed or evaded. When we speak to God, we must speak to him out of a forgiving heart. If we do not forgive those who have wronged us, then God will not forgive us. This is not the arbitrary will of a despot, but the operation of an eternal law. Prayer is communion with God. God is love, and hate cannot commune with love. A spiteful heart cannot hold fellowship with a heart of pity. A forgiving God cannot dwell in a heart made foul by grudges. Revengeful people cannot pray. They can say prayers, but receive no answers.[4]

Let us humbly seek forgiveness for all that has stood between us and our God during the days past. For

138

My failure to be true even to my own accepted standards:
My self-deception in face of temptation:
My choosing of the worse when I know the better:
O Lord, forgive.
My failure to apply to myself the standards of conduct I demand
of others:
My blindness to the suffering of others and my slowness to be
taught by my own:
My complacence toward wrongs that do not touch my case
and my over-sensitiveness to those that do:
My slowness to see the good in my fellows and to see the evil
in myself:
My hardness of heart toward my neighbors' faults and my
readiness to make allowance for my own:
My unwillingness to believe that Thou hast called me to a
small work and my brother to a great one:
O Lord, forgive.[5]

PERIOD OF SILENCE

MUSICAL INTERLUDE: "Dear Lord and Father of Mankind."

LEADER:

Here at the gate of another year we pause in deep concern—concern for our world, faltering in a darkness of hate and fear, seething with conflicting greeds, strife between races and creeds, nations warring against nations. There is so much that stands in the way of peace this New Year's Eve. Let us be silent as we lift up these problems to God. Let us pray for his spirit of love to work with great power through us and all who believe, during the year to come. Let us pray in faith, believing with our whole hearts that God in his infinite wisdom and might and love can accomplish the miracle of peace on earth, good will among men.

PERIOD OF SILENCE

POEM:

I cannot think that God would be content
To view unmoved the toiling and the strain,

139

The groaning of the ages, sick and spent,
The whole creation travailing in pain.
The suffering God is no vast cosmic force,
That by some blind unthinking, loveless power
Keeps stars and atoms swinging in their course,
And reckons naught of men in this grim hour.
Nor is the suffering God a fair ideal
Engendered in the questioning hearts of men,
A figment of the mind to help me steel
My soul to rude realities I ken.
God suffers with a love that cleanses dross;
A God like that I see upon the cross.[6]

HYMN: "God of Grace and God of Glory."

LEADER:

Before another hour has passed the bells will ring out the birth of a new year. For many of us they will ring in new hope, new opportunities, new joys. But all of us will listen to their peals in the consciousness that here is a time for new dreams, new beginnings, no matter how dark the past may have been, or how sobering is the present hour. Always, there is a new hope, a new way of life for those who will, in faith, seek out the Christ and accept his guidance for the future. Let us be in prayer as we shape in our minds our plans and objectives for the year ahead. Let us evaluate our desires in the light of Jesus' teaching, and cast out all unworthy aims.

PERIOD OF SILENCE
MUSICAL INTERLUDE: "Holy Spirit, Truth Divine."
LEADER:

Quiet now
Close the mind's door
On business of the day
And for this brief moment
Clear the way
For God.

· · · · · · ·

Quiet now
No need for words
Listen . . . and be still . . .
His voice will direct,
His spirit fill
Your soul.[7]

PERIOD OF SILENCE

SCRIPTURE READING:

Thy word is a lamp unto my feet
And light unto my path.

  . . . .

Open thou mine eyes, that I may behold
wondrous things out of thy law.
    —Ps. 119:105, 18 R.S.V.

Teach me, O Jehovah, the way of thy statutes;
And I shall keep it unto the end.
Give me understanding, and I shall keep thy laws;
Yea, I shall observe it with my whole heart.
    —Ps. 119:33-34 R.S.V.

With my whole heart have I sought thee:
Oh, let me not wander from thy commandments.
Thy word have I laid up in my heart,
That I might not sin against thee.
    —Ps. 119:10-11 R.S.V.

LEADER:

Our work, our problems, our thoughts and dreams, our every day of living, our hope for peace and brotherhood in the coming year—let us commit them all into his hands, believing in his wisdom and love.

SOLO: "The Lord's My Shepherd."

BENEDICTION:

Now may the God of peace who brought again from the dead

141

our Lord Jesus, the great shepherd of the sheep . . . equip you with everything good that you may do his will, working in you that which is pleasing in his sight through Jesus Christ; to whom be glory for ever and ever. Amen. (Heb. 13:20 r.s.v.)

Worship Moments at a New Year's Party or Dinner

The New Year's party or dinner is always an especially gay affair. Dressed in his best party outfit, each person comes prepared to have a big evening. But after the fun, the noise-making, the special food or refreshments, the group may want to pause for a few moments to be serious, to think of what possibilities may lie ahead in the new year; to seek God's guidance in whatever may come; to listen for his direction as you undertake the responsibilities ahead or make decisions that are pending. Here is a suggested plan for such moments of worship.

The leader may bring the group together for these quiet moments with the following or some other selected poem:

> Standing at the portal
> Of the opening year,
> Words of comfort greet us,
> Hushing every fear;
> Spoken through the silence
> By our Father's voice,
> Tender, strong and faithful,
> Making us rejoice.
>
> . . . .
>
> He will never fail us,
> He will not forsake;
> His eternal covenant
> He will never break!
> Resting on His promise,
> What have we to fear?
> God is all-sufficient
> For the coming year.[8]

The leader might then say something like this: "As we stand at the gateway of a New Year, each of us has some special concerns—some of us are making decisions that will affect our entire lives; others are involved in situations where they need strength and guidance; all of us are in need of daily strength and guidance in living our lives as Christians. In these moments, let us turn to God, each of us lifting up to God our particular concern, and then listening in the silence for his voice.

PERIOD OF SILENCE

The leader may bring the period of meditation to a close by a prayer similar to the following:

O God, our gracious heavenly Father, who gives us gifts far beyond our deserving; as we look ahead to a new year, help us to put aside past disappointments and discouragements and failures, and help us to use the days and months ahead in discovering and applying your will for our lives, so that we may be more like the persons we were born to be and worthier to receive your good gifts. This we ask in the name of Jesus the Christ whom you gave us to point the way to the abundant life. Amen.[9]

Then the entire group may sing the following hymn, or if this is not practical, the words may be read as a poem:

> Another year is dawning,
> Dear Master, let it be,
> In working or in waiting,
> Another year with Thee.
>
> . . . .
>
> Another year of progress,
> Another year of praise,
> Another year of proving
> Thy presence all the days. Amen.
> —FRANCES R. HAVERGAL

New Year's Worship in the Church School Group

Sometimes the church school group meeting either at the church or elsewhere during the New Year's season will want to plan for brief seasonal moments of worship. The following is a suggested pattern for developing such worship.

MUSIC: "Finlandia."

PRAYER:

O God, our help in ages past,
Our hope for years to come,
Our shelter from the stormy blast,
And our eternal home!

Before the hills in order stood,
Or earth received her frame,
From everlasting Thou art God,
To endless years the same.

—ISAAC WATTS

HYMN: "From All That Dwell Below the Skies."

A READING (may be read by two readers):

FIRST READER: I am as one caught, trapped in time of transition —I and the others of my generation. The ancient walls of knowledge and of custom built by our fathers and their fathers before them lie crumbling about us.

SECOND READER: And we of this generation have been eager to see them fall. We have even helped to tear them down.

FIRST READER: But now—now we stand as in the path of an oncoming storm—unprotected, fearful, trembling. A strange new age surges about us. It beckons, challenges, draws us into itself. It is frightening, dark. . . .

SECOND READER: Yes, dark from this point of view. But perhaps there is light beyond.

FIRST READER: It is an age in which the tiny atom has become a giant, a giant that stalks our world and terrifies us all. The normal life—home, family, friends—become something we dare not hope for in the face of total annihilation.

SECOND READER: Your view is limited. Look once again. Do you not see the whole new way of life that same atom opens to us— new wonders in industry, more miracles in medicine and science, new modes of transportation and communication, more comfortable homes for families, to name a few. And it could be that the very threat of the atom's power would in itself turn the world to peace.

144

FIRST READER: Peace in our world may not be enough. Think what it means if even part of what we read these days is true of space. Suppose those dots on our radar screens, the unidentified flying objects, actually are space ships cruising about our planet, spying on us.

SECOND READER: Yes, suppose all that is true, and it may well be. What could be more exciting, more challenging to human thought and effort?

FIRST READER: Exciting, perhaps, but what of us and the families that are reared in this world? Shall sons and daughters of this nation be sacrifices to the great god science?

SECOND READER: Some will, of course. For in every age there must be those who dedicate their lives to searching out the secrets of the universe. But always there are others who, just as avidly, explore in other fields. Music and the arts will always claim their followers. And think of the possibilities for those who will adventure with the mind and spirit into space and time!

There will be more to challenge those who come after us in this new age than we can dream of now. We need not fear for ourselves or for them. We cannot hold back the changes that we see emerging, but we can accept them as a part of a wonderful, constantly evolving plan. We can maintain poise in the realization that "new occasions teach new duties," and remain secure in the knowledge that this is still our Father's world.[10]

SCRIPTURE READING (by the leader):
    The Lord is my light and my salvation;
        whom shall I fear;
    The Lord is the stronghold of my life;
        of whom shall I be afraid?
                —Ps. 27:1 R.S.V.

When I look at thy heavens, the work of thy fingers,
    the moon and the stars which thou hast established;
what is man that thou art mindful of him,
    and the Son of man that thou dost care for him?
Yet thou hast made him little less than God,
    and dost crown him with glory and honor.

145

Thou hast given him dominion over the works of thy hands;
thou hast put all things under his feet.

—Ps. 8:3-6 R.S.V.

Wait for the Lord;
be strong, and let your heart take courage;
yea, wait for the Lord!

—Ps. 27:14 R.S.V.

PRAYER HYMN: "Spirit of Life, in This New Dawn."

SOME ADDITIONAL RESOURCES

Scripture Selections

SET YOUR HEART ON HIS KINGDOM

No one can be loyal to two masters. He is bound to hate one
and love the other, or support one and despise the other. You cannot serve God and the power of money at the same time. That is
why I say to you, Don't worry about living—wondering what you
are going to eat or drink, or what you are going to wear. Surely
life is more important than food, and the body more important
than the clothes you wear. Look at the birds in the sky. They never
sow nor reap nor store away in barns, and yet your Heavenly
Father feeds them. Aren't you much more valuable to him than
they are? Can any of you, however much he worries, make himself an inch taller? And why do you worry about clothes? Consider
how the wild flowers grow. They neither work nor weave, but I
tell you that even Solomon in all his glory was never arrayed like
one of these! Now if God so clothes the flowers of the field, which
are alive today and burned in the stove tomorrow, is he not much
more likely to clothe you, you "littlefaiths"?

So don't worry and don't keep saying, "What shall we eat, and
what shall we drink or what shall we wear?" That is what pagans
are always looking for; your Heavenly Father knows that you need
them all. Set your heart on his kingdom and his goodness, and all
these things will come to you as matter of course.

(Matt. 6:24-34 PHILLIPS)

THE NEW YEAR

PUT THESE THINGS BEHIND YOU

Give your heart to the heavenly things, not to the passing things of earth. . . . have nothing to do with sexual immortality, dirty-mindedness, uncontrolled passion, evil desire, and the lust for other people's goods, which last, remember, is as serious a sin as idolatry. It is because of these very things that the holy anger of God falls upon those who refuse to obey him. And never forget that you had your part in those dreadful things when you lived that old life.

But now, put all these things behind you. No more evil temper or furious rage: no more evil thoughts or words about others, no more evil thoughts or words about God, and no more filthy conversation. Don't tell one another lies any more, for you have finished with the old man and all he did and have begun a life as a new man, who is out to learn what he ought to be, according to the plan of God.

(Col. 3:2, 5-10 PHILLIPS)

SOME SCRIPTURE REFERENCES

Rom. 12:1-2 — Renew Your Mind
Matt. 7:7-8 — Help is Available
II Tim. 2:15 — Do Your Best

Hymns

"The God of Abraham Praise"
"Come, Let Us Anew Our Journey Pursue"
"O God, Our Help in Ages Past"
"Ring Out, Wild Bells"
"Come, Let Us Use the Grace Divine"
"Father, Let Me Dedicate"

Prayers

PRAYER FOR GUIDANCE

And now, O our Father, as we turn our steps down the path of the new year, grant that we may go forward as those to whom has been given the power of an endless life. Help us to live the eternal life here and now—the life of faith, of love, of fellowship, of service. Help us to measure by eternal values and to live for eternal things. So shall all of life be full of meaning and of beauty.

147

So shall we share in carrying out the purpose that shaped thy world. So shall we think thy thoughts after thee. So shall we be eager only to do thy will, whether tomorrow find us toiling here, or in the City on the Hill. Into this life eternal and victorious, O Lord of Light, lift all our hearts today! Amen.[11]

BE RULER OF OUR LIVES

O God, who hast set before us the great hope that thy kingdom shall be established upon earth: so rule our lives by thy spirit that all our thoughts, desires, and acts may be made obedient unto thee; and that through us thy power, thy glory, and the mightiness of thy kingdom may be made known unto men; grant this, O merciful Father, for thy great love's sake. Amen.[12]

NEW YEAR'S PRAYER

O Lord,
We are grateful
For gadgets, gimmicks and gold,
But must we always
Lust for the ephemeral,
When thou hast for us the Eternal
Gift of the Grace of God?

Teach us
To meditate
Contemplate
Worship and wait—
The Voice and the Fire
O Lord—

For of what use
Are the stretched-out days
The stretched-taut mind
The jet-smalled world,

But to love
Thee,
The next-door man,
And serve humbly in Thy Name.
Amen.[13]

—JAMES WILLIAM SELLS

A NEW YEAR'S PRAYER

Thou, O God, art our Father.
Humbly we bow before thee
Eternally grateful for thy goodness and love.

New days open before us.
Earnestly we pray that we may be equal to the tasks
  entrusted to us.
We ask for guidance as we seek to do thy work.

Yesteryear is gone. We would build on that which is past,
Ever seeking to become more Christlike persons.
Arouse in us new faith, new enthusiasms, new
  determination to serve thy children everywhere.
Reveal thyself and thy will to us that we may
  help to build thy Kingdom on earth. Amen.[14]

—EMMA JANE KRAMER

Poems

TIME AND SEASONS

Life is as bright and sweet and gay
And swiftly run as a summer's day.

Or bitter and barren of delight,
Long and cold as a winter's night.

But long or short or swift or slow,
Love or the lack of it makes it so.[15]

—OLIVE STANTON

THIS NEW YEAR

There is no magic crystal that can show
This New Year to me, there is none can say
Which way the variant winds of life will blow,
Boding me ill, or whisking clouds away—
So I shall not do wrong to meet the year
With certain preparation. I shall go
With ample stock of bravery, who fear,
With a lamp of faith, down roads I cannot know.
And I shall not forget that often laughter
Has power within it, that a song secure

149

Within the breast is beyond price. And after
Some interval when little more seems sure,
I must remember beauty has rebirth,
And God is never unmindful of his earth.[16]
—ELAINE V. EMANS

A LIGHTED CHURCH

Should all the good resolves inspired
Within that lighted church
Be kept by those who made them there,
We'd not have far to search
To find that many ills were healed
And burdened hearts made light;
That lonely ones found happiness
More darkened lives made bright.
Not just resolves on New Year's Day,
Each morning one should claim,
Then we could know true brotherhood
More beautiful than name.[17]
—RUTH ROANE STARKEY

THE RICH YOUNG RULER

We know not what became of him,
The rich young ruler, high and proud,
Who ran to Jesus in the way
And knelt before him in the crowd.

"Good Master," murmured he, but when
Jesus with love and yearning cried,
"Sell all thou hast and follow me!"
The splendor from his dark eyes died.

As back to ease and power he turned
I wonder if a deep unrest
Would nevermore let him forget
That he had forfeited life's best.

Or did the slowly gathering dust
Of worldly cares his spirit dim,
Till visions of the perfect way
No longer heard or troubled him?

Somber, against the centuries
He stands, who heard the call supreme,
Who loved, but did not own, his Lord,
Who saw, but followed not, truth's gleam.[18]

—EFFIE SMITH ELY

Meditations

THIS IS THE NEW YEAR

The beginning of a new chapter in the book of life, threshold of a house that has never been entered, opening of a drama that none has ever witnessed—*this is the new year.*

Opportunity for undreamed-of experiences, personality growth, promise of more abundant living—*this is the new year.*

Use for unused energies and neglected powers, investment of treasures corroding from disuse, exercise of talents whose possibilities none knows—*this is the new year.*

A new outlook on the world and all life, a new glimpse of what the Creator meant for his human creatures to become, new and clearer vision of the vastness that beckons men to achievement—*this is the new year.*

God's grace proffered all men, his love demonstrated and proven, his invitation to achieve likeness unto himself, his mandate to come into our inheritance, his wooing to acquire heavenly benediction and untarnished happiness—*this is the new year.*

Dream of that which eye hath not seen, nor ear heard, but which is already coming to reality, the voice of the Almighty bidding all who will to come drink of the fountain of life freely and to inherit the kingdom prepared for them—*this is the new year.*[19]

—CHARLES J. LOTZ

A MEDITATION ON NEWNESS OF LIFE

If any man be in Christ, he is a new creature: old things are passed away; behold, all things are become new.

Let us rejoice in the power of Christ to recreate our manhood, to give us a new status before God, to bring forth powers we never suspected within ourselves, and to redeem us from the drag of the past.

151

Let us ask forgiveness if we have preferred the familiarity of the old: old ways, old thoughts, old relationships, and old roads to tread in.

Let us meditate afresh upon the newness of Christ's life, the freshness of each day's response to the Father's love and to the world's need, the newness of his grasp of truth, the newness of his surrender to love.

Let us ask that we may be made new now in his latest encounter with his life and love.

Jesus said: *Behold, I make all things new.*

Let us give thanks that the living Christ makes all things new, that he takes the stale stuff of daily life—its worn routine, its shabby tiredness—and give it vitality and freshness, that he is able to show us new sights to see, new thoughts to think, new tasks to essay, that he makes unfamiliar what was commonplace and gives us new eyes to see people, things, and the hand of God in life.

Jesus said: *Every scribe which is instructed unto the kingdom of heaven is like unto a man that is an householder, which bringeth forth out of his treasure things new and old.*

Let us pray so to be instructed in the kingdom of God that we also might have the power to bring forth things new and old, to communicate with those whose thoughts are in the past, to share with those whose eyes are on the future, to reconcile in one fellowship the conservatives and the radicals, and to make both at home within the kingdom of love.

Jesus said: *A new commandment I give unto you, That you love one another; as I have loved you, that ye also love one another. By this shall all men know that ye are my disciples, if ye have love one to another.*

Let us place ourselves anew into the living hands of Christ and seek to embody and express his love.

Let us look with new eyes upon the faces of our fellow men that we may see them with the compassion of Christ; let us learn that every situation is a new one when we see God in it: Let us trust in the power of Christ's crucified and risen life to cleanse and renew our love for one another.

O come, let us sing a new song unto the Lord! Amen.[20]

—W. B. J. MARTIN

152

A BRAND NEW WORLD!

The cowboy had been quite a guy. All over his section of the territory, he was known as a tough fighter and a fast man with a gun. You stayed out of his way unless you wanted trouble. But one night the cowboy went to a tent revival, and was converted.

Several weeks later he rode into town, and his horse, knowing his habits, took him straight to the saloon. The cowboy hopped off and threw the reins around the hitching rail. Just then the preacher came by. "If you're gonna follow Jesus, cowboy," he said, "you'll hafta find yourself a new hitching rail!"

When we decide we are going to live our lives as Christ directs, we have to find ourselves new hitching posts, too. Becoming a Christian makes everything new for us.

We begin to see the world through new eyes! Before, the world was just the place we happen to inhabit. But when we hear what Christ has to say about life, we realize that this world is God's. We know that it is good and that it offers a good life to us.

We see the people around us in a new light! Before, they just happened to be around: one day, they were helpful to us; the next day they were problems. But when we begin to live as Christ's followers, we discover that people around us are all God's children, and that he has called us to love them into loving him.

And we even see ourselves as brand new—almost as if we hadn't ever seen ourselves before. For now we begin to understand ourselves. We know that God has a purpose in creating us. We know that he has a plan for us in his bright, challenging world. We know that we belong to him, and that he is our Father.

When God helps us to see these things, then we know that the old way of seeing and knowing and living won't do any more. We begin to look for a new hitching rail, a new place to tie up while we go about the business of every day.[21]

THE NEW WITHIN YOU

"The kingdom of God is not coming with signs to be observed; nor will they say, 'Lo, here it is!' or 'There!' for behold, the kingdom of God is in the midst of you." (Luke 17:20)

Year after year we have looked for new things to do and new

153

tasks to perform. We want to get to work building a better world, but we have forgotten to start with ourselves. This year, before we attempt to build the kingdom of God in the whole world, let us begin to dwell in the kingdom of God within ourselves.

We need to come in repentance to God and ask Him with earnest and humble hearts for the gift of the kingdom's spirit. With all of our modern science and mass production lines, we know that our civilization cannot even survive materially unless it is redeemed spiritually. Jesus Christ is still the world's Savior.

Like sheep we have all gone astray from the fold of the Good Shepherd of life. We have said, "Look, here . . . there," and we have looked, sometimes indifferently, sometimes in frantic search for the signs of God's coming kingdom. But Jesus still is saying to those who will be quiet long enough to listen: . . . *the kingdom of God is in the midst of you.*

Why make plans so feverishly? God has plans for you. Why stand in the darkness of a world which struggles to the death with itself? God has light for His children who seek Him. Why search for the new treasures of God's unfolding universe in the world of things about you? Look for the new within yourself; it's as old as God![22]

IN THE BEGINNING

In the beginning God. . . . (Gen. 1:1)

In the beginning of all life, of all beauty, of all truth; in the beginning of every great service, behind every noble personality. For that which was begun and *built* with and *in* Him has led to achievements which physical riches have never reached and the minds of men have never conceived.

As we begin a new year of experiences and adventure, let us begin it with Him. Let each one of us look squarely to our heavenly Father—give Him our burdens, pour our hearts out to Him and be cleansed of self, let Him free us from doubt and fear. Not looking behind, let us leave Him in complete charge . . . for he too is seeking to do for us beyond all that we may ask or think . . .

May we watch our decisions that they may be found in His will and speak of His love . . .

154

May we realize the joy and peace in the present moment that new opportunities may be ours . . .

The omnipotent power of the almighty is manifest in the present hour. Live each eternal minute fully aware of God's presence . . .

What no eye has seen, nor ear heard, nor the heart of man conceived, what God has prepared for those who love him (I Cor. 2:9) . . .

In the beginning God . . . and God saw every thing that he had made, and, behold, it was very good (Gen. 1:1, 31).[23]

—NORMA DUKE

CHAPTER 8

National Holidays and Celebrations

*Many times during the year we stop—as citizens of our country
—to remember heroes or recall special moments in our history. This
stopping for such holidays helps hold us together as a nation, for
we hold before ourselves the same high goals and ideals that have
drawn our people ever since our nation was founded—and indeed
even before!*

*On many of these occasions, we slow down long enough to
realize that our celebration is not complete unless as a part of it
we say "Thank you" to the One who has placed us here in the midst
of a land that lives and moves as a part of His Providence. And so
we worship . . . just after our Fourth of July picnic . . . when our
club happens to meet on Lincoln's birthday . . . when we sadly
recall those who gave their lives in combat . . . And we say our
thanks to God, who has great plans yet for us, and for our land.*

Remembering Our Nation's Heroes

Many occasions arise when we find it good gratefully to remember leaders who have endeared themselves to our nation. On such
occasions, the leaders of worship will find a wealth of material
available to help them reach a high moment of thanksgiving and
remembrance. Sometimes the occasion will be a specific celebration:
Lincoln's birthday, for example, or a commemoration of a president's inauguration. And sometimes there is a need to pause to
remember heroes both famed and unknown. For such an occasion,
the following service will be useful—and it will suggest several approaches for similar occasions.

PRELUDE: Hymn tune, "Truro."

156

PRAYER-HYMN:

Great God of nations, now to Thee
Our hymn of gratitude we raise;
With humble heart and bending knee
We offer Thee our song of praise.

Thy Name we bless, Almighty God,
For all the kindness Thou hast shown
To this fair land the pilgrims trod,
This land we fondly call our own.

Here freedom spreads her banner wide
And casts her soft and hallowed ray;
Here Thou our fathers' steps didst guide
In safety through their dangerous way.

Great God, preserve us in Thy fear;
In danger still our guardian be:
O spread Thy truth's bright precepts here;
Let all the people worship Thee. Amen.
—ALFRED A. WOODHULL

A CALL TO REMEMBRANCE

Today we come to remember the heroes of our nation—men
and women whose devotion to their fellow men issued in the
growth of our land. Their dreams set our direction, and their courage put us on our course.

We remember many whose names are lost today. . .
Sturdy venturers who faced death in order to find freedom on
our shores. . .
Strong pioneers who moved across frontier after frontier,
settling our land from shore to shore. . .
Soldiers, preachers, prophets, poets. . .
Lawyers, housewives, scouts, and teachers. . .
All stood in their day and faced their own world, and marked
the trail for us. . .
We remember many whose names are chiseled deep in our monu-
ments as well as in our hearts:

157

Giant leaders of men—Franklin, Washington, Lincoln,—who accepted the challenge of their day with devoted dedication to our land and our God—and to us. . .

Great poets who sang our disharmonies into a great national symphony of brotherhood. . .

Men who kept before us the stern and stirring demands of our God. . .

Today, as inheritors of their steadfastness, we remember them, and come to dedicate ourselves to the service of God and our country, remembering that the strength and hope of every land and every man in his salvation, in the freedom found in his truth.

SCRIPTURE:

We have heard with our ears, O God,
  our fathers have told us,
what deeds thou didst perform in their days,
  in the days of old:
thou with thy own hand didst drive out the nations,
  but them thou didst plant;
thou didst afflict the peoples,
  but them thou didst set free;
for not by their own sword did they win the land,
  nor did their own arm give them victory;
but thy right hand, and thy arm,
  and the light of thy countenance;
for thou didst delight in them.
                    —Ps. 44:1-3 R.S.V.

LITANY FOR OUR COUNTRY:

LEADER: O God, the Ruler of the universe, without whom nothing is great, nothing is strong,
GROUP: Have mercy upon our country.
LEADER: O God, who in thy Son, Jesus Christ, didst reveal a way of life for us and for all men, wherein we might walk as children of one Father,
GROUP: Have mercy upon our country.
LEADER: O God, who not by might nor by power but by thy Spirit dost move the hearts of men,

158

GROUP: Have mercy upon our country.

LEADER: From the love of gain and possession, from materialism and the worship of Mammon,

GROUP: O Lord, deliver us.

LEADER: From all cruelty and oppression of our fellow men, from the evils of our industrial system, from all subordination of human life and labor to selfish ends,

GROUP: O Lord, deliver us.

LEADER: From overbearing national pride, from thinking that Thou dost love our own nation more than any other, from all false patriotism,

GROUP: O Lord, deliver us.

LEADER: From racial injustice, from religious prejudice, from all disloyalty to truth and justice,

GROUP: O Lord, deliver us.

LEADER: Almighty God, whose service is perfect freedom, for all those who, in high place or low, have labored that our country may be grounded and established in freedom, in freedom for human life, in freedom for thought and opinion, for religion and worship,

GROUP: We thank thee.

LEADER: From all that from time to time threatens this heritage,

GROUP: O Lord, deliver us.

LEADER: For all those who, in high place or low, have labored to establish justice in our land, justice that shall deliver us from all domination of class, or wealth, or race,

GROUP: We thank Thee.

LEADER: From all that threatens in our land the impartial administration of this justice,

GROUP: O Lord, deliver us.

LEADER: For all those who have labored to guard and secure the homes of our land, that they may be saved from vice, selfish indulgence, and anything that endangers child life,

GROUP: We thank Thee.

LEADER: From all that threatens the homes of our land,

GROUP: O Lord, deliver us.

LEADER: By remembrance of all who have truly served our country, the remembrance of their life and labors, their sufferings, their devotion and their martyrdom, confirm in us the determination

159

that we shall not be found unworthy of our heritage. Govern us,
O God, and lift us up forever. Amen.[1]

BENEDICTION (may be said or sung):
As Thee their God our fathers owned,
So Thou art still our King:
O, therefore, as Thou didst to them,
To us deliverance bring!

To Thee the glory we ascribe,
From whom salvation came;
In God, our shield, we will rejoice,
And ever bless Thy Name. Amen.

—Ps. 44 TATE AND BRADY

Celebrating Our Nation's Birth

The Fourth of July is a day full of many kinds of experience—
firecrackers popping, politicians speaking, flags waving—all reminding us of the day long ago when it all started in the midst of the
trembling courage of a few men. The nation raises its heart to
God on this day, remembering, thanking, hoping, dedicating. The
worship experience can be informal if the situation calls for it—
no more than a bright singing of "O Beautiful for Spacious Skies"
and the quiet offering of sentence prayers by a group by a lakeside,
as they picnic. Or the many poems and prayers that have come
into our tradition can be called upon for something of a more
formal service. The suggested service that follows—it is intended
to help you find just the right way to plan worship for your group
—makes use of one of the famous stories of Benjamin Franklin,
whose towering intellect and spirit helped to bring the nation to
birth. The service will enable his words even at this distance to remind us all that ours is indeed a nation "under God."

PRELUDE: Hymn tune, "National Hymn."

CALL TO WORSHIP:
Thine, O Lord, is the greatness, and the power, and the glory,
and the victory, and the majesty; for all that is in the heavens and

in the earth is thine; thine is the kingdom, O Lord, and thou art exalted as head above all. Amen.

HYMN: "God of Our Fathers, Whose Almighty Hand."

SCRIPTURE:

"Every one then who hears these words of mine and does them will be like a wise man who built his house upon the rock; and the rain fell, and the floods came, and the winds blew and beat upon that house, but it did not fall, because it had been founded on the rock. And every one who hears these words of mine and does not do them will be like a foolish man who built his house upon the sand; and the rain fell, and the floods came, and the winds blew and beat against that house, and it fell; and great was the fall of it." (Matt. 7:24-27 R.S.V.)

STORY:

He was seventeen when he decided to leave his brother's printing shop in Boston and find work on his own in Philadelphia. Looking the runaway he was, he arrived one Sunday morning at the Market Street wharf, tired, dirty, and hungry. With his last few cents he bought three loaves at a nearby bakery and carrying one under each arm and munching the third, started out to look for a place to live.

Deborah Read saw him coming down the street. When he had passed her house she turned and laughed at him. How was she to know she was laughing at her future husband: that in just seven years she would be Mrs. Benjamin Franklin? None of the people passing him on their way to church guessed that this shabby young man was going to change life for all of them because along with the crumpled shirts bulging from his coat pocket, he was bringing with him his own ten talents and a priceless eleventh.

As time went on it was clear enough that Mr. Franklin had started more than a new printing shop in Philadelphia. People acquired a habit of reading a new paper, *Poor Richard's Almanac*. Franklin stoves and chair ladders were taking the pain out of their chores. The fame of his scholarship and his library added to the prestige of the whole town.

161

But his most remarkable talent, a kind of eleventh to his other ten, was the way he had of getting people to work together. Pooling time and money, Philadelphians were soon able to boast of well-lighted and cobbled streets. They had a hospital, and a subscription library. And everyone slept better because of their do-it-yourself police and fire department.

It was this genius for human relations that gave him his long-range influence as co-framer and signer of the *Declaration of Independence*, and as the first ambassador of American democracy to the courts of Europe. How much depended on it, was revealed during the convention that met to draft a constitution for the new nation. It opened in May. June came and still opposing self-interests wrangled with increasing bitterness. Had the delegates forgotten the life-price paid by Washington's underfed, ragged armies? Quickly, Mr. Franklin—an old man now but easily one of the best minds there—rose to speak:

"How has it happened, Sir (he addressed Washington as president), that we have not once thought of humbly applying to the Father of light to illuminate our understandings? The longer I live the more proofs I see that God governs in the affairs of men. I believe that without his aid we shall succeed in this political building no better than the builders of Babel. We shall be divided by our little particular interest, and we ourselves be a reproach and byword down to future ages. And, what is worse, mankind may hereafter from this unfortunate instance despair of establishing governments by human wisdom and leave it to chance, war, and conquest."

The delegates failed to act on his resolutions. But Mr. Franklin had his victory. The air cleared. There was a lift to good will. A constitution was worked out. A new experiment in democracy got its chance to become ours.[2]

PERIOD OF QUIET MEDITATION, WITH MUSICAL BACKGROUND

POEM:

Peace in our time, O Lord,
To all the peoples—Peace!
Peace surely based upon Thy Will

And built in righteousness.
Thy power alone can break
The fetters that enchain
The sorely-stricken soul of life,
And make it live again.

Too long mistrust and fear
Have held our souls in thrall;
Sweep through the earth, keen breath of heaven,
And sound a nobler call!
Come, as thou didst of old,
In love so great that men
Shall cast aside all other gods
And turn to Thee again!

O shall we never learn
The truth all time has taught,—
That without God as architect
Our building comes to naught?
Lord, help us, and inspire
Our hearts and lives, that we
May build, with all Thy wondrous gifts,
A Kingdom meet for Thee!

Peace in our time, O Lord,
To all the peoples—Peace!
Peace that shall build a glad new world,
With Thy High Sovereignties.
O Living Christ, who still
Dost all our burdens share,
Come now and dwell within the hearts
Of all men everywhere! [3]

UNISON PRAYER, FROM THE BIBLE:

O God, bless us with thy favor,
    may thy face smile on us,
that so thy purpose may be plain to men,
    thy saving power to every nation.
O God, may the world praise thee,
    may all races praise thee!

163

may the nations sing for joy,
for thou rulest the world justly,
thou guidest the nations on earth!
O God, may the world praise thee,
may all races praise thee!
The land has yielded the harvest
by the blessing of God, our God;
bless us, O God, bless us,
till men revere thee to the world's far end.

—Ps. 67 MOFFATT

BENEDICTION:

Our Father, whose power has brought our land into being and whose love has kept it through the years, grant to all of us thy peace, call us to thy work, and strengthen us to do thy will. In the name of Christ we pray. Amen.

Considering Our Nation's Role in a New World

When we—as Christians—look upon the world in which we live, we are distressed at what we see. The wide world over men fight their brothers, selfishness reigns, and peace is only a wisp of a dream. Yet we know that our Lord—whose world looked strangely like ours does—has offered hope and love and peace to those who can accept his Way and have faith in his Father's love. For that reason, we look with compassion upon this "new world" we hear so much about. We hear Christ calling all of us within this world to come to him so that men can learn to trust each other, so that love can begin to reign, and peace become a reality. Every sign of man's coming together is a sign of hope to us. And for that reason, the United Nations and other organizations that have served to make our world smaller can be considered as parts of God's providence in our day, a sign of his working among us all to bring us together to his throne. The service that follows can help a group focus its concern upon the fractured world we live in, and upon the hope offered by the United Nations to bring men together.

PRELUDE

A CONFESSION:

O God, we confess to thee the sinful, fractured ways that have kept us long asunder. In this day when groups and institutions beyond the walls of the Church are calling men together, we confess that we have often lagged behind, dreading the encounter that will open us to new life and new horizons as we come to know our brothers. As thy disciples in the world, we seek thy forgiveness and come now to consider thy ways in a new and strange earth that is finding itself a smaller and smaller part of the scheme of things. Hear us as we seek thy grace. Forgive us, O God. Forgive us. And lead us into thy ways. Amen.

SCRIPTURE:

> Is not this the fast that I choose:
> to loose the bonds of wickedness,
> to undo the thongs of the yoke,
> to let the oppressed go free,
> and to break every yoke?
> Is it not to share your bread with the hungry,
> and bring the homeless poor into your house;
> when you see the naked, to cover him,
> and not to hide yourself from your own flesh?
> Then shall your light break forth like the dawn,
> and your healing shall spring up speedily;
> your righteousness shall go before you,
> the glory of the Lord shall be your rear guard.
> Then you shall call, and the Lord will answer;
> you shall cry, and he will say, Here I am.
> —Isa. 58:6-9a R.S.V.

MOMENTS OF CONCERN: (*An optional, but powerful, element in this service of worship is the viewing of the fifteen-minute United Nations film "Overture," presenting the plight of millions of persons in the world today, and indicating the hope offered to them through the work of the United Nations. Fuller description and information about availability are to be found on page 193.*)

PRAYER FOR ALL MEN:

Our Father, the people of the world need so many things. We are thankful that the United Nations gives us a chance to help them. We pray for the work of the United Nations, realizing that it serves thy children, our brothers. We pray too, for all of the people of the world, for we do not forget that even as they come to have better food and clothing and shelter they can miss thy greatest gift to them: thy love, as shown to us in Christ. Make each one of us here today true evangelists of thine, carrying the word of thy love along as we seek to bind wounds and feed hungry mouths. In Jesus' name we pray. Amen.

PRAYER FOR CLOSER FELLOWSHIP:

Father of infinite mercy, humbly we come before thee. We know that thou callest us with a holy calling, but we know too that without thy help we shall fail before we reach our goal.

We pray—

That thy power may be shown in our day, filling us with the desire to live only for thee.

That thy word may reach the depths of our hearts and also touch the hearts of those who have not yet heard the Good News.

That the light of thy gospel may infiltrate more and more into the life of our nation and find a place in our traditions.

That our belief in the name of thy Son may help us draw nearer to our neighbor, helping him in his needs.

That thy unifying spirit may lead us into a sharing fellowship with other people in Africa, Europe, Asia, the Americas, and Australia.

And so, all united in the same Christian purpose, let us fight against the shadows that torment us in this world. Amen.[4]

BENEDICTION:

May thy enfolding love grow more and more in the world so that thy name will be known; and may we who know thy love hold it warmly and share it gladly. Amen.

Honoring Those Who Labor

Labor Day gives many groups the opportunity to focus their attention on the meaning of vocation and the significance of work.

The opportunities for worship on this occasion are sometimes limited, so the "order" of the service will have to adapt itself to the demands of the day. On nearly any occasion, with the proper setting of hymns and Scripture (see the list in the latter part of this chapter), the following story can become the center of memorable worship on Labor Day.

HIS BREAD TASTED SWEET

If you had been passing the St. John's Catholic Church in the steel town of Aliquippa, Pennsylvania, one day in the spring of 1939, you would have seen crowds of people, seven hundred or more of them, going inside. The cars in front of the church would have told you that it was a funeral that had brought such throngs of people there.

"What a very important person it must be to have so many people going to his funeral!" you would have thought. "It must be the mayor, or the president of the largest bank, or a famous explorer, or perhaps the richest man in town."

If you were curious enough, you might have asked someone, "Whose funeral?"

"Mario Ezzo's" the answer would have been.

"But who is Mario Ezzo?" you might well have asked.

The answer would have surprised you. "He's the shabby little old man who was always cleaning the streets."

After such a strange answer, you would have made a business of finding out why so many people were honoring a shabby old street cleaner. And this is what you would have learned.

Seven years before, Mario Ezzo had left Italy to make his home in America. This country was good to him, and he learned to love it. He still loved Italy, but there was room in his loyal old heart for the love of two countries. He was glad of work to do, even though his wages were so small that he could not lay aside much money for the time when there might be no way for him to earn, for the time when his feet would be less quick and his arms less strong.

The time finally came when no one seemed to need his help. He went from place to place, looking for work, but there were enough

167

younger men to do all the work for which there was money to be paid. Finally, there was nothing for him to do but tell the men who gave out relief money that he, Mario Ezzo, could find no way to earn. When the relief agents looked at the little old man, they did not hesitate to put him on the relief rolls. He was so shabby and so wizened that they were sure he must be very poor. They wondered why he had not come to them sooner.

"Here are three dollars and sixty cents," said the relief agent. "Come each week and you will receive the same amount."

Mario thanked him and went away.

Now so far this story is just like the story of hundreds and thousands of other people. But here comes the part that is different. Some men would have grumbled because three dollars and sixty cents a week is such a wee amount of money. They would have wondered how the government expected them to live on so little. They would have been sure that never again would they do any harder work than bringing a loaf of bread home from the bakery.

That was not Mario's way. When he thanked the relief agent, he really meant that he was grateful. When people are really grateful, they think of some way to show it. The first thing that Mario did when he left the relief office was to get a huge stiff brush. Then he went out into the dirtiest street he could find and began to sweep. He swept and he swept. Six days of the week and eight hours of the day, Mario Ezzo could be found sweeping the streets of Aliquippa. Each day he worked, rain or shine, and was seen at different times going beyond the town limits to repair sewers and dig surface water drains. He whistled as he worked, for he was a happy man. Why should he not be? He had work to do for others.

"Why do you work so hard?" people would ask him. "You get your relief money without working. Why bother to work?"

And Mario would stop whistling long enough to give an answer in English that was hard to understand. Italian was so much easier for him to speak. "I think this is a wonderful country," he would say. "I decide I will be an honest man with this country. They give me money to live. So I keep this town clean like table. It makes my bread taste sweeter. I am a man because I work." Then Mario Ezzo would bend to his work again, sweeping and sweeping as he whistled old Italian melodies.

168

This was the little old street cleaner whose funeral was packing the church. The people of Aliquippa, most of them steelworkers, later erected a monument for this man who worked for others so humbly, yet so usefully. The inscription on the stone reads, "Work makes me feel good inside, My bread it tastes tweet." [5]

Remembering Those Who Have Died in War

Memorial Day and Veterans Day are among the occasions when we pause to remember men and women who sacrificed their lives in line of duty in time of war. Their gift of themselves calls forth from us varied expressions of gratitude—gratitude not only to them but also to God whose love kept them and keeps them still.

Since the occasions for worship will vary considerably, it is suggested that this opportunity for worship be taken as a challenge to a group to make its worship expression on this occasion specific and personal.

Several steps will help any group achieve this aim.

First, the choice of hymns and scripture readings can serve as a prelude to further thought about the content of the worship service. By turning to the hymnal used by the group, and searching the section dealing with "National Life" or "America" or "Patriotism," appropriate hymns can be found; a partial list is found in the latter part of this chapter. Scripture readings can appropriately come from those parts of the Bible that find men concerned with their relationship to their nation, or with their remembrances of their heroes. See who in the group can recall such instances, and refer to them. For further help, there are suggested readings given in the latter half of this chapter. Beyond this preliminary effort, the group might want to consider several possibilities that will enable them to relate this special occasion directly to the community, or to specific events the group may want to commemorate. A litany might be created, in which the group would thank God specifically for heroes known to the group—or for the unsung heroes who have served so well. Or perhaps a committee could prepare a directed meditation that begins with the words, "We remember . . . ," and then filling in details that would be of special memory to the group. Or perhaps there is a poet in the group whose simple but sincere

169

offering might be just the thing to bring the group to full consciousness before God as they stop to remember those who have died in war.

And be sure to keep that main point always before you as you plan. We are pausing not to praise men alone. And we do not here merely celebrate our country's greatness. In worship on this occasion we come together before God to remember and to praise. We begin by confessing, and we end by expressing gratitude. And in so doing, we honor our heroes in the highest possible manner.

SOME ADDITIONAL RESOURCES

Scripture Selections

GOD JUDGES A NATION

Cry aloud, spare not,
  lift up your voice like a trumpet;
declare to my people their transgression,
  to the house of Jacob their sins.
Yet they seek me daily,
  and delight to know my ways,
as if they were a nation that did righteousness
  and did not forsake the ordinance of their God;
they ask of me righteous judgments,
  they delight to draw near to God
Why have we fasted, and thou seest it not?
  Why have we humbled ourselves,
  and thou takest no knowledge of it?
Behold, in the day of your fast you seek your own pleasure,
  and oppress all your workers.
Behold, you fast only to quarrel and to fight
  and to hit with wicked fist.
Fasting like yours this day
  will not make your voice to be heard on high.
Is such the fast that I choose,
  a day for a man to humble himself?
Is it to bow down his head like a rush,
  and to spread sackcloth and ashes under him?

Will you call this a fast,
and a day acceptable to the Lord?
Is not this the fast that I choose:
to loose the bonds of wickedness,
to undo the thongs of the yoke,
to let the oppressed go free,
and to break every yoke?
Is it not to share your bread with the hungry,
and bring the homeless poor into your house;
when you see the naked, to cover him,
and not to hide yourself from your own flesh?
Then shall your light break forth like the dawn,
and your healing shall spring up speedily;
your righteousness shall go before you,
the glory of the Lord shall be your rear guard.
Then you shall call, and the Lord will answer;
you shall cry, and he will say, Here I am.
If you take away from the midst of you the yoke,
the pointing of the finger, and speaking wickedness,
if you pour yourself out for the hungry
and satisfy the desire of the afflicted,
then shall your light rise in the darkness
and your gloom be as the noonday.
And the Lord will guide you continually,
and satisfy your desire with good things,
and make your bones strong;
and you shall be like a watered garden,
like a spring of water,
whose waters fail not.
And your ancient ruins shall be rebuilt;
you shall raise up the foundations of many generations;
you shall be called the repairer of the breach,
the restorer of streets to dwell in.

—Isa. 58:1-12 R.S.V.

GOD IS THE NATION'S RULER

We have heard with our ears, O God,
our fathers have told us,

171

what deeds thou didst perform in their days,
in the days of old:
thou with thy own hand didst drive out the nations,
but them thou didst plant;
thou didst afflict the peoples,
but them thou didst set free;
for not by their own sword did they win the land,
nor did their own arm give them victory;
but thy right hand, and thy arm,
and the light of thy countenance
for thou didst delight in them.
—Ps. 44:1-3 R.S.V.

THE THINGS THAT ARE CAESAR'S

And they sent to him some of the Pharisees and some of the Herodians, to entrap him in his talk. And they came and said to him, "Teacher, we know that you are true, and care for no man; for you do not regard the position of men, but truly teach the way of God. Is it lawful to pay taxes to Caesar, or not? Should we pay them, or should we not?" But knowing their hypocrisy, he said to them, "Why put me to the test? Bring me a coin, and let me look at it." And they brought one. And he said to them, "Whose likeness and inscription is this?" They said to him, "Caesar's." Jesus said to them, "Render to Caesar the things that are Caesar's, and to God the things that are God's." And they were amazed at him. (Mark 12:13-17 R.S.V.)

OTHER APPROPRIATE SCRIPTURE SELECTIONS

Prov. 6:6-11 or Prov. 24:30-34. A contrast between the life of industry and the life of idleness—for Labor Day.

Isa. 2:1-4. God the judge of all nations.

Ps. 33:1-12. The blessings of a nation whose God is the Lord.

Hymns
"God the Omnipotent."
"God of Our Fathers, Whose Almighty Hand."
"Lord, While for All Mankind We Pray."
"O God, Beneath Thy Guiding Hand."
"Great God of Nations, Now to Thee."

172

"In Christ There Is No East or West."
"O Beautiful for Spacious Skies" ("America").
"Men, Whose Boast It Is."
"Life of Ages, Richly Poured."

Prayers

FOR OUR LAND

Almighty God, we beseech thee to look with favor upon our land and people. All undeserving, thou has made us great among the nations of the earth. Let us forget that this place and this power have come from thee, and that we have them as a trust to use in thy service. Save us from pride and arrogance; make us quick to see the needs of those less fortunate than ourselves, and to be resolute in purpose to promote goodwill and fellowship among all men; through Jesus Christ our Lord. Amen.[6]

A PRAYER FOR NATIONAL GUIDANCE

O God, bless our country. Show her the way to walk, and give us the courage to help her walk in it. Hold before her the hope of peace and brotherhood, and give us the faith to move toward that hope. Make her contrite for her sins and penitent for her pride. But continue to bless her that she may in humility learn to serve thee as she opens her heart to all the men of the world. In Jesus' name. Amen.

PRAYER FOR GOOD LEADERS

O God, send us leaders who aren't too easy on us—who hold up before us things to do that are entirely too hard for us (but we try, anyway!) . . . who let us know in no uncertain terms that they expect nothing less than our best (and they always seem to expect more than we think is our best) . . . who show us what it is to be strong, and not to give in to little disappointments or pains and aches or failures (and by their own strength, we seem to have more ourselves). Send us, O God, leaders who are *good* for us! Amen.[7]
—CLARICE M. BOWMAN

A PRAYER FOR TRUE FREEDOM

O God of all lands, and of our land, make us free with the freedom that is rooted in thy truth and granted as a gift to those who

173

know thee. Unloose us from the bonds of our narrow timid, and false liberties so that we can move widely in the freedom of thy love. To this freedom thou hast called us. We pray that thou wilt strengthen us, that we might not use our freedom as an opportunity for selfishness, but that through love we may become servants of all men. In Christ's name we pray. Amen.

A PRAYER OF THANKS FOR THE NATION

Almighty God, who hast given us this good land for our heritage; We humbly beseech thee that we may always prove ourselves a people mindful of thy favour and glad to do thy will. Bless our land with honourable industry, sound learning and pure manners. Save us from violence, discord, and confusion; from pride and arrogancy, and from every evil way. Defend our liberties, and fashion into one united people the multitudes brought hither out of many kindreds and tongues. Endue with the spirit of wisdom those to whom in thy Name we entrust the authority of government, that there may be justice and peace at home, and that, through obedience to thy law, we may show forth thy praise among the nations of the earth. In the time of prosperity, fill our hearts with thankfulness, and in the day of trouble, suffer not our trust in thee to fail; all which we ask through Jesus Christ, our Lord. Amen.

—THE BOOK OF COMMON PRAYER

A PRAYER FOR GOD'S BLESSING ON LABOR

We thank Thee, O God, for the worship of this day and for the restoration of the body and soul which comes to us through communion with Thee. We rejoice that Thou hast permitted us to be coworkers with Thee in the unfolding of Thy divine plan. Thou hast set Thy blessing upon labor, and hast enabled us to promote the well-being of all by the faithful work we do. Strengthen in us, O God, the spirit of service and sacrifice. May we never be tempted to profit by impoverishing and degrading the lives of others. Make us realize the wrong of letting others hunger while we are surfeited with the bounties of nature. Implant in our hearts, we pray Thee, a sense of responsibility and comradeship. Reveal to us the divine glory that abides in every soul, and the high dignity that invests all honest labor. Help us so to live that, by our own endeavors, we may hasten the day when all shall toil and serve side by side as

174

brothers; when love and sympathy shall stir every heart, and greed and want no longer mar the beauty of Thy creation. Amen.[8]

—THE UNION PRAYER BOOK

A MORNING PRAYER
(Copied by George Washington at age twenty.)

Almighty God, and most merciful Father, who didst command the children of Israel to offer a daily sacrifice to Thee, that thereby they might glorify and praise Thee for Thy protection both night and day; receive, O Lord, my morning sacrifice which I now offer up to Thee; I yield Thee humble and hearty thanks that Thou hast preserved me from the dangers of the night past, and brought me to the light of this day, and the comforts thereof, a day which is consecrated to Thine own service and for Thine own honor. Let my heart, therefore, Gracious God, be so affected with the glory and majesty of it, that I may not do mine own works, but wait on Thee, and discharge those weighty duties Thou requirest of me; and since Thou art a God of pure eyes, and wilt be sanctified in all who draw near unto Thee, who dost not regard the sacrifice of fools, nor hear sinners who tread in Thy courts, pardon, I beseech Thee, my sins, remove them from Thy presence, as far as the East is from the West, and accept of me for the merits of Thy son, Jesus Christ, that when I come unto Thy temple, and compass Thine altar, my prayer may come before Thee as incense; and as Thou wouldst hear me calling upon Thee in my prayers, so give me grace to hear Thee calling on me in Thy word, that it may be wisdom, righteousness, reconciliation and peace to the saving of my soul in the day of the Lord Jesus. Grant that I may hear it with reverence, receive it with meekness, mingle it with faith, and that it may accomplish in me, Gracious God, the good work for which Thou hast sent it. Bless my family, kindred, friends and country; be our God and guide this day and forever for His sake, who lay down in the grave and rose again for us, Jesus Christ, our Lord. Amen.

A PRAYER FOR OUR NATION

God of our nation and of all the nations, we grope for thy hand in these confused days. Suffer us not to wander from our faith in thee and in the truths upon which our fathers founded the laws of our land. Grant us a sense of thy presence with us as we encounter new experiences that are fraught with both great opportunity and great danger.

Help us to remember that nations, as individuals, break themselves upon the stones that are thy just and unchangeable laws when they dare to ignore or to violate them. Convince us that ultimately justice must prevail. Illuminate our minds and the minds of all men to understand that those nations are blessed whose God is the Lord. Grant us patience to endure when our spirits are tried by disagreements between nations and between rulers.

Bid the men of God in every land to rise up and devote themselves to the building of a new order that shall be founded upon foundations of justice and truth and brotherhood and good will. Forbid that any of us should be so greatly disturbed by the strange and unaccustomed forms that the purposes of men take that we shall forget or neglect or postpone to build the commonwealth of God among men. Stab our spirits broad awake to realize that unless we sow the seeds of justice and peace we shall be sowing to the wind only to reap the whirlwind of yet fiercer strife and more deadly warfare than has ever ravaged the earth.

May our blessed America stand at the head of the forces of reconstruction. Help her to prove herself the good Samaritan to the devastated lands of the earth. Grant us courage and purpose to validate the faith of our fathers. So shall all the earth be blest. Amen.[9]

—CHARLES J. LOTZ

Litanies
A LITANY OF THANKS FOR AMERICA'S HEROES

LEADER: For all the leaders of our country, men and women of today and of the years gone by, we pray.

GROUP: Hear our prayer, O God.

LEADER: For heroic leaders whom we proclaim as giants in our land, we pray, and ask thy blessing on us as we follow in their way.

GROUP: Hear our prayer, O God.

LEADER: For leaders now in the line of duty, whose ideals and dreams are being challenged by the demand of expediency and selfishness, we pray, and ask thy blessing that they may stand for truth and right.

GROUP: Hear our prayer, O God.

LEADER: For lonely men now serving us in high places, we pray, and ask thee to send thy loving fellowship that their loneliness may become light with new meaning and dedication.

GROUP: Hear our prayer, O God.

LEADER: For men lost and wandering before thee, dishonest to their calling to serve our land, we pray, and beg thy forgiveness for them, even as we seek it daily for ourselves.

GROUP: Hear our prayer, O God.

LEADER: For all who serve our land, we pray, and for all who follow them.

GROUP: Hear our prayer, O God. Amen.

A RESPONSIVE AFFIRMATION OF DUTY

LEADER: Because it is our right in this bright land to have full life—food enough for our needs, shelter above our heads, and rest from the day's toil—

GROUP: It is our duty to offer the full life to all other men, children of God, our brothers on the face of the earth.

LEADER: Because it is our right in this bright land to have an open road before us as we seek the happiness that pulls us forward all our days,

GROUP: It is our duty to point the open road to other men, children of God, our brothers on the face of the earth.

LEADER: Because it is our right in this fair land to be free men and women, standing unbound before all the world, freed by God's love in Christ's sacrifice,

GROUP: It is our duty to proclaim this gracious gift of life to all other men, children of God, our brothers on the face of the earth.

A LITANY FOR LABOR DAY

LEADER: For the honest toil that refreshes our lives and sweetens our rest,

GROUP: We thank thee, Lord.

LEADER: For thy continuing call to us to serve Christ in the daily round of our labor,

GROUP: We thank thee, Lord.

LEADER: For reward after labor and the joy of a job well done,

GROUP: We thank thee, Lord.

177

LEADER: Because thou has sent thy Son before us as a worker, not ashamed,

GROUP: We thank thee, Lord.

LEADER: When hungry mouths cry for food, and we can heed their cries through our labor,

GROUP: We thank thee, Lord.

LEADER: When we daily join thy whole creation in praising thee through our work, we remember thy mercies to us, and we sing our praises with hammer, anvil, plow, and pen; needle, cradle, voice, and hand.

GROUP: We thank thee, Lord, we thank thee.

Poems

I THINK CONTINUALLY OF THOSE WHO WERE TRULY GREAT

I think continually of those who were truly great.
Who, from the womb, remembered the soul's history
Through corridors of light where the hours are suns,
Endless and singing. Whose lovely ambition
Was that their lips, still touched with fire,
Should tell of the spirit clothed from head to foot in song.
And who hoarded from the spring branches
The desires falling across their bodies like blossoms.

What is precious is never to forget
The delight of the blood drawn from ageless springs
Breaking through rocks in worlds before our earth;
Never to deny its pleasure in the simple morning light,
Nor its grave evening demand for love;
Never to allow gradually the traffic to smother
With noise and fog the flowering of the spirit.

Near the snow, near the sun, in the highest fields
See how those names are feted by the waving grass,
And by the streamers of white cloud,
And whispers of wind in the listening sky;
The names of those who in their lives fought for life,
Who wore at their hearts the fire's centre.
Born of the sun they traveled a short while towards the sun,
And left the vivid air signed with their honour.[10]

—STEPHEN SPENDER

178

NOW PRAISE WE GREAT AND FAMOUS MEN

Now praise we great and famous men,
The fathers, named in story;
And praise the Lord, who now as then
Reveals in man his glory.

Praise we the wise and brave and strong
Who graced their generation;
Who helped the right, and fought the wrong,
And made our folk a nation.

Praise we the great of heart and mind,
The singers sweetly gifted,
Whose music like a mighty wind
The souls of men uplifted.

Praise we the peaceful men of skill,
Who builded homes of beauty,
And, rich in art, made richer still
The brotherhood of duty.

Praise we the glorious names we know,
And they whose names have perished—
Lost in the haze of long ago—
In silent love be cherished.

In peace their sacred ashes rest,
Fulfilled their day's endeavor;
They blessed the earth, and they are blessed
Of God and man, for ever.

So praise we great and famous men,
The fathers named in story;
And praise the Lord, who now as then
Reveals in man his glory.[11]

—WILLIAM GEORGE TARRANT

INSCRIPTION AT MOUNT VERNON

Washington, the brave, the wise, the good,
Supreme in war, in council, and in peace,
Valiant without ambition, discreet without fear,
Confident without presumption.

179

In disaster, calm; in success, moderate; in all, himself.
The hero, the patriot, the Christian,
The father of nations, the friend of all mankind,
Who when he had won all, renounced all,
And sought in the bosom of his family and of nature, retirement,
And in the hope of religion, immortality.

THE INEVITABLE

I like the man who faces what he must
With step triumphant and a heart of cheer;
Who fights the daily battle without fear;
Sees his hopes fail, yet keeps unfaltering trust
That God is God; that somehow, true and just
His plans work out for mortals; not a tear
Is shed when fortune, which the world holds dear,
Falls from his grasp; better, with love, a crust
Than living in dishonor; envies not,
Nor loses faith in man; but does his best
Nor ever mourns over his humbler lot,
But with a smile and words of hope, gives zest
To every toiler; he alone is great
Who by a life heroic conquers fate.[12]

—SARAH K. BOLTON

AMERICA

God built Him a continent of glory and filled it with treasures untold;

He carpeted it with soft-rolling prairies and columned it with thundering mountains;

He studded it with sweet-flowing fountains and traced it with long-winding streams;

He planted it with deep-shadowed forests, and filled them with song.

Then He called unto a thousand peoples and summoned the bravest among them.

They came from the ends of the earth, each bearing a gift and a hope.

180

The glow of adventure was in their eyes, and in their hearts the
glory of hope.

And out of the bounty of earth and the labor of men,
Out of the longing of hearts and the prayer of souls,
Out of the memory of ages and the hopes of the world,
God fashioned a nation in love, blessed it with a purpose sublime—
And called it America! [13]

—ABBA HILLEL SILVER

THE HIGHER CITIZENSHIP

Athenians, I hold you in the highest regard and love,
But I will obey God rather than you;
And as long as I have breath and strength
I will not cease from philosophy, and from exhorting you,
And declaring the truth to every one of you whom I meet,
Saying, as I am wont, You are a citizen of Athens,
A city which is very great and famous for wisdom and power of
mind.
Are you not ashamed of caring so much for the making of money,
And for reputation?
Will you not think or care about wisdom,
And truth, and the perfection of your soul?

—SOCRATES

FREEDOM EVERMORE

For He that worketh high and wise,
Nor pauses in his plan,
Will take the sun out of the skies
Ere freedom out of man.

—RALPH W. EMERSON

EACH DAILY HAPPENING

A man I know has made an altar
Of his factory bench,
And one has turned the counter of his store
Into a place of sacrifice and holy ministry.
A Martha in our midst has made
Her kitchen table a communion table;
A postman makes his daily round

181

A walk in the temple of God:
To all these, each daily happening
Has come to be a whisper from the lips of God,
And every common circumstance
A wayside shrine.[14]

—RITA F. SNOWDEN

DEAR LAND OF ALL MY LOVE

Long as thine Art shall love true love,
Long as thy Science truth shall know,
Long as thin Eagle harms no Dove,
Long as thy Law by Law shall grow,
Long as thy God is God above,
Thy brother every man below,
So long, dear Land of all my love,
Thy name shall shine, thy fame shall grow.

—SIDNEY LANIER

CENTENNIAL HYMN

Our fathers' God! From out whose hand
The centuries fall like grains of sand,
We meet today, united, free,
And loyal to our land and Thee,
To thank Thee for the era done,
And trust Thee for the opening one.

Here, where of old, by Thy design,
The fathers spake that word of Thine
Whose echo is the glad refrain
Of rended bolt and falling chain,
To grace our festal time, from all
The zones of earth our guests we call.

Be with us while the New World greets
The Old World thronging all its streets,
Unveiling all the triumphs won
By art or toil beneath the sun;
And into common good ordain
This rivalship of hand and brain.

Thou, who hast here in concord furled

The war flags of a gathered world,
Beneath our Western skies fulfill
The Orient's mission of good-will,
And, freighted with love's Golden Fleece,
Send back its Argonauts of peace.

For art and labor met in truce,
For beauty made the bride of use,
We thank Thee; but, withal, we crave
The austere virtues strong to save,
The honor proof to place or gold,
The manhood never bought nor sold!

Oh make Thou us, through centuries long,
In peace secure, in justice strong;
Around our gift of freedom draw
The safeguards of Thy righteous law:
And, cast in some diviner mould,
Let the new cycle shame the old!
—JOHN GREENLEAF WHITTIER

THE TUFT OF FLOWERS

I went to turn the grass once after one
Who mowed it in the dew before the sun.

The dew was gone that made his blade so keen
Before I came to view the levelled scene.

I looked for him behind an isle of trees;
I listened for his whetstone on the breeze.

But he had gone his way, the grass all mown,
And I must be, as he had been,—alone,

"As all must be," I said within my heart,
"Whether they work together or apart."

But as I said it, swift there passed me by
On noiseless wing a bewildered butterfly,

Seeking with memories grown dim o'er night
Some resting flower of yesterday's delight.

And once I marked his flight go round and round,
As where some flower lay withering on the ground.

And then he flew as far as eye could see,
And then on tremulous wing came back to me.

I thought of questions that have no reply,
And would have turned to toss the grass to dry;

But he turned first, and led my eye to look
At a tall tuft of flowers beside a brook,

A leaping tongue of bloom the scythe had spared
Beside a reedy brook the scythe had bared.

I left my place to know them by their name,
Finding them butterfly weed when I came.

The mower in the dew had loved them thus,
By leaving them to flourish, not for us,

Nor yet to draw one thought of ours to him,
But from sheer morning gladness at the brim.

The butterfly and I had lit upon,
Nevertheless, a message from the dawn,

That made me hear the wakening birds around,
And hear his long scythe whispering to the ground,

And feel a spirit kindred to my own;
So that henceforth I worked no more alone;

But glad with him, I worked as with his aid,
And weary, sought at noon with him the shade;

And dreaming, as it were, held brotherly speech
With one whose thought I had not hoped to reach.

"Men work together," I told him from the heart,
"Whether they work together or apart." [15]

—Robert Frost

FROM "PASSAGE TO INDIA"

Have we not stood here like trees in the ground long enough?
Have we not groveled here long enough, eating and drinking,
like mere brutes?

Have we not darkened and dazed ourselves with books long
   enough?
Sail forth—steer for the deep waters only.
Reckless, O soul, exploring, I with thee, and thou with me,
For we are bound where mariner has not yet dared to go,
And we will risk the ship, ourselves and all!

O my brave soul!
O farther, farther sail!
O daring joy, but safe! are they not all the seas of God?
O farther, farther, farther sail!

                    —WALT WHITMAN

FREEDOM

The time has come for us to analyze
The great word "freedom," we who have been free
To walk upright beneath the arching skies
With no hard hand held out detainingly
To bar our way. We have walked proudly here
As is man's right upon the earth's good sod:
Free to speak forthrightly, free from fear,
And free in our own way to worship God.

So precious is that freedom, we would pay
The price for it no matter what the cost.
The cries across the world are loud today—
When nations lose their freedom, all is lost!
God stay the menace, blot it from the earth,
That men may hold this thing of vital worth.[16]

                —GRACE NOLL CROWELL

THOUGHTS UPON SEEING THE UNITED NATIONS BUILDING

Today
I saw a building made for peace
And it was wondrous fair.
Its walls were made of glass
And there was sunshine everywhere.
Its doors were made of burnished steel
Yet none need feel

185

Afraid to enter, for within was brotherhood.
And midst the sounds of many tongues
All understood.

I know
Another building made for peace.
Its ceiling is the sky.
I wonder why
Man built the walls of hate and greed,
And with a golden key
Locked doors to human need?

And yet
I know that with a patient, endless faith
The Architect holds fast
To blueprint incomplete—until at last
His workmen shall rise up anew
To make His dream of peace come true.[17]
—FRANCES G. TOWER

LET US HAVE PEACE

The earth is weary of our foolish wars.
Her hills and shores were shaped for lovely things,
Yet all our years are spent in bickerings
Beneath the astonished stars.

April by April laden with beauty comes,
Autumn by Autumn turns our toil to gain,
But hand at sword-hilt, still we start and strain
To catch the beat of drums.

Knowledge to knowledge adding, skill to skill,
We strive for others' good as for our own—
And then, like cavemen snarling with a bone,
We turn and rend and kill. . . .

With life so fair, and all too short a lease
Upon our special star! Nay, love and trust,
Not blood and thunder, shall redeem our dust.
Let us have peace! [18]
—NANCY BYRD TURNER

186

PEACE ON EARTH

Peace, peace on earth! the heart of man forever
Through all these weary strifes foretells the day;
Blessed be God, the hope forsakes him never,
That war shall end and swords be sheathed for aye.

Peace, peace on earth! for men shall love each other,
Hosts shall go forth to bless and not destroy;
For man shall see in every man a brother,
And peace on earth fulfill the angels' joy.

—SAMUEL LONGFELLOW

Meditations

THE PATRIOTISM OF PEACE

Ever since Stephen Decatur defined the arrogant patriotism of war the world has waited for a universal conception of the patriotism of peace.

The point too seldom stressed is that such a patriotism has its roots in simple things—in trees and earth and rivers, in homes and children, the schools we go to and the jobs we work at.

All of us are quick to associate patriotism with the mood of an heroic moment—watching an endless file of troops marching on and ever on, down to death and glory; seeing the flags go by, or cherishing the last dying note of "taps" echoing away on the horizon. We reserve our feelings for public occasions and let them burst in swelling triumph at an Inaugural, or the observance of Armistice Day and the Fourth of July.

It should be understood that these moments bear testimony to intensely brief and triumphantly desolate interludes in our country's history. The patriotism of peace plays no part in them. It cannot be encompassed in a fire-cracker, nor betrayed in a flight of oratory. It cannot be limited to a day, nor yet a year. It is a matter of the spirit, expressed in action, throughout our lives.

It is the spirit which moves men to go calmly and quietly about the task of conserving our waning forests, our minerals, our water power; harnessing the destructive power of floods; cleansing our rivers; embracing our new citizens; improving the cities in which we live and the industries in which we labor; creating healthier and happier and more prosperous homes; bringing education and enlightnment to young and old, to rich and poor.

187

These are the campaigns of peace, waged quietly, often un-
heroically. Victory holds no fruits of undying fame nor everlasting glory for the leaders—no frame but the happiness of our
fellow, no glory but the glory of progress.[19]

LINCOLN

Noah Brooks, in a speech in 1860 at Cooper Union, New
York, spoke of Abraham Lincoln in these words:
"When Lincoln rose to speak, I was greatly disappointed. He
was tall, tall—oh, how tall!—and so angular and awkward that I
had, for an instant, a feeling of pity for so ungainly a man. His
clothes were black and ill-fitting, badly wrinkled—as if they had
been jammed carelessly into a small trunk. His bushy head, with
stiff black hair thrown back, was balanced on a long and lean head-
stalk, and when he raised his hands in an opening gesture, I
noticed that they were very large. He began in a low tone of
voice—as if he were used to speaking outdoors, and was afraid of
speaking too loud. He said, 'Mr. Cheerman,' instead of 'Mr.
Chairman,' and employed many other words with an old-fashioned
pronunciation. I said to myself:
" 'Old fellow, you won't do; it's all very well for the wild West,
but this will never go, down in New York.'
"But pretty soon he began to get into his subject; he straightened
up, made regular and graceful gestures; his face lighted as with an
inward fire; the whole man was transfigured. I forgot his clothes,
his personal appearance, his individual peculiarities. Presently, forgetting myself, I was on my feet with the rest, yelling like a wild
Indian, cheering this wonderful man. In the closing parts of his
argument, you could hear the gentle sizzling of the gas-burners.
When he reached a climax the thunders of applause were terrific.
It was a great speech.
"When I came out of the hall, my face glowing with excitement and my frame all a-quiver, a friend, with his eyes aglow,
asked me what I thought of Abe Lincoln, the rail-splitter. I said:
" 'He's the greatest man since St. Paul.' And I think so yet."

A CHRISTIAN'S RESPONSIBILITY ON A CHANGING PLANET

Christians have seen basic responsibilities in a changing world.
1. They must study and know the facts as profoundly as pos-

sible. This means thousands of hours of hard, responsible work; and this includes especially knowledge of the laws of change. The Christian has no excuse whatsoever to be shallow and sentimental. The Christian thinker must be the deepest thinker in the world; his aim is to overcome all stupid superficiality of analysis.

2. They must feel profound concern for the state of the world. They are makers of history and not mere on-lookers, and God will hold them strictly accountable for the course of events. Profound and troubled concern is an absolute Christian necessity.

3. They must be in close touch with situations. They must think, act and react from within these situations. To think and talk from outside is a very grievous sin these days. And this "closeness of touch" must include taking the poor, lonely, weak, distracted, over-worked and over-burdened leaders into the inner warm fellowship of the Church. The Church cannot assume responsibility for political decisions; it can only criticize, inspire, commend, set up norms in accordance with the will of its Lord.

4. Prayer is a fourth requisite. The Christian must daily invoke several times God's will on earth as it is in heaven. Nothing is more potent before the throne of God than the sincere prayer of a contrite heart.

5. A Christian has responsibilities to Jesus Christ, over and above any other responsibilities he may be shouldering in this life. He must therefore witness to him, amidst every change and despite every change. A most grievous sin is to allow the change so to overwhelm us as to cause us to forget our witnessing duties. Our direct knowledge of the grace of Christ is infinitely more important than all the world and all its changes.

6. The Christian must seek the unity of the Church. This is the urge at ecumenicity. If the Christians really become one, the world will be suddenly transfigured. This takes infinite humility. No greater scandal exists than that of the separation of those who were baptized in the name of the Father, of the Son and of the Holy Ghost.

7. Christians must remain faithful to their faith, in all the plentitude of its fundamental tenets as they have received them from the Apostles, from the Fathers and from the Saints. This holy deposit of faith regarding man, history and God is above all

189

systems, all ideologies and all economic and political orders. It is most important to achievement, no matter how noble and true. Jesus Christ, the Cross, the Gospel, the Church, the Freedom of the children of God—these things cannot be subject to any "change" in any "changing planet." The primary Christian responsibility on a changing planet is to be humbly faithful to Jesus Christ.

If we know the truth in all its depths, if we are genuinely troubled and concerned about the world, if for any situation we learn to speak from within, if we pray and pray and pray, if we never faint in witnessing to Jesus Christ despite our dullness and preoccupations, if we seek the original unity of the Church according to the will of Christ, and if we remain faithful to the full plenitude of our faith, then there is hope that a changing planet will in God's time be captured to the glory of God in Jesus Christ.[20]

—CHARLES MALIK

THE PLAIN AND POWERFUL PILGRIMS

Some regard the settling of New Plymouth as the sowing of the seed from which the crop of Modern America has grown. For all the Mayflower's sailing there is, perhaps, little existing in modern England or America "according to the Primitive Pattern in the Word of God." It would be healthful could either country see herself through the eyes of those pioneers, or see the pioneers as they were. The Pilgrims leave no impression of personality on the mind. They were not "remarkable." Not one of them had compelling personal genius, or marked talent for the work in hand. They were plain men of moderate abilities, who, giving up all things, went to live in the wilds, at unknown cost to themselves, in order to preserve to their children a life in the soul.[21]

—JOHN MASEFIELD

A FEAR-FILLED PEOPLE

"I will show you fear in a handful of dust."—T. S. Eliot.

Why are our lives, indeed the whole of America, seemingly so filled with fear and mistrust today? Could the chief reason be that America has neglected God?

We have driven God to the outer fringes of life, and in his

place we have made our culture our god. We want things to remain as they are because we are on top! We are like the cartoon character who said, "Well, sir, reforms are all right so long as they don't change anything."

We fail to distinguish between values which are worth living for and life's rubbish. We place "possessions above persons, position above perfection, and power above principle." There come moments of moral and spiritual strength from God stimulating us to acts of Christian love, but our wills are paralyzed and we respond not to the highest within us, but to our own selfish desires.

We destine ourselves for defeat both as individuals and as a nation when we live by physical power alone, and neglect the spiritual power. From his study of the rise and fall of twenty-one civilizations preceding ours in America, Arnold Toynbee concludes that the temptation to use military power is a sign of coming destruction.

Father, help us to trust in you knowing that fears vanish and the peace which passes all understanding comes only when we dedicate our wills to yours. Amen.[22]

—FINLEY EVERSOLE

THE LIFE BEHIND THE STATISTICS

He was working as an office boy that day the man came in and started talking with him, asking him what his plans were, what he really wanted to do, "You ought to take up engineering," he said, putting the idea, and with it, the possibility, into the boy's mind.

Herbert thought about it. He liked the idea. But what did he have to go on?

Certainly not money for a college education. After the death of his parents he had left his hometown, West Branch, Iowa, and come out here to Oregon to live with his uncle, a country doctor. Worse still, he had never been to high school.

But he had been to night school and picked up some Latin and mathematics, so when he came across a notice that Stanford University was opening in the fall and tuition was free he decided to try to pass the entrance exams.

While studying at Stanford he spent his summers working with the United States Geological Survey. With that experience and his diploma, he expected to land a job the minute he graduated.

He was in for a rude shock. Nobody was impressed by his diploma. Recalling that time many years later, ex-president Herbert Hoover told NBC's Ray Henle in an interview: "I got to a condition where I took a job underground in a gold mine. I didn't even have the distinction of being a miner. I was started loading trucks. A miner is a fellow who runs a drill. I rose to that eminent position only two or three months later." And he worked a ten-hour day, six days a week, for two dollars a day.

From this princely salary, he finally saved enough to make it to San Francisco and a better job. His first ten-thousand-dollar job was in Australia. Then as a partner in an international engineering firm he managed mines in China, India, Burma, Australia, Russia, Canada, and the United States.

In the first seven years of our century, his work took him around the world seven times.

He came to know it and its people as few other men could. And he acquired unusual skill in organizing and financing large scale projects. When the first World War broke out, engineer Herbert Hoover was the man for the enormous job of Food Administrator of the United States, to which Woodrow Wilson called him. With the Quaker's habit of understandment, he explained to Ray Henle: "You had to transport a tremendous volume of food overseas with a fleet of 300 ships . . . distribute and transport it . . . ration the populations; . . . in fact it was the first food administration in the history of the world."

Later the Allied governments called him back to Europe to take over the rehabilitation and food supply of some 350 million people in Eastern Europe.

In 1923 Russia was hit by a severe drought. And it was Mr. Hoover who was sent over to administer seventy million dollars of American money for Russian relief.

During World War II, he was called back into service again to shoulder the task of famine relief. He visited thirty-eight nations by plane. As a result of his work, instead of 800 million people dead of starvation, no mass starvation occurred anywhere.

What a work score for one lifetime! All this and the years in the White House too. Did he ever accept any compensation for it? You may have heard the interview in which he said: "I prospered in my profession . . . I was able to have a competence; and I felt that I owed my country a debt that was unpayable. I felt that I had no right to ask her to pay me. That has been my practice right up until this moment." [23]

—ELEANOR B. STOCK

Audio-Visuals

Overture. In a short nine-minute period this film, without speaking a word, carries us out across the world to witness the waste and destruction that follow war. Then we see a hint of hope as United Nations forces begin to help the world rebuild. A powerful musical score and deeply sensitive selection of photography make this a powerful inspirational meditation, to which the worship leader will want to append his own statement concerning the role of the love of Christ in reconstruction. For information concerning availability, write your denominational film library or Contemporary Films, 614 Davis Street, Evanston, Illinois or 267 West 25th Street, New York City.

Sound of a Stone. In a worship setting, this distressing story of a midwestern high school teacher accused of "subversive activities" can open the matter of civil rights for Christian meditation and prayer. The film is twenty-seven minutes in length, and is available in color or black and white. For information concerning availability, write Cokesbury, 201 Eighth Avenue South, Nashville 3, Tennessee.

Alternatives. This twenty-four minute color film uses animation and the narration of a motion picture star (Don Murray) to tell the story of the conscientious objector to military service. The story is told in such a way that the film can be integrated into a service of worship in which the worshipers are concerned to explore the ways in which a young Christian can walk today as he faces military service. An excellent leader's guide can be ordered so that a group can determine ahead of time if it can make good use of the film. For information about availability, write denominational film libraries or the Fellowship of Reconciliation, Nyack, New York.

The Face of Lincoln. This twenty-minute film classic presents an almost spiritual portrayal of Lincoln as a sculptor executes his

193

work of this great president and tells us of his life. There is quiet simplicity here that catches us and enables us to see Lincoln grow from thoughful youthfulness to deep maturity. This black and white film can be used imaginatively in worship on the occasion of Lincoln's birth. For information about availability, write the University of Southern California, Department of Cinema, Los Angeles 7, California.

The Bible and the Presidents. This excellent series of sound filmstrips shows the ways in which the Bible has profoundly influenced four of our presidents. The material is treated in an inspirational manner, and the resources are therefore easily adaptable for use in worship settings. The titles are *Inspiration to Greatness: George Washington; We Hold These Truths: Thomas Jefferson; A Man and His Book: Abraham Lincoln; and Doer of the Word: Theodore Roosevelt.* The filmstrips are in color. They each require seventeen minutes playing time. They may be ordered from The American Bible Society, either from its branch offices, or from headquarters, P. O. Box 98, New York 16, New York. They are also distributed by some denominational film libraries.

194

CHAPTER 9

Lent and Easter

The Lenten season is celebrated in many ways by different churches. Many Protestant denominations do not have regular, prescribed orders in which all their members participate. But every church has its own way of offering special opportunities for worship in this time of penitence that precedes the joy of the Easter season. Your denominational resources present a rich source of guidance every year, so do not neglect to find and use them.

Groups within a church will want to plan their own worship experience so that it is an appropriate part of the whole plan of worship in the church, and it is with that fact in mind that the following suggestions are offered. None of the services or ideas below are intended to be used as substitutes for the regular and essential congregational worship that nourishes the Christian life as nothing else can. But they can serve you and your group if you feel a special need to take part—within your group—in the happiness and seriousness of this season of the church's life.

For the Beginning of Lent

At the beginning of Lent, Christians will be reminding themselves that they have an opportunity for soul-searching and for rededication to the way of Christ. The following service can serve to help a group plan its own way of entering this season. Some groups might find the occasion of enough importance to set aside a special time—a week-night, or an early morning period—for the purpose of preparing for the journey to Easter.

195

PRELUDE

INVOCATION:

Hear us, O God, for we come to thee asking for help. We want to enter the lean days that precede our celebration of Christ's victory over death. We know that we need to pause to look deeply within ourselves, and we ask thee to help us look with honesty and courage. We want to see ourselves as we are, and we want the brightness of Jesus Christ to illumine our way so that we can become the persons thou hast destined us to be.

HYMN: "All Glory, Laud, and Honor."

SCRIPTURE:

Surely he has borne our griefs
    and carried our sorrows;
yet we esteemed him stricken,
    smitten by God, and afflicted.
But he was wounded for our transgressions,
    he was bruised for our iniquities;
upon him was the chastisement that made us whole,
    and with his stripes we are healed.
All we like sheep have gone astray;
    we have turned every one to his own way;
and the Lord has laid on him
    the iniquity of us all.

—Isa. 53:4-6 R.S.V.

MEDITATION:

Another Lenten season is here. All over the world Christian men and women are reminded of the forty dark days preceding the Crucifixion.

It all happened such a long, long time ago, and in such a faraway country. To the people then alive, large and important events were in progress. There was money to be made, trading to be done, taxes to be gathered, and wars to be fought. As today, fame, glory, love were sweet.

A strange man called the Nazarene was reported to be saying foolish things. In a universe of competition and hate, He spoke

196

of love. In a land bristling with soldiers, He talked of peace. Where the rich and powerful were masters, He emphasized the dignity of the humble and the poor. Cruelty, greed, ambition, arrogance, lust and all manner of evil spread a blackness over the then known earth. In its midst for a short while, a Light glowed—Jesus walking among men.

Then, when men had scourged, mocked and crucified Him, nothing happened. He was gone, and things appeared to be as usual. The friends who loved Him most began to forget the miracle of the Resurrection. The old evil life of the Romans went on.

Yet nearly 2000 years later other men of other races speak of those days with a catch in their throats. Their hearts move with mysterious longing. Now and then, some memory of that time returns to haunt them and their souls yearn for the love of which the Nazarene spoke. A resurgence of the ancient hope lightens their spirits. For down the years and through the mists of time, they hear the echo of a Voice that said—

"To this end was I born, and for this cause came I into the world, that I should bear witness unto the truth. Everyone that is of the truth heareth My voice."

Yes, the Lenten season is here again. And He whom we call our Saviour endures once more the ancient agony. While the few weep, the many crucify Him.[1]

SCRIPTURE:

Surely he has borne our griefs
    and carried our sorrows;
Yet we esteem him stricken,
    smitten by God, and afflicted.
But he was wounded for our transgressions,
    he was bruised for our iniquities;
upon him was the chastisement that made us whole,
    and with his stripes we are healed.
All we like sheep have gone astray;
    we have turned every one to his own way;
and the Lord has laid on him
    the iniquity of us all.

—Isa. 53:4-6 R.S.V.

197

Let us then with confidence draw near to the throne of grace, that we may receive mercy and find grace to help in time of need.

(Heb. 4:16 R.S.V.)

SILENT MEDITATION

POEM:

Now let the body fast a while,
The shelf and board grow lean,
And man lift up his hungry heart
To find a world unseen.

Now let him know his beggared state,
What starveling fare is bread,
What sparse and bitter herbs are his
Unless the soul be fed.[2]

SILENT MEDITATION

HYMN:

Lift up your heads, ye mighty gates,
Behold, the King of glory waits;
The King of kings is drawing near;
The Saviour of the world is here!

Fling wide the portals of your heart;
Make it a temple, set apart
From earthly use for Heaven's employ,
Adorned with prayer and love, and joy.

Redeemer, come, we open wide
Our hearts to Thee; here, Lord, abide.
Thine inner presence let us feel;
Thy grace and love in us reveal. Amen.

—GEORG WIESSEL

BENEDICTION:

The Lord bless you and keep you; the Lord make His face to shine upon you and be gracious unto you; the Lord lift up His countenance upon you and give you peace. Amen.

For Holy Week

Some groups have the opportunity to spend some time in worship during each day of Holy Week. In order to achieve a unity in the worship for this period, it is a good idea to develop a special order, into which appropriate scriptures, hymns, and meditations can be integrated. Below there is one suggested order, and some possible meditations that might be used for each day. If possible, the order of service should be duplicated and made available to every worshiper so that the litany can be fully participated in.

PRELUDE

INVOCATION:

O God, we have come to walk again the last days in the life of our Lord. Guide our steps. Enable us to meet the Master day by day as we recall his sacrificial love for us. In his name we pray. Amen.

HYMN (*Use the appropriate hymn from the following list*):
Monday: "Lift Up Your Heads, Ye Mighty Gates."
Tuesday: "All Glory, Laud, and Honor."
Wednesday: "O Thou Eternal Christ of God."
Maundy Thursday: "Into the Woods My Master Went."
Good Friday: "O Sacred Head, Now Wounded."

SCRIPTURE:
Monday: Mark 11:12-21.
Tuesday: Mark 12:38-44.
Wednesday: Matt. 26:14-16.
Thursday: Matt. 26:36-50.
Friday: Luke 23:32-38.

LITANY:
LEADER: Lord, Have mercy upon us.
GROUP: Christ, have mercy upon us.
LEADER: Lord, have mercy upon us.
LEADER: Blessed Saviour: By thy entry into Jerusalem:
GROUP: Give us courage to accept the issues of our faith.

199

LEADER: By thy cleansing of the Temple:

GROUP: Give us zeal for righteousness and for thy holy church.

LEADER: By thy breaking of the bread and giving of the cup:

GROUP: Help us to give ourselves for the life of the world.

LEADER: By thy washing of the disciples' feet:

GROUP: Take away our pride, and endue us with the spirit of true humility.

LEADER: By thy acceptance in the Garden of the will of God:

GROUP: Help us to seek to learn the will of God, and to surrender our own will to it.

LEADER: By thy forgiveness of those who nailed thee to the Cross:

GROUP: Make us steadfast in our faith to our life's end, for thy Name's sake.

LEADER: Almighty and everlasting God, who, of thy tender love towards mankind, has sent thy Son, our Saviour Jesus Christ, to take upon him our flesh, and to suffer death upon the cross, that all mankind should follow the example of his great humility; Mercifully grant, that we may both follow the example of his patience, and also be made partakers of his resurrection; through the same Jesus Christ our Lord. Amen.[3]

MEDITATION (See below for texts of meditations):

Monday: A Tree Without Fruit

Tuesday: More Blessed to Give

Wednesday: What Will You Give?

Thursday: Why Are You Here?

Friday: He Saved Others

PRAYER:

O God, as we recall the last days of our Master and dwell upon his life and his teachings, send thy Spirit upon us so that the saving grace of our Lord and Savior can become powerful in our lives. With penitence we remember the love that has loved us, the life that was lived for us, the blood that was shed for us. Forgive us our easy forgetfulness, our careless indifference, and help us to become thy servants.

THE LORD'S PRAYER, IN UNISON:
Our Father, who art in heaven: hallowed be thy name. Thy kingdom come, thy will be done, on earth as it is in heaven. Give us this day our daily bread. And forgive us our trespasses, as we forgive those who trespass against us. And lead us not into temptation, but deliver us from evil. For thine is the kingdom, and the power, and the glory, for ever. Amen.

BENEDICTION:
The grace of the Lord Jesus Christ, and the love of God, and the communion of the Holy Spirit, be with you all. Amen.

Texts of Meditations for Holy Week

MONDAY: A TREE WITHOUT FRUIT

If you can isolate any one incident which leads directly to the crucifixion of Christ, it is probably the cleansing of the temple. For in this act Jesus reveals His true intention—to bring all men into one fellowship with God.

The court of the Gentiles had been built into the temple at Jerusalem as a promise. For the people of Israel were called to be a light to the Gentiles, to bring all nations to the Lord. But it is in the court of the Gentiles that the temple money-changers and livestock agents have set up their business. The mission of the Jews had been forgotten; these men are out to make a profit for themselves out of religion.

So the fury of Jesus is unleashed, and the meaning of His anger is unmistakable.

A church that does not turn its eyes outward to serve the world is a tree without fruit. The haughty self-righteousness and pride that so easily infiltrate the church are the seeds of death and decay.

We are called to throw our lives away in the service of mankind. We receive an invitation to become the servants of all. We are not offered wealth and prestige; we are offered a cross.

Prayer: God, let me not turn down the cross of life for any worldly security. Amen.[4]

TUESDAY: MORE BLESSED TO GIVE

There is a kind of piety which is really disguised self-seeking. It is easy to parade your goodness before men, seeking admiration and applause. The noblest act can become the vehicle of our selfish pride.

But true piety seeks no reward; it seeks only to do the will of God. Christ is never anxious for the praise of men. He is only anxious that He fail neither His Father nor His brother.

He watches the men who come to give their gifts to God. The rich come and, with a great show, give large sums. A widow comes and puts in a penny. And it is the widow whom He praises.

He does not measure our gifts by their size. He measures by how much the gift costs the giver. The widow gave all that she had.

He watches through this day as you and I give of ourselves and our goods to God's service. And as we answer our neighbor's need, as we participate in the work of the church, as we speak with friends, let us remember how He evaluates our service. It is not the impression we make which counts with Him. He longs to see us give all that we have to God.

Prayer: Lord, let my giving be free from pride and self-seeking. Amen.[5]

WEDNESDAY: WHAT WILL YOU GIVE?

Judas asks this fateful question of the chief priests: "What will you give me if I deliver Him to you?" At one time or another we all ask that question.

You know the kind of things a man is promised if he will betray the Christ. Some do it for safety. Judas may well have bargained for this. He could avoid suffering himself if he joined the other side. That kind of betrayal is something we know about. Are there not times when you are afraid to witness for Him?

Some betray Him for cheap popularity. We are anxious to be one of the gang. We do not want to be different because of Him. We fear the disapproval of our friends more than the disappointment of God.

Perhaps the most common reason of all is that we want to be our own Master. We want to do what we please. We want freedom to determine our own destiny, and for this we betray Him.

But all these things that seem so attractive turn into ashes in our hands. Judas finally threw down the money and took his own life. Safety, popularity, freedom are all worthless apart from Christ. Life itself has no meaning for the betrayer.

Prayer: God, keep me from betraying my Savior. Amen.[6]

THURSDAY: WHY ARE YOU HERE?

The shadowy garden of Gethsemane has many visitors tonight. There comes a man who brings His friends with Him and then goes apart from them to pray. His prayer is agonizing and painful, for He accepts the crushing burden of the world's sin upon His shoulders. And most terrible of all, He sees that He can atone for the sin He carries only by death. The victory of God can only be won by apparent defeat. God is about to deliver Him over to the condemnation and judgment of unrighteous men. Yet if this is the will of God, Jesus will accept it.

Where are the Master's friends? They have been singled out to share in the redemptive work of Christ—called to follow Him. But when His greatest crisis comes, they are asleep.

And now another comes into the garden. He leads a group of soldiers. In false devotion he greets Christ as "Master." In mock love he kisses Him. But the Lord with infinite love looks into his eyes and asks, "Friend, why are you here?"

Why have you come to the Garden of Gethsemane? Why do you call Him Lord? What will you do when He most needs you?

Prayer: Lord Jesus, let me watch with Thee and share Thy grief. Amen.[7]

FRIDAY: HE SAVED OTHERS

There was one thing Jesus could not do. He could not save Himself. The people chanted in derision, "He saved others; let Him save Himself, if He is the Christ of God, His chosen One!" And in their mockery they hit upon the fundamental truth of His life.

The whole tragic history of man's alienation from God, beginning in the Garden of Eden and leading to the present day, is the struggle of man to save himself. We want to control our destiny.

Jesus is always absolutely dependent on His Father. At the beginning of His ministry He firmly put down the temptation to use His God-given power for His own advantage. Here, at the

203

end of His ministry, He cannot do anything to lighten the suffering and shame of death on a cross. He cannot save Himself.

See Him there upon the cross, ridiculed by the passing crowd. His will is perfectly one with that of God. His confidence is supremely in God and in what God will do with His act.

It is not what we do that matters in life. It is what God does with what we do. It is not our work that shall save the world—it is God working through us.

Prayer: Father, keep me from seeking to save myself. Amen.[8]

A Service for Good Friday

PRELUDE

PRAYER:

Most merciful Father, we thank thee for thy lavish generosity to us, the children of men. We who deserve nothing but judgment are called this day into fellowship with thee through thy Son Jesus Christ. We stand in perpetual amazement of thy love, manifested in the life and death and resurrection of Jesus Christ, else we could not believe it. But thou hast placarded it before our eyes. Thanks be to thee! Help us now to abandon our craven fears and to turn in faith to the love revealed on Calvary. Suffer us not to rely upon our own feelings, but give us courage to trust what we have seen in his outstretched arms, the love that will not let us go.

And this we ask for his sake. Amen.[9]

HYMN: "O Sacred Head, Now Wounded."

SCRIPTURE:

So they took Jesus, and he went out, bearing his own cross, to the place called the place of a skull, which is called in Hebrew Golgotha. There they crucified him, and with him two others, one on either side, and Jesus between them. Pilate also wrote a title and put it on the cross; it read, "Jesus of Nazareth, the King of the Jews." Many of the Jews read this title, for the place where Jesus was crucified was near the city; and it was written in Hebrew, in Latin, and in Greek. The chief priests of the Jews then said to

Pilate, "Do not write, 'The King of the Jews,' but, 'This man said, I am King of the Jews.'" Pilate answered, "What I have written I have written."

When the soldiers had crucified Jesus they took his garments and made four parts, one for each soldier. But his tunic was without seam, woven from top to bottom; so they said to one another, "Let us not tear it, but cast lots for it to see whose it shall be." This was to fulfill the scripture.

"They parted my garments among them,
and for my clothing they cast lots."

So the soldiers did this; but standing by the cross of Jesus were his mother, and his mother's sister, Mary the wife of Clopas, and Mary Magdalene. When Jesus saw his mother, and the disciple whom he loved standing near, he said to his mother, "Woman, behold your son!" Then he said to the disciple, "Behold your mother!" And from that hour the disciple took her to his own home.

After this Jesus, knowing that all was now finished, said (to fulfill the scripture), "I thirst." A bowl full of vinegar stood there; so they put a sponge full of the vinegar on hyssop and held it to his mouth. When Jesus had received the vinegar, he said, "It is finished"; and he bowed his head and gave up his spirit. (John 19:17-30 R.S.V.)

THE LORD'S PRAYER:

Our Father, who art in heaven: hallowed be thy Name, Thy kingdom come, thy will be done, on earth as it is in heaven. Give us this day our daily bread. And forgive us our trespasses, as we forgive those who trespass against us. And lead us not into temptation, but deliver us from evil. For thine is the kingdom, and the power, and the glory, for ever. Amen.

MEDITATION:

On a Friday during the middle of what we call the first century an itinerant lay preacher and healer from Galilee, found by the rulers of the day to be politically dangerous and by the churches to be heretical, was executed outside the walls of Jerusalem on a wooden crossbeam in the manner of the times. In some ways it was a common event; crosses were so numerous during the procuratorship of Pilate that even a sensitive man could pass them by with hardly a glance. But this cross, flung against a lowering sky, has posed questions and put claims which men have not been able to ignore. No answer to those questions, no response to those claims, has been at once so audacious and yet so acceptable as the Petrine explanation that this cross came by the "definite plan and fore-knowledge of God." If you say that the cross is unutterable cruelty, you are right; if you say that it is magnificent heroism, you are right; but you are wrong if you say no more. For there was something more here than extreme brutality on the one side and futile courage on the other. God took this matter out of the hands of both crucifiers and crucified and wrought the miracle which was for the salvation of the world. This is either ghastly lie or glorious truth. To say it, one must either strut on the edge of utmost blasphemy or bow before a mystery too deep for thought. When men are seized by this truth on the inside of their being, they call this day not evil or brave but Good Friday.[10]

SOLO: "O Thou Eternal Christ of God."

PRAYER (The Gloria in Excelsis, to be said or sung):

Glory be to God on high, and on earth peace, good will toward men. We Praise Thee, we bless Thee, we worship Thee, we glorify Thee, we give thanks to Thee for Thy great glory, O Lord God, Heavenly King, God the Father Almighty!

O Lord, the only-begotten Son Jesus Christ: O Lord God, Lamb of God, Son of the Father, that takest away the sins of the world, have mercy upon us. Thou that takest away the sins of the world, have mercy upon us. Thou that takest away the sins of the world, receive our prayer. Thou that sittest at the right hand of God the Father, have mercy upon us. For Thou only art holy; Thou only art the Lord; Thou only, O Christ, with the Holy Ghost, art most high in the glory of God the Father. Amen.

BENEDICTION:

And now may our God, the Father of our Lord and Savior, Jesus Christ, grant us his peace, that our hearts and minds may be kept in his knowledge and love; and may the blessing of God

206

—the Father, the Son, and the Holy Spirit—be among us and remain with us always. Amen.

A Brief Service for Easter Sunday

All groups will want to join together with their entire congregations for worship on this highest occasion of our Christian year. But many will also want to spend a few moments together within the warm fellowship of their own group. These moments together will not need to be especially formal, and they certainly do not need to be long. The following suggestion is built around one of the hymns we like to sing on Easter Sunday. The brief meditation will lead the group to a joyful expression of its faith in song—and the group will have sung its Easter praises together and be prepared to join their fellow Christians at the congregational worship hours.

PRELUDE

PRAYER:

On this glad Easter day, our Father, we come together here in the fellowship that means so much to us to praise thee and thank thee for thy Son, Jesus Christ, who has died for us, and who was raised from the dead so long ago, to become thy living Son and our ever-living Lord. Hear our prayers this day, and grant us thy love. Hear our songs of praise, and make us truly thine. In Jesus' name we pray. Amen.

MEDITATION:

As each year comes and goes, all of us wonder a little bit more about that strange event that each and every person knows he must face: death.

Even when we are young, death begins to haunt us with its threat. We know relatives and sometimes even close friends who come face to face with death; some live through such events, but others die. And we begin to wonder what death is all about.

Job wondered. And the more he wondered the angrier he got. To him, it was wicked of God to create man, give him life and happiness, children and land, and then allow him to be destroyed.

207

... there is hope for a tree,
    if it be cut down, that it will sprout again,
    and that its shoots will not cease. ...

.   .   .   .

But man dies, and is laid low;
    man breathes his last, and where is he?
As waters fail from a lake,
    and a river wastes away and dries up,
So man lies down and rises not again;
    till the heavens are no more he will not awake,
    or be roused out of his sleep. ...
If a man die, shall he live again?
                                —Job 14:7; 10-12, 14 R.S.V.

This very question that has always haunted us was answered with great joy on the first Easter.

For Christ, tortured and killed by his enemies, did not let death conquer him. God raised him from his tomb into the world again where he entered the hearts of those who loved and accepted him. And by his own conquest of death, his followers believe that they too will live again after their bodies die and are seen no more on earth.

For those who know Christ, this grand hope is cause for rejoicing. And it was to celebrate this hope and to express joy that Charles Wesley wrote the triumphant hymn, "Christ the Lord Is Risen Today, Alleluia!" [11]

Christians have sung it joyfully for many years. This morning our voices will join thousands who sing it again with loud alleluias!

HYMN: "Christ the Lord Is Risen Today."

POEM:
The Head that once was crown'd with thorns
    Is crown'd with glory now;
A royal diadem adorns
    The mighty Victor's brow.

The highest place that heaven affords
    Belongs to Him by right,

The King of kings, and Lord of lords,
And heaven's eternal Light:

The Joy of all who dwell above,
The joy of all below,
To whom He manifests His love
And grants His Name to know.

The Cross He bore is life and health,
Though shame and death to Him,
His people's hope, His people's wealth,
Their everlasting theme.
—THOMAS KELLY

BENEDICTION:

Now the God of peace, that brought again from the dead our
Lord Jesus, that great shepherd of the sheep, through the blood of
the everlasting covenant, make you perfect in every good work to do
his will, working in you that which is well-pleasing in his sight,
through Jesus Christ; to whom be glory for ever and ever. Amen.
(HEB. 13:20-21 K.J.V.)

SOME ADDITIONAL RESOURCES

Scripture Selections

THE MESSIAH

Who has believed what we have heard?
And to whom has the arm of the Lord been revealed?
For he grew up before him like a young plant,
    and like a root out of dry ground;
he had no form or comeliness that we should look at him,
    and no beauty that we should desire him.
He was despised and rejected by men;
    a man of sorrows, and acquainted with grief;
and as one from whom men hide their faces
    he was despised, and we esteemed him not.

209

Surely he has borne our griefs
and carried our sorrows;
yet we esteemed him stricken,
smitten by God, and afflicted.
But he was wounded for our transgressions,
he was bruised for our iniquities;
upon him was the chastisement that made us whole,
and with his stripes we are healed.
All we like sheep have gone astray;
we have turned every one to his own way;
and the Lord has laid on him
the iniquity of us all.

He was oppressed, and he was afflicted,
yet he opened not his mouth;
like a lamb that is led to the slaughter,
and like a sheep that before its shearers is dumb,
so he opened not his mouth.
By oppression and judgment he was taken away;
and as for his generation, who considered
that he was cut off out of the land of the living,
stricken for the transgression of my people?
And they made his grave with the wicked
and with a rich man in his death,
although he had done no violence,
and there was no deceit in his mouth.

—Isa. 53:1-9 r.s.v.

HE GAVE POWER

There was a man sent from God, whose name was John. He came for testimony, to bear witness to the light, that all might believe through him. He was not the light, but came to bear witness to the light.

The true light that enlightens every man was coming into the world. He was in the world, and the world was made through him, yet the world knew him not. He came to his own home, and his own people received him not. But to all who received him, who believed in his name, he gave power to become children of God; who were born, not of blood nor of the will of the flesh nor of the will of man, but of God. (John 1:6-13 r.s.v.)

FROM DEATH TO LIFE

What shall we say then? Are we to continue in sin that grace may abound? By no means! How can we who died to sin still live in it? Do you not know that all of us who have been baptized into Christ Jesus were baptized into his death? We were buried therefore with him by baptism into death, so that as Christ was raised from the dead by the glory of the Father, we too might walk in newness of life.

For if we have been united with him in a death like his, we shall certainly be united with him in a resurrection like his. We know that our old self was crucified with him so that the sinful body might be destroyed, and we might no longer be enslaved to sin. For he who has died is freed from sin. But if we have died with Christ, we believe that we shall also live with him. For we know that Christ being raised from the dead will never die again; death no longer has dominion over him. The death he died he died to sin, once for all, but the life he lives he lives to God. So you also must consider yourselves dead to sin and alive to God in Christ Jesus.

Let not sin therefore reign in your mortal bodies, to make you obey their passions. Do not yield your members to sin as instruments of wickedness, but yield yourselves to God as men who have been brought from death to life, and your members to God as instruments of righteousness. (Rom. 6:1-13 R.S.V.)

JESUS' LAST WEEK, AND THE EASTER STORY

The story of the passion, death, and resurrection of Jesus Christ is found in the Gospels as follows:

Matt. 21:1 through 28:20.
Mark 11:1 through 16:20.
Luke 19:29 through 24:53.
John 12:1 through 21:25.

Hymns

"Ride On! Ride On in Majesty."
"All Glory, Laud, and Honor."
"O Thou Eternal Christ of God."
" 'Tis Midnight; and on Olive's Brow."
"O Sacred Head, Now Wounded."

211

"Beneath the Cross of Jesus."
"When I Survey the Wondrous Cross."
"Christ the Lord Is Risen Today."
"Come, Ye Faithful, Raise the Strain."
"O Come and Mourn With Me Awhile."
"Near the Cross Her Vigil Keeping."

Prayers

A PRAYER FOR THE LENTEN SEASON

Our Father, with humble and contrite spirit we enter the glorious portals of another holy season. Our needs are concrete; therefore our desires and expectations are definite, for Thy promises are sure, and Thou dost desire only our good. Graciously lead us into the divine mysteries of our Lord's Passion. Grant us patient endeavor and heart-searching devotion to follow Him in the journey toward the Cross. Make each of us to know: "It was for me He died." In Jesus' name. Amen.[12]

A PRAYER FOR GUIDANCE DURING HOLY WEEK

O God, our father and the father of our Lord, Jesus Christ, we come to this Holy Week with a prayer in our hearts. We know that many who were in Jerusalem with Jesus in his last days misunderstood and distrusted him and deserted him. We ask thee to enable us to stand with his spirit in these days. We do not understand Christ even now—but he has won our trust, and we want to be loyal to him forever. Help us to walk again the anxious days of long ago, facing the cross with thee, and with thy Son. If we seek to desert him, call us back. Look upon us once more with thy grace so that we cannot fail to continue in thy love.

In darkness Thou art our God, and we know that thou providest light for heavy hearts. Keep us moving through the darkness that will become dawn, and through the somber days of this week, help us to remember the brightness of the resurrection morn and the warmth of thy sacrificial love for all men. Thy salvation keeps us, and we praise thy goodness to us. Amen.

A GOOD FRIDAY PRAYER

O God, on this Friday of defeat, hear our prayer. We seek to praise thee for thy gift of Christ upon the cross. Those who seized

LENT AND EASTER

and slew him could not accept his love—forgive them. Even today we walk with uncertainty below his cross. Above us he looms to remind us that we, too, have sinned against him and against the people of his love. Our downcast eyes see the brightness of his fresh-spilled blood, and we know that thou hast continued to surrender thy son to our meanness and spite. Forgive us, O God. Forgive us, Christ, our Lord and Master. We have failed, and continue to fail. But thy love redeems us, and we give thee thanks. Lift us now from the sorrow and frustration of that other Friday and point our hearts toward the Sunday garden that has made this Friday good. In His name we pray. Amen.

A PRAYER FOR GOD TO AWAKEN US AT EASTER

You have done so much, God—like sending us a Master to lead our way, and making him so straight he wouldn't even dodge death for his own sake but took death for ours. He was your Son, and you gave him to us. But just look at us now, God, just look!

You have done so much, God—could you do just one more thing this Easter day? Wake us up! With your whole world flaming into life, and the universe singing choruses of Alleluia, can't you wake us up and show him to us again? Help us remember you gave him to us. And that he is still alive, ready to lead and command. Ready to love—and to be loved.

We forget so easily, God. Won't you wake us up and give us your gift just one more time?

Litanies

A LITANY OF PENITENCE

LEADER: Lent is for remembrance of Christ's suffering and death and discovering afresh the significance of these. It is a divine call for individual spiritual examination, renewal, and dedication. It requires one to utter his own prayer, and repent of his own sin.

GROUP: In this season of penitence, O God, forgive us our sins.

LEADER: Lent is an agonizing experience for earnest Christians because it requires us to bare our souls before God; to confess the sin which colors our lives; to recognize in a mood of penitence our fear of living without self-concern, and to re-examine the totality of our lives in light of our Master's utter devotion to God.

GROUP: In this season of penitence, O God, forgive us our sins.

213

LEADER: The presence of God in the person of Christ confronts us with our stale piety, our self-righteous thoughts, our feet of clay.

GROUP: In this season of penitence, O God, forgive us our sins.

LEADER: We are made uncomfortable in the presence of Christ, because we are caught short by our reflection in the mirror of His matchless life. His complete devotion to God shames us for trifling with less than this. His utter trust in God confronts us with our lack of certainty that God does reign supreme on earth.

GROUP: In this season of penitence, O God, forgive us. Amen.[13]

—JACK BELTON

A LITANY FOR PALM SUNDAY

LEADER: Blessed be the King who comes in the name of the Lord. His dominion shall be from sea to sea, and from the River to the ends of the earth.

GROUP: Blessed be he who comes in the name of the Lord!

LEADER: Behold, your king is coming to you, humble and mounted on an ass, and on a colt, the foal of an ass.

GROUP: Blessed be he who comes in the name of the Lord!

LEADER: Hosanna to the Son of David!

GROUP: Blessed be he who comes in the name of the Lord!

LEADER: The very stone which the builders rejected has become the head of the corner; this was the Lord's doing, and it is marvelous in our eyes.

GROUP: Blessed be he who comes in the name of the Lord!

LEADER: In the wilderness prepare the way of the Lord, make straight in the desert a highway for our God.

GROUP: Blessed be he who comes in the name of the Lord!

LEADER: Every valley shall be lifted up, and every mountain and hill be made low; the uneven ground shall become level, and the rough places a plain.

GROUP: Blessed be he who comes in the name of the Lord!

LEADER: For you shall go out in joy, and be led forth in peace; the mountains and the hills before you shall break forth into singing, and all the trees of the field shall clap their hands.

GROUP: Blessed be he who comes in the name of the Lord!

LEADER: Hosanna to the Son of David. Blessed be he who comes in the name of the Lord.

GROUP: Blessed be he who comes in the name of the Lord!

A GOOD FRIDAY LITANY

LEADER: The soldiers stripped him and placed a scarlet robe on his shoulders. They spat upon him and beat his head with the mock-scepter they had forced into his hands, so that their thorn crown pierced his forehead. The man of peace was marred, disfigured. His agony had begun.

GROUP: "Many were astonished at him—his appearance was so marred, beyond human semblance, and his form beyond that of many men—"

LEADER: Up the long avenue of spite he carried his cross. At the top of Skull Mountain they spiked him to it and thumped him into the hole dug between the other two. Those who loved him were sickened at his countenance; even his enemies were taken aback. But from his grisly visage there was power, and peace so sweet as to seem cruel. Blood and forgiveness, with the stench of sweat and death! All were startled.

GROUP: "So shall he startle many nations; kings shall shut their mouths because of him; for that which has not been told them they shall see, and that which they have not heard they shall understand."

LEADER: For out of this sweat and death, from this blood and forgiveness flowing on Golgotha, salvation comes, as a clap of thunder unexpected or a rainstorm undeserved. Out of ugliness comes this beauty—out of death, new life.

GROUP: "Surely he has borne our griefs and carried our sorrows."

LEADER: "Yet we esteemed him stricken, smitten by God, and afflicted."

GROUP: "But he was wounded for our transgressions, he was bruised for our iniquities."

LEADER: "Upon him was the chastisement that made us whole, and with his stripes are we healed."

GROUP: "All we like sheep have gone astray; we have turned every one to his own way; and the Lord has laid on him the iniquity of us all."

LEADER: Lord, have mercy upon us.

GROUP: Christ, have mercy upon us.

LEADER: Lord, have mercy upon us.

GROUP: "He was oppressed and he was afflicted, yet he opened not his mouth.

215

LEADER: "Like a lamb that is led before its shearers is dumb, so he opened not his mouth."

GROUP: O Lamb of God that takest away the sins of the world, have mercy upon us.

LEADER: O Lamb of God that takest away the sins of the world, have mercy upon us.

GROUP: O Lamb of God that takest away the sins of the world, grant us thy peace. Amen.[14]

A RESPONSIVE THANKSGIVING FOR NEW LIFE

LEADER: As the fragrant softness of spring rain touches all growing things, bringing freshness and growth,

GROUP: Touch our lives with the gentle freshness of thy love, O Father, that we may grow according to thy will.

LEADER: As tall trees put on new leafage, outward signs of continuous growth from sturdy roots,

GROUP: May our every act be evidence of growth in Christian stature that is deep-rooted in knowledge and in love of thee.

LEADER: As we attend the planting of our crops and gardens in order that we may have food for another season,

GROUP: Let us be mindful of the need to share with others both our knowledge of thee and our material wealth.

LEADER: As the lengthening grasses bend and sway, sensitive to the slightest breeze,

GROUP: May we be keenly aware of thy whispered directions in the hurry of our daily living,

LEADER: As all beasts and birds without fear, build anew their homes and rear their young each season,

GROUP: May we learn to live in peace according to thy plan, placing our days in thy hands with perfect trust.

ALL (in unison): Our Father, we thank thee for all the signs in the world around us that tell us of the new life that comes from thee. As we have thanked thee for the awakening world, we now thank thee for thy Son, Jesus Christ, whose coming, dying, and rising have given us life eternally new in thee. Unto his way we commit ourselves as we enter this lenten period again. Guide our steps through these weeks so that we may find ourselves in thy love. In his name we pray. Amen.[15]

Poems

LET ME KEEP LENT

Let me keep Lent—
Let me not kneel and pray,
Forego some trifle every day,
Fast, take sacrament,
And then
Lend tongue to slander, hold ancient grudge, deny
The very law which I would glorify.

Let me keep Lent—
Let my heart grow in grace;
Let God's light shine till my illumined face
Will be a testament
Read by all men
That hate is buried, self-crucified.
New born
The spirit that shall rise on Easter morn.

—AUTHOR UNKNOWN

ON ASH WEDNESDAY

Ashes are everywhere, to mock the pride
That raged and leaped and perished in its flame,
Yet vanity within us has not died;
The cautery has left us much the same.

Before our bones are ashes, and our wills
Have forfeited all power to repent,
God, bend our stubborn spirits and our skills
To uttermost obedience this Lent! [16]

—ELINOR LENNEN

PALM SUNDAY—A BOY'S MEDITATION

I wish I had been near when Jesus came
  Riding toward Jerusalem that day
Upon a lowly colt—the beast of peace—
  While people sang hosannas by the way.

217

I think the longing in his quiet face,
His earnest need to have all people see
He was God's Son now bringing peace and love,
Would have shown plainly to a boy like me.

They sang for joy, and waved palm branches high,
Thinking He came to conquer soldier-wise.
They paved His path with leaves, but that He came
Through love alone, they did not realize.

The Palm reminds us of that holy day:
We view His humble ride, remembering
How Jesus proved great heroes come in peace
To make God's love a real and pulsing thing.[17]

—WEBB DYCUS

NOTHING FAIR ENOUGH

Lord, we would fain some little palm branch lay
Upon Thy way;
But we have nothing fair enough or sweet
For holy feet
To tread, nor dare our sin-stained garments fling
Upon the road where rides the righteous King.

Yet, Lord, our stubborn wills we first will break,
If Thou wilt take;
And next our selfishness and then our pride,
And what beside?
And hearts, Lord, poor and fruitless though they be,
And quick to change and nothing worth to see.

—SARAH CHAUNCEY WOOLSEY

MAUNDY THURSDAY

It does not feel like Holy Week to me
But the church's hours do not await my feelings
So leafing, hymning, standing, confessing, kneeling,
Familiarly I wait upon the Lord, with an absent mind.

218

I hear and nod, like a disciple preparing to flee.
Sounds, disengaged, intoned from the leather book
On the altar (". . . when he had given thanks, he
   took. . .")
Toll in the background, vaguely distress, wind

Around my petulant rememberings, current gods,
Unparadoxical sufferings. Then like a rod
Across my lips I taste the bread, the wine.[18]

                   —STEPHEN CRITES

GETHSEMANE NOW

Woe, a man cast askew on a mossy mound,
Speaks with twelve unwanted mouths
Each, reluctant, put the crimson question forth,
"Is this Thy cross for me? Lord,
Is this Thy cross for me!"

Behold, the end was not yet at Calvary.
Mallow now, the cries match the
Creeping shroud—poured, like sap, from the rupted
   vine—
"Is this Thy cross for me, Lord?
Is this Thy cross for me!"

Now the cringing night weaves furtively a pall
Whilst twice twelve lips cadence the
Fleeing footfall of Cain, and saints, martyrs join the
   plea
"Is this Thy cross for me? Lord,
Is this Thy cross for me!" [19]

                 —BOBB HAMILTON

GOOD FRIDAY

Am I a stone, and not a sheep,
   That I can stand, O Christ, beneath Thy cross,
   To number drop by drop Thy blood's slow loss,
And yet not weep?

                       219

Not so those women loved
   Who with exceeding grief lamented Thee;
Not so fallen Peter weeping bitterly;
   Not so the thief was moved.

Not so the Sun and Moon
   Which hid their faces in a starless sky,
A horror of great darkness at broad noon—
   I, only I.

Yet give not o'er,
   But seek Thy sheep, true Shepherd of the flock;
Greater than Moses, turn and look once more
And smite a rock.
          —CHRISTINA ROSSETTI

WE WOULD NOT

We would not crucify the Christ—
Not us.
We would not nail him to a tree—
Not us.
We would not see him suffer, would
not have him feel the pain, would
never leave him on a cross—
Not us.
   What's that?
   We gorge while others starve?
   We like our friends but hate
   our enemies?
   We take so little time to help
   the ones who really need our help,
   the least of these our brethren?
   Well, that may be true.
   We're only human after all.
   What do you expect—perfection?
But don't forget,
We would not crucify the Christ—
Not us.[20]
          —IAN J. McCRAE

JESUS OF NAZARETH

Would you see the marks of the Roman scourge,
  And the pits where the nails were driven?
They are all hidden under fresh wounds.

Much more than forty lashes have I borne since Calvary;
Blows aimed at striking labor have bruised my body sore;
I've known the torture of my kinsmen by the gentile mob;
My back is raw from lashings by heroes, masked, at night.
Wherever man was beaten, I was whipped.

You see this scar?
  'Twas a bayonet in Flanders.
You see this bruise?
  A slave's chain pinched me there.
My shoulders stoop?
  Under the heavy load of labor.

You would see the marks of the Roman scourge,
And the pits where the nails were driven?
They are all hidden under fresh wounds.[21]
                    —ERNEST CADMAN COLWELL

FRAGMENT FROM GOLGOTHA

My mind is ever splintered
on the anvil of Time
and my spirit wanders restlessly
through the caverns of Eternity.
You ask me why?

I was an ordinary legionary in Jerusalem
nigh two thousand years ago.
One chill, windy morning
we nailed a Man to a cross.
(It was a routine job.)
He died rather soon.
I remember throwing down the dice
(we were gambling for His clothes),
and, picking up my spear, a trusty weapon

221

that had seen me through many a skirmish
in Gaul and Libya,
I thrust it into His side
to make certain before telling the centurion.
I saw water and blood trickle down the haft
gripped in my hands.
I saw more—though, by the bird of Jupiter,
I wish I hadn't.
Looking into His deathless eyes
I saw His heart was broken
for me.[22]

—CHANDRAN DEVANESEN

PERHAPS

Dear God, I wonder, when You climbed
The hill of Calvary—
Where were the children that You used
To take upon Your knee?
Where were they? In among the crowd?
And did they, too, not care
What happened to You, God, dear God,
But only came to stare?
Where were the children that You loved?
They do not seem to be
Around as You begin to climb
The hill of Calvary!
O God, I wish that I had been
A child that day! I might
Have done some little thing for You
To make the Cross more light!
I might have given you a glass
Of water on the way—
"I love You," whispered, as You passed,
"I love You so today!"
I might have done this—and yet—O!
Perhaps I would have hid
Among the people and done just
What other children did.[23]

—MARY DIXON THAYER

IN THINE OWN HEART
Though Christ a thousand times
In Bethlehem be born,
If he's not born in thee
Thy soul is still forlorn.
The cross on Golgotha
Will never save thy soul,
The cross in thine own heart
Alone can make thee whole.
—ANGELUS SILESIUS

SEND YOUR ROOTS DEEP DOWN
O Tree of Calvary,
send your roots deep down
into my heart.
Gather together the soil of my heart,
the sands of my fickleness,
the stones of my stubbornness,
the mud of my desires.
Bind them all together,
O Tree of Calvary,
interlace them with Thy strong roots,
entwine them with the network
of Thy love.[24]
—CHANDRAN DEVANESEN

SING, SOUL
Sing, soul of mine, this day of days.
The Lord is risen.
Toward the sunrising set thy face.
The Lord is risen.
Behold he giveth strength and grace;
For darkness, light; for mourning, praise;
For sin, his holiness; for conflict, peace.

Arise, O soul, this Easter Day!
Forget the tomb of yesterday,
For thou from bondage are set free;
Thou sharest in his victory

223

And life eternal is for thee,
Because the Lord is risen.
—AUTHOR UNKNOWN

EMPTY TOMB

Come see the silent empty tomb,
The place where Jesus lay,
The place from which, triumphantly,
He rose and went His way.

Come hear the silence as it speaks,
A Resurrection voice,
The emptiness, proclaiming life,
Commands: Rejoice, rejoice.[25]
—FLORENCE PEDIGO JANSSON

LOVE IS THE LESSON

Most glorious Lord of Lyfe! that, on this day,
Didst make Thy triumph over death and sin;
And having harrowed hell, didst bring away
Captivity thence captive, us to win:
This joyous day, deare Lord, with joy begin,
And grant that we, for whom thou diddest dye,
Being with Thy deare blood clene washt from sin,
May live forever in felicity:
And that Thy love we weighing worthily,
May likewise love Thee for the same againe;
And for Thy sake, that all lyke deare didst buy,
With love may one another entertayne!
So let us love, deare Love, lyke as we ought:
—Love is the lesson which the Lord us taught.
—EDMUND SPENSER

EASTER SUNRISE

Today we rise early and greet the dawn.
(This will be no ordinary day.)
In pulsing silence and awareness we will wait . . .
The rain-washed air is cool and fresh upon the cheek.
Breathe deeply . . . smell the green things growing—
224

New life from winter's death they speak.
Listen . . . birdsongs fill the gray—
Joyful, telling of new life, knowing.
Look now . . . the red clouds part . . . here comes the sun!
The same that greeted those who turned to run
On that first Easter and proclaim "He lives!"
How that cry thunders down through time and gives
On this new day new joy, new life to you and me!
Here is a center for our faith—here wondrous certainty! [26]

—HELEN F. COUCH

SYMBOL

My faith is all a doubtful thing,
　Wove on a doubtful loom,
Until there comes, each showery spring,
　A cherry tree in bloom.

And Christ, who died upon a tree
　That death had stricken bare,
Comes beautifully back to me,
　In blossoms everywhere.[27]

—DAVID MORTON

EASTER CANTICLE

In every trembling bud and bloom
　That cleaves the earth, a flowery sword,
I see Thee come from the tomb,
　Thou risen Lord.

In every April wind that sings
　Down lanes that make the heart rejoice,
Yea, in the word the wood-thrush bring,
　I hear thy voice.

Lo! Every tulip is a cup
　To hold thy morning's brimming wine;
Drink, O my soul, the wonder up—
　Is it not thine?

225

The great Lord God, invisible,
   Hath roused to rapture the green grass;
Through sunlit mean and dew-drenched dell
   I see Him pass.

His old immortal glory wakes
   The rushing streams and emerald hills;
His ancient trumpet softly shakes
   The daffodils.

Thou art not dead: Thou art the whole
   Of life that quickens in the sod;
Green April is thy very soul.
   Thou great Lord God! [28]
          —CHARLES HANSON TOWNE

LIFE WITHOUT END

I planted a weathered seed one day
   Out by the garden path.
Time took me out to recollect
   Elemental's conception out of earth
A green beam balancing a cup,
   Virtuous white, opalescent with dew.
And God spake to me; "Behold!
   I make all things new." [29]
          —ELLEN LINNEA JENSEN

IF A MAN DIE SHALL HE LIVE AGAIN?

I will repudiate the lie
Men tell of life;
How it will pass
As fragile flower, or butterfly,
Whose dust shall nourish
April grass.

Since one, for love, died on a tree
And in the stony
Tomb was lain,

226

Behold I show a mystery:
All sepulchres
Are sealed in vain! [30]
—JOHN RICHARD MORELAND

CHRIST IN THE UNIVERSE

With this ambiguous earth
His dealings have been told us. These abide:
The signal to a maid, the human birth,
The lesson, and the young Man crucified.

But not a star of all
The innumerable host of stars has heard
How He administered this terrestrial ball.
Our race have kept their Lord's entrusted Word.

Of His earth-visiting feet
None knows the secret, cherished, perilous,
The terrible, shamefast, frightened, whispered, sweet,
Heart-shattering secret of His way with us.

No planet knows that this
Our wayside planet, carrying land and wave,
Love and life multiplied, and pain and bliss,
Bears, as chief treasure, one forsaken grave.

Nor, in our little day,
May His devices with the heavens to be guessed,
His pilgrimage to thread the Milky Way,
Or His bestowals there be manifest.

But in the eternities
Doubtless we shall compare together, hear
A million alien Gospels, in what guise
He trod the Pleiades, the Lyre, the Bear.

O, be prepared, my soul!
To read the inconceivable, to scan
The million forms of God those stars unroll
When, in our turn, we show to them a Man.[31]
—ALICE MEYNELL

227

THE CALL

Come, my way, my truth, my life:
  Such a way as gives us breath;
  Such a truth as ends all strife;
  Such a life as killeth death.

Come, my light, my feast, my strength:
  Such a light as shows a feast;
  Such a feast as mends in length;
  Such a strength as makes his guest.

Come, my joy, my love, my heart:
  Such a joy as none can move;
  Such a love as none can part;
  Such a heart as joys in love.
                    —GEORGE HERBERT

EASTER

What is Easter?
  It is a joy different from other
    joys.
  It is a tulip opening in a garden.
  It is a bird singing, singing, sing-
    ing.
  It is a white lily before a stained-
    glass window.
  It is great music ringing,
    "Alleluia."
  It is a wondrous happiness.
  It is a deep quietness in the heart.
  It is a knowing that our Lord
    Christ lives.
        He lives!
  All this is Easter! [32]
                    —MURIEL GESSNER

Meditations

JESUS SETS HIS FACE

Jesus knows what waits for Him in Jerusalem—His death. And
still He sets His face toward the terrible city of man, for there

God leads Him. His brother's need calls out to Him, and He must go.

Think carefully before you dare to follow. For he who follows this Lord must follow Him on this journey. We each have our Jerusalem.

Jerusalem is the place where it is hard to make a witness. Jerusalem is the place where you must die to yourself in order to let God's work be done. Jerusalem is the place of suffering, the place where it seems almost too much to ask that you act as a Christian. It could be in your school, the gang, your church, your home. Wherever it is, God needs you there.

When Jesus arrives at the city, He goes to a hill outside the gates. There He can look into the busy streets and see men rushing about. Their lives have no purpose and no joy. He puts His head in His hands and weeps for mankind.

Be prepared to weep with Him if you follow to Jerusalem. And more than weeping must be done. He moves from tears to sacrifice.[33]

—SAM CLARK

THOUGHTS ON PALM SUNDAY

Two mighty, tragic characters enter on the wide stage of the world: man and God. Here they are, Act I, in the city streets at high noon, confronting one another. Quickly they shift about, from temple court to the little village of Bethany; until on Good Friday, with dry eyes and parched lips, one comes upon Act II, "Man's Way with God." After that the hours drag by from dusk to dawn to dusk again: when there, in the dim twilight of morning, the last Act opens, "God's Way with Man." We thrust him away and he comes back, like "the eager, terrible spring." And it goes on and on. Always, late or soon, man, with the gods he makes—Baal for his crops, Venus for his lust, Mars for his anger—meets the God who makes him! Never until then does he know himself for what he is: harried and hectored by grandeur and meanness; always halfway between heaven and hell, between the abyss of his own sin and the boldest, hungriest hopes that ever strode up and down through the human soul. Nor until then does he know what God is. This turbulent, ugly thing called humanity, princely and

229

full of heartache, Jesus loved—and left on it forever the mark of his hand, and the seal of his unbroken dominion.[34]

—PAUL SCHERER

A PALM SUNDAY MEDITATION

When Jesus rode into Jerusalem on the back of a donkey, "Hosanna in the highest!" was the cry of the people raised. But what did they really think? A peasant on a donkey—not much royalty in that.

Maybe that was the day Judas became disgusted with Jesus. It must have occurred to him: "This man isn't out for a thing. Following Him won't get me anywhere."

For the greatness of Christ is His humility. He waits on His disciples at the table like a butler; He washes their feet like a slave. He touches a leper and becomes Himself ceremonially unclean, but Jesus doesn't care—He is empty of pride and self-seeking. An adulteress is not afraid to talk to Him, for He is empty of condemnation and self-righteousness.

Five days from now Pilate will bring Christ out onto a balcony. And Pilate will turn to the crowd—to us—and ask, "What shall I do with your King?" They answer, "We have no king but Caesar."

Caesar's greatness we understand—power, money, popularity, comfort. But Jesus' greatness is strange and terrible—suffering, humility, lowliness.

Prayer: God, let me lose my life, for I would learn the greatness of humility. Amen.[35]

—SAM CLARK

A CURTAIN TORN

"The curtain of the temple was torn in two." The temple tore its gown as the mourners did because He, to whom the temple belonged more than to anybody else, was thrown out and killed by the servants of the temple. But the temple—and with it, all temples on earth—also complained of its own destiny. The curtain which made the temple a holy place, separated from other places, lost its separating power. He who was expelled as blaspheming the temple, had cleft the curtain and opened the temple for everybody, for every moment. This curtain cannot be mended any more,

230

although there are priests and ministers and pious people who try to mend it. They will not succeed because He, for whom every place was a sacred place, a place where God is present, has been brought on the Cross in the name of the holy place. When the curtain of the temple was torn in two, God judged religion and rejected temples. After this moment temples and churches can only mean concentration on the holy which is the ground and meaning of every place.[36]

—PAUL TILLICH

THE CROSS, AND THE CROSSES

Jesus' death upon the cross was not enough; there must be many more crosses raised before the world can be redeemed. Within the heart of every Christian there must be a cross upon which he crucifies the evil desires of his own soul. Within every church there must be a cross upon which the congregation crucifies its worldliness. Within every nation there must be a cross upon which the people crucify their un-Christian attitudes. Salvation cannot come to any man until he raises his own cross.[37]

—ROY L. SMITH

BREAKTHROUGH TO LIGHT

George Frederick's musical career began with a flat "No" from Papa Handel. Music was no way to get on in the world. But the law: that was different matter, and pushed you up a rung or two on the social ladder. George disagreed but consented to a compromise. He'd go to the university and register as a law student, but at the same time he'd spend a year as probationer-organist at the local church. At the end of the year, his playing won him a definite appointment as organist and whatever his father might still think, he decided for a life of music and dropped out of law school.

After his father's death, George went to Hamburg and got a job at the opera house as second violinist. By the time he was twenty he had written his first opera. Five years later he was conducting. He made a hurried visit to London where his opera Rinaldo won him an ovation. The following year he went to London again and decided to stay.

At first, his luck was extraordinary. He not only had the patronage of the king, but he had the people too as an admiring and enthusiastic audience for the operas he turned out. He worked at top speed, writing an opera in two or three weeks and producing and directing it himself.

As his success mounted so did the number of enemies who envied it. And he plunged into deeper and deeper debt to meet the cost of his lavish productions. You didn't need to be a prophet to predict catastrophe as dark as his success had been brilliant.

At fifty-two, Handel's health was broken by a stroke. His creditors clamored for the thousands he owed them. He went back to the continent to recover his health. Returning to London he produced five more operas. All turned into costly failures. George Handel's enemies gloated.

But they hadn't measured their man. The bishop of London forbade representing biblical characters on the stage. Handel hit upon the idea of writing oratorios instead of operas. They required no scenery and no expensive foreign singers. Here, at last, he was free to give himself wholly to the creation of the music. Here, at the point where he seemed finally defeated, he reached out to take up the work for which he had been born. In that double darkness of blindness and failure he had come to the breakthrough into light that was the *Messiah*.

He wrote it down in twenty-four days. His servant found him finishing the *Hallelujah Chorus*. Tears running down his face, Handel explained: "I did think I did see all heaven before me, and the great God himself!"

Shortly after his seventy-fourth birthday, and after conducting ten major works in a little more than a month to packed houses, Handel closed the series with the *Messiah*. And no one in that huge audience could say whether he was more deeply moved by the sight of the blind composer sitting by the organ, or by the splendor of the music and the victory of that mighty *chorus*.

A few days later, George Frederick Handel was dead. People from all walks of life followed his body to Westminster Abbey.

That was two hundred years ago. And still choral groups, amateur and professional, sing the great solos and choruses. Here in our Atomic Age, for us too—as when blind Handel wrote it—his

Messiah opens a breakthrough to light. It has become one with the world's celebration of Easter.[38]

—Eleanor B. Stock

LIFE OUTRUNS DEATH

Easter calls attention to the way life outruns death. You bury a bulb in the ground; in a few days the resurrection brings forth a hyacinth. A girl buries herself in her studies; God brings her forth a trained nurse. A Schweitzer buries himself in the African jungles, and he does not die when the jungle is brought to life.

Perhaps we need to think again about what it means for us to have eternal life. It means that we will live forever. We are of such value to God he will not let our spirits die.

In this perspective we see that the life we are building now is the life that goes with us through eternity! This realization puts new light on the decisions we make and the way in which we live.

What a difference it makes—in friendships, in international relations, in growing as a Christian—when we know that we live forever. Nothing is more important than your real life—the life of the spirit within you! The message of Easter is—"You will live forever!" You are of the utmost worth to God. Therefore, glorify God! Know Him and follow His Christ! Seek to be and do all that Jesus expects of you.[39]

—David and Martha Ash

WHAT DOES EASTER MEAN?

Last year one of the many exchange students studying in the United States was a lovely, intelligent girl from India. Although she was a Hindu, she had heard of Christ while in her country and was eager to learn more of him while she was in our country. She, like many foreigners, assumed that since America was called a Christian nation all Americans would be Christians.

She arrived at mid-semester at an Eastern college and immediately began her search of knowledge. After about a month she began hearing about a day called Easter that was to take place. So she listened and looked to observe what this day would be. She saw advertisements in the paper and on TV saying "Get fitted for Easter now," and "Buy your Easter outfit from us," Supermarkets announced sales on Easter hams and reminded people to buy their

233

Easter eggs, baskets, and candy from them. Florists urged everyone to remember loved ones with flowers. Newspapers printed "Lenten suggestions" that turned out to be different ways to fix fish and cheese dishes. By the time Easter arrived she was completely confused and did not know what Easter really meant.

What *does* Easter mean? Surely no one will object to the wearing of new clothes, and enjoying some of the festivities of the Easter season. But is this all Easter means to us? Years ago Dr. L. P. Jacks said one trouble with the churches is that too many people want to have Easter without Calvary.

How right he was. Most of us are thrilled over the story of Christ's resurrection from the dead. But how many of us remember that Easter came only after the sacrifice on Calvary?

During this Lenten season, let us take a new look at Jesus on the cross as well as the risen Christ.[40]

—BETTY H. COX

CHRIST LIVES!

To the discouraged disciples, whose leader had been crucified, the realization of Christ's new life with them brought a joy and strength that could not be downed. Where they had been weak and fearful of their opposition among the Roman and Jewish leaders, now they were strong and fearless.

Something wonderful happened after Good Friday! I do not know how to describe the radiant amazement of the disciples on that Easter morning. I do not know what the picture was like at the grave where Jesus was laid. The stories in the different Gospels tell us many things about this greatest of days. The Gospels tell of angels at the tomb. They tell of Jesus appearing to Mary Magdalene in the garden. While we cannot be sure of the details of what happened on that Easter morn, we can be sure of one central truth —that Christ did return to his disciples. Through the Easter experiences the disciples were made into new men with a new outlook on life. They were sure now that evil was not triumphant. They saw that Jesus was stronger than those who had put him to death. They knew that he was alive and that he could live in them and always be with them.

The Easter season helps us to face the fact that Christ is alive in the world today. His Way is the one true way of life. If we take

234

Christ with us and follow His Way then life begins to have purpose and meaning.[41]

—DAVID AND MARTHA ASH

ETERNAL LIFE

History . . . finds its consummation in the kingdom of God. The Christian rejoices in his personal fulfillment in life eternal. Faith in eternal life is not based upon the belief that man has some element or "soul" within him which is, by nature, immortal and incapable of dying. The Christian believes in life after death because he believes in the love and goodness of God. Our Eternal life is a gift of God; we will live beyond death because God himself, by the power with which he created the world and life in the first place, will provide for us as persons eternal life with him.

As a result, the Christian does not rest his faith primarily on philosophical attempts to prove the immortality of the soul. Nor can the Christian faith be based upon findings of spiritualists who claim to call back the dead to communicate with the living. The Christian faith is far more than a belief that life will continue. The mere continuance of life could be a curse as well as a blessing. The Christian looks forward to life after death only because it will be life with God revealed in Christ. We can trust him to fulfill our human existence with himself. In short, our hope is from the beginning to the end a hope and trust in God experienced in community in the Church triumphant.

It is significant that when Jesus spoke about life after death or the last judgment, he did it in the context of teaching man his duty to love his neighbor in this life. . . . When we believe that the lives we are building in ourselves and the lives we are influencing in others are not for threescore and ten years but forever, this belief adds a whole new dimension of importance and significance to what we do.[42]

Audio-Visuals

Great Stories of the New Testament. Eight beautiful and reverent filmstrips present the life and teachings of Christ. The titles in the series that are of special relevance to Lent and Easter are: "The

235

Triumphal Entry and Last Supper," "The Trial of Jesus," "The Story of the Crucifixion," and "The Story of the Resurrection." These filmstrips are accompanied by a reading script that makes them easily adaptable for worship purposes. They are produced by Encyclopaedia Britannica Films, 1114 Wilmette Avenue, Wilmette Illinois, and are available from denominational audio-visual distributors.

The Life of Christ in Art. The color version of this exploration of the world's great art can be used as the central element in a worship service. The camera moves over many great masterpieces, giving us (through the words of the Revised Standard Version of the Bible) an inspiring portrayal of the life of Christ. Produced by Coronet Films, 65 East South Water Street, Chicago 1, Illinois, this twenty-one minute film is available for rent from many denominational film libraries, and from some state universities.

Barabbas the Robber. This thirty-eight minute, black and white film is a fictional story of Barabbas and of how he might have been influenced by the life of the man who died in his place. Its high inspiration makes it an excellent worship resource. It is distributed by United World Films, 105 East 106th Street, New York 29, New York, and is available for rent from most denominational film libraries.

Power of the Resurrection. One of the finest full-length resources among all the Bible films, this hour-long presentation shows us the exciting story of Simon Peter's conflicts and victories during Jesus' last days, and up until the birth of the Church on the day of Pentecost. The story of the hesitating, frightened follower as he becomes a true disciple will provide a good center for worship in Lent or at Easter. Produced by Family Films (5823 Santa Monica Boulevard, Hollywood 38, California) and the Broadcasting and Film Commission of the National Council of Churches (475 Riverside Drive, New York 27, New York), this film, available in both black and white and in color, can be rented from most denominational film libraries.

A Meditation for Holy Week and Easter. This color filmstrip is based on significant scenes from the Passion Play at Oberammergau. With prayers, and the story of the passion, crucifixion, and resurrection told from the pages of the Gospels, it will provide

236

a moving forty-five minute service of worship. The script (there is no recorded narration) lends itself well to choral reading. Produced by the Christian Education Press. 1501 Race Street, Philadelphia 2, Pennsylvania, it is offered for sale by most denominational film distributors.

Advent and Christmas

There are many occasions centering around Advent and Christmas when groups want to plan for worship. Sometimes this may be only a moment of worship before the group goes caroling. Or, it may be that you will want to pause before leaving the Christmas party or dinner to give a moment's thought to the Great Event that is the reason for your festivity. Often the group will want a longer, more formal time of worship at this season, too. The suggestions given here may be adapted for many types of worship, either the brief worship times or the longer service.

SOME WORSHIP SUGGESTIONS

A Service of Worship for Advent

This worship service is a sample of the kind you can develop to make the Advent season more meaningful for your group. Choose other materials from this section or from other sources, combine them, and create your own Advent worship service.

WORSHIP SETTING: A tall white candle is burning on a table at the front of the room. The table is covered with a white cloth, and greenery is arranged around the candle base.

MUSIC (played softly by the pianist): Tune of "Come, Thou Long-expected Jesus."

SCRIPTURE READING:
> In the wilderness prepare the way
> of the Lord,

> make straight in the desert a
> highway for our God.
> Every valley shall be lifted up,
>   and every mountain and hill be
>   made low;
> the uneven ground shall become level,
>   and the rough places a plain.
> And the glory of the Lord shall be
>   revealed,
> and all flesh shall see it together,
>   for the mouth of the Lord has
>   spoken.
>
> —Isa. 40:3-5 R.S.V.

MEDITATION:

This is a busy time of year for all of us. Christmas is in our thoughts, and we find ourselves involved in a rush of activities. Actually, however, we have not yet come to the season in the Christian Year that is known as Christmas. We are now observing the season of Advent.

Just as the New Year is brought in with New Year's Day on January first, so the Christian Year is brought in with the first Sunday of Advent. This comes on the Sunday nearest November 30 each year. Advent includes four Sundays and extends to Christmas.

In the early Christian church Advent was observed much as Lent is now observed. It was a time of penitence, of fasting, and church attendance. In all this people were trying to prepare themselves for Christmas, for receiving God's gift of love, the Christ.

Through the centuries, however, customs of observance of the Advent season have changed. But Advent is still the season of preparation, the time when we open our hearts and minds to prepare ourselves for new experiences of the spirit, new understandings of what Christ's coming means in our lives. Advent is a season of joyous expectancy, of waiting, of preparation. It is a season of singing, a season of prayer, a season of searching the Scriptures.

Let us observe this season here and now. Let us join together in

239

preparing to receive the Christ. Let us sing joyfully and let us also bow our heads in prayer.

HYMN: "Come, Thou Long-expected Jesus."

LITANY:

LEADER: That we may be prepared for the coming of thy Son, the Babe of Bethlehem, help us to rid our hearts of selfishness, thoughtlessness, and vain pride.

GROUP: We pray thee, our Father.

LEADER: As the ever-watchful shepherds saw thy glory in the skies, may we too be mindful of thy glories.

GROUP: We pray thee, our Father.

LEADER: May the message of the heavenly host, Peace on earth, good will toward men, ever find echo in our hearts, and be practiced in our lives.

GROUP: We pray thee, our Father.

LEADER: Touch our hearts, O Lord, that we may feel thy divine presence, that we may be strong and of good courage, that we may speak helpful words and do good deeds.

GROUP: We pray thee, our Father.[1]

HYMN: "O Come, O Come, Immanuel."

POEM:

Love came down at Christmas,
Love all lovely, Love Divine;
Love was born at Christmas,
Stars and angels gave the sign.

. . . .

Love shall be our token,
Love be yours and love be mine,
Love to God and all men,
Love for plea and gift and sign.[2]

HYMN: "Joy to the World! The Lord Is Come."

BENEDICTION:

As with gladness men of old
Did the guiding star behold;
As with joy they hailed its light,
Leading onward, beaming bright;
So, most gracious God, may we
Evermore be led by Thee.[3]

Amen.

A Service of Worship with Living Pictures [4]

Here is a sample of the dramatic worship service which may be lengthened, shortened, or otherwise adapted to fit your needs. Although this service calls for living pictures, it is only one possibility. For example, the shepherds might pantomime the action during the reading or, if you prefer, they might speak the words themselves. And in the last picture you might prefer to have Mary move about some, arrange the blanket over the baby, then take him in her arms. The living pictures are described here:

I. Three shepherds in traditional costume are gathered about a campfire. Two may be seated, one may be standing and looking at the sky.

II. The shepherds are transfixed in a beam of bright light coming from overhead. One may be standing, another crouching, and the third one half-rising.

III. Mary is seated by the baby in the manger. She wears a blue robe and head covering.

MUSIC:

Arrange the music according to the talents of your group. All music can be sung or played by soloists or by a group of singers. Or, the entire group may sing the well-known carols from memory, following the lead of two or three in the group who have been cued in advance to start the singing.

READER:

The Reader may wear a choir robe and read from a lectern at the front of the room. Or, you may prefer to have him read from the back of the room or from behind a screen.

If you decide to do the shepherds scene as a living picture you

241

will need three additional readers, each with a voice quite different from the others. These persons should not be seen.

LIVING PICTURES:
Persons pose as in a picture, and the scene is spotlighted. A frame about the "picture" helps, but is not necessary. Your imagination can help you here. Pictures can be arranged at opposite sides of the room or platform and remain in darkness until lights come up on them.

LIGHTS:
Spotlights will be necessary for lighting the scenes or pictures. In the second picture the light comes from overhead and a little to one side. The room in which the program is given might be decorated with lighted candles. The Reader will, of course, need a candle or small reading light at the lectern.

MUSIC (instrumental or by hidden singers): "O Little Town of Bethlehem."

READER:
And in that region there were shepherds out in the field, keeping watch over their flock by night.
(Spotlight comes up on Shepherds, Picture I. Three Readers read the following.)
FIRST SHEPHERD: The stars are very clear tonight . . . "The heavens declare the glory of God, and the firmament showeth his handiwork."
SECOND SHEPHERD: Out here, under the stars, the Lord seems very real and very near. But when I go down into the town to sell my wool in the market place, I wonder whether some of the people there ever think of him. They would do well to spend some quiet night here on the hillside, remembering their Creator.
THIRD SHEPHERD: It is true. Last week, every buyer tried to cheat me out of a fair price for my wool. They cannot be remembering the law of Moses—when they try to steal the food from my children's mouths.
FIRST SHEPHERD: Sometimes I think our people need more help from God. It is not enough to go to the synagogue on the Sabbath

and be reminded of his loving care. We need a better understanding of how he wants men to live.

SECOND SHEPHERD: You are right—it is the very men who try to cheat us in the market place that are most reverent in the synagogue. They say prayers and sing psalms with their lips, but their lives cannot be pleasing to God. They do not understand what God really wants of men.

THIRD SHEPHERD: Perhaps what we need is a pattern—someone to show us how God would act if he were living as a man.

FIRST SHEPHERD: We need only to study the words of our great teachers. Did not the prophet Micah warn us that the costliest sacrifice at the temple altar would not be acceptable to God as a substitute for righteous living?

SECOND SHEPHERD: These great teachings have not been enough —men are still sinful. . . . Perhaps we do need a pattern—a man who could show us how God would change our lives.

THIRD SHEPHERD: Could it be that the Messiah will be such a man? We have always thought of him as a king—but . . . perhaps he will be a common man like one of us. . . .

FIRST SHEPHERD: If he were not a king, how would we recognize him? Where would he get his authority . . . his power . . . ?

SECOND SHEPHERD: His understanding of God's truth might be his authority. . . .

THIRD SHEPHERD: Yes, and his goodness might be more powerful than a king's army. . . .

(Spotlight off.)

READER:

And the angel of the Lord appeared to them, and the glory of the Lord shone around them, and they were filled with fear.

(Spotlight up on Living Picture II.)

READER:

And the angel said to them, "Be not afraid; for behold, I bring you good news of a great joy which will come to all the people; for to you is born this day in the city of David a Saviour, who is Christ the Lord. And this will be a sign for you: you will find a babe wrapped in swaddling cloths and lying in a manger." And suddenly there was with the angel a multitude of the heavenly host praising

243

God and saying, "Glory to God in the highest, and on earth peace among men with whom he is pleased."

MUSIC: "Hark! the Herald Angels Sing."

(Spotlight off.)

READER:
When the angels went away from them into heaven, the shepherds said to one another, "Let us go over to Bethlehem and see this thing that has happened, which the Lord made known to us." And they went with haste and found Mary and Joseph, and the babe lying in a manger.

(Lights up on Mary and child during following conversation.)

FIRST SHEPHERD: This is beyond me. I cannot understand why the Savior is born in a manger.

SECOND SHEPHERD: It's all just as the angel said—wrapped in swaddling cloths and lying in a manger.

FIRST SHEPHERD: But—a manger!

THIRD SHEPHERD: Does it really matter where he is born? It's the kind of person he grows up to be that really counts, I think.

SECOND SHEPHERD: But it does seem strange—

THIRD SHEPHERD: Yes, it does. But the ways of God are always strange to us. We can never understand completely. But we can believe in his plan behind everything he does. And we can rejoice when we see his wonders (Pause). Let us kneel down before this child, the Savior who has been given to us this night. Let us welcome him and worship him with rejoicing.

MUSIC: "O Come, All Ye Faithful."

PRAYER:
Our loving, giving Father, who planned for us the amazing miracle of thy Son who would come to earth to show us what thy love would be like, send thy light from the star into our hearts this Christmastime. Burn away any selfishness, wrongness. Make us clean and new. Turn our eyes toward tasks thou hast for us, even as

Jesus grew into your manhood and turned to tasks thou didst have for him. . . .

And . . . if it be thy will, may a bit of "peace on earth, good will toward men" come into living reality through us. In the name of the Babe of Bethlehem. Amen.[5]

MUSIC: "Joy to the World! the Lord Is Come." (This may be played as a postlude, or the group may leave singing.)

A Christmas Service of Worship [6]

Often a longer, more formal type of worship is needed by church groups at the Christmas season.

The service given here can be adapted easily to your needs, or may serve as idea material for creating your own service of worship. Be sure to check the section when the Voices mention problems in the U. S.—this may need updating and reference to the current scene. The number who come to kneel at the altar can, of course, be reduced or expanded.

The church is dimly lighted as audience gathers. Organist or pianist is playing Christmas music. Lights go down as Candle Lighters enter from rear, light candles on table or altar and on lecterns at either side of chancel, if light is needed. Two Readers in choir robes take their places at lecterns. A manger scene has been arranged in the darkness in the center of the chancel.

MUSIC (*by choir seated in balcony or behind audience*): "Deck the Halls with Boughs of Holly."

MEDITATION, PART I:

FIRST READER: Again the candles have been lighted! The greens have been hung! Christmas music fills the air! Only a little while now until the great day will be here!

SECOND READER: Yes, it's Christmas time again.

FIRST READER: O I'm glad it's Christmas time! Everyone is so busy and gay. People forget their sorrows and troubles at this time of year. There is happiness everywhere at Christmas.

245

SECOND READER: Christmas is indeed a happy time. Great joy is abroad. But . . .

FIRST READER: But—what? Surely we all love this season.

SECOND READER: We do love this season. But one cannot help wondering just a little . . .

FIRST READER: Wondering? Wondering about what?

SECOND READER: One cannot help wondering if what we call Christmas joy could be just a shallow, thoughtless gaiety . . .

FIRST READER: Actually, I suppose it is rather thoughtless. But there is so much going on and so much to do at this time of year that we don't have time to think.

SECOND READER: That is what I'm wondering about. Are we experiencing a deep joyousness because God's love for His world was manifested in flesh that first Christmas, or are we allowing ourselves from year to year to become more and more involved in a breathless confusion of pleasant activities and bright, traditional symbols?

FIRST READER: Oh, but we always put the manger at the center of our Christmas celebrating.

(Lights up on manger scene)

SECOND READER: Do we . . . really? Is the manger at the center of our Christmas symbolic of the birth of a Savior for the world, or have we made it only a part of our decorations and tableaux, possibly giving us a few moments to indulge in a bit of sentiment about a baby born in a manger?

FIRST READER: But that is Christmas—the baby in the manger, the Wise Men, the shepherds—

SECOND READER: That is true. To many of us that is Christmas— the color, the pageantry, the symbols. But Christmas is so much more than that—so much more!

FIRST READER: I'm afraid I don't see what more it could possibly be.

(Lights go down slowly on manger scene.)

SECOND READER: After that night when Jesus was born in Bethlehem—do you remember?—there were thirty-three years that he spent in a land where there was no peace—always going about his Father's business, learning, living, teaching, preaching, healing.

(Voices come in rapidly from behind a screen
or from loud speakers.)

VOICE 1: This man is no ordinary man, I tell you, neighbor. He is a worker of miracles. Only yesterday I saw him cure a blind man. He spat upon the ground and placed the moistened clay upon the blind man's eyes. Now the man sees.

VOICE 2: "And the eyes of the blind shall be opened and the ears of the deaf unstopped."

VOICE 3: And they do say that he heals the crippled and infirm. Some say he even cleanses lepers.

VOICE 2: "Then shall the lame man leap as an hart and the tongue of the dumb shall sing."

VOICE 4: He tells strange tales to the multitudes—simple, homely tales that even the uneducated can understand. Yet, they are filled with great meaning.

VOICE 2: "What man of you, having a hundred sheep, if he lose one of them, doth not leave the ninety and nine in the wilderness, and go after that which is lost, until he find it? And when he hath found it, he layeth it on his shoulders rejoicing. And when he cometh home, he calleth together his friends and neighbors, saying unto them, 'Rejoice with me; for I have found my sheep which was lost.' I say unto you, that likewise joy shall be in heaven over one sinner that repenteth, more than over ninety and nine just persons, which need no repentance.'"

VOICE 3: There is such tenderness, such compassion in Him.

SOLO (by hidden singer): "The Lord's My Shepherd."

VOICE 4: I stood in a great company when he was teaching and it seemed suddenly that he was speaking directly to me—that he was asking me to leave the life I had been living and follow Him.

VOICE 2: "Come unto me all ye that labour and are heavy laden and I will give you rest. Take my yoke upon you and learn of me."

VOICE 1: If only you could have heard the sermon he preached on the mountain! Never have I heard such preaching! Quarreling and wrongdoing among the people of a nation, or warfare among nations of the world could never be again if all of us could grasp the true meaning of that message—if we could truly follow the way he pointed out.

VOICE 2: "Love your enemies, bless them that curse you, do good to them that hate you, and pray for them which despitefully use you and persecute you."

VOICE 3: And he taught us how each of us might speak to the

247

Father. He gave us a prayer so simple, yet so full of might and power, that we must be careful lest we use it unthinkingly.

THE LORD'S PRAYER (led by choir group without announcement).

MEDITATION, PART II:

FIRST READER: Yes, I know this Jesus was a great teacher and preacher. His was a wonderful ministry. But look at our world today. We stand at the very brink of destruction. Did it really make any difference that He lived at all? If Jesus himself were to come back tonight, what would he find? Where could he find that his teachings were being followed? He would not know where to start. . . .

(Voices come in fast as above)

VOICE 1: Not in the United States!

VOICE 2: Not in the East—definitely! The coast out there is in terrible confusion—all sorts of labor-management bitterness in the big industrial cities—strikes, riots, violence.

VOICE 1: Not in the West—definitely! The coast out there is a breeding place for godless "isms!"

VOICE 3: Nor the South! It's all mixed up with hatred and prejudice.

VOICE 2: Perhaps Russia?

VOICE 3: No, not Russia! Communism does not recognize a power higher than itself. No, not there!

VOICE 2: China, then?

VOICE 1: Not China! China is a nation red with the blood of innocent people sacrificed to conflicting greeds and desire for power.

VOICE 2: Surely the other nations of the world . . .

VOICE 3: No! They are all struggling for power, for wealth, for position in world affairs. Their hands are bloody with warfare and their minds black with suspicion and hate.

VOICE 2: "Behold the nations are as a drop of a bucket, and are counted as the small dust of the balance . . . the nations before him are as nothing."

FIRST READER: I'm afraid it is rather hopeless. Jesus' teachings are being ignored in the world today. But how can we expect anything else? Even the people of his own generation did not accept

248

him. His own countrymen shouted, "Crucify Him! Crucify Him!"

SECOND READER: Yes . . . And they nailed him to a cross. . . .

FIRST READER: With his death his teachings died, too. Perhaps, after all, he was just a figure in history—perhaps he was just another great teacher who lived and died two thousand years ago.

SECOND READER: It is true that even in his own day only a few recognized him as the Son of God. And they did crucify him. But you have forgotten one very important fact.

FIRST READER: I do not know what I could have forgotten.

SECOND READER: You have forgotten that his death was not the end—because he was not dead. He conquered death. He arose from the tomb to give all who would believe definite and positive proof that life is eternal.

VOICE 2: "I am the resurrection and the life: he that believeth in me, though he were dead, yet shall he live, and whosoever liveth and believeth in me shall never die."

SECOND READER: His cross has become a symbol of hope for all mankind. He is no mere figure of history. He has lived all through the centuries and he lives today.

FIRST READER: He lives in this world of war and suffering and sadness? In this world where our only escape is in the brief brightness of Christmas?

SECOND READER: Even in this confused, stumbling world of ours he lives. He is the light toward which the nations are groping. He lives in the hearts of all the men and women and children everywhere of every race and creed who truly believe in him. His kingdom is here among us, even though we cannot see it.

FIRST READER: Perhaps . . . perhaps there is still hope, but. . . .

SECOND READER: There is always hope for those who have a faith in a power greater than themselves. Truth is eternal.

VOICE 2: "The grass withereth, the flower fadeth: but the word of our God shall stand forever."

SECOND READER: Jesus talked constantly about the kingdom of God—do you remember?—it was a kingdom of love, of peace. That was the message the world had been waiting for so long that first Christmas—a world as war-torn, as sad, and confused as our world today. Its people were crying out for a message of hope.

CHOIR: "O come, O Come, Immanuel."

MEDITATION, PART III.

FIRST READER: My world, too, is crying out for a message of hope, of peace. If ever the world needed such a message it is today.

SECOND READER: And the message is here for us, if we will but hear it. Do you recall the angel's message?

VOICE 2: "And the angel said unto them, 'Fear not! for behold I bring you good tidings of great joy, which shall be to all people. For unto you is born this day in the city of David a Saviour, which is Christ the Lord' . . . and suddenly there was with the angel a multitude of the heavenly host praising God, and saying, 'Glory to God in the highest, and on earth peace, good will toward men.' "

SECOND READER: The peace the angels told of that night can come to our world. But it can come only as we find peace ourselves. We, too, must be born again—become as little children—even though some of us are old in years and rigid in our thinking. We must begin our lives again by seeking new knowledge, by accepting new ideas, by developing new and Christlike attitudes.

VOICE 2: "Verily I say unto you, Except ye be converted, and become as little children, ye shall not enter into the kingdom of heaven. Whosoever shall humble himself as a little child, the same is the greatest in the kingdom of heaven."

(Lights up on manger)

SECOND READER: God's love shone out to all the world from a humble stable manger that first Christmas. Through the life of His Son he revealed His plans and purposes for His world.

FIRST READER: Mankind has done very little about it!

SECOND READER: Yes, mankind has made only feeble attempts to put His teachings into practice, but God has been patient.

VOICE 2: "Hast thou not known? Hast thou not heard, that the everlasting God, the Lord, the creator of the ends of the earth fainteth not, neither is weary. There is no searching of his understanding."

FIRST READER: I believe I am beginning to understand a little of what you are trying to tell me.

SECOND READER: We can all understand if we will but pause long enough in the busyness of this time—if we will but look beyond the tinsel, the store windows, the Christmas dinners, the Santa

250

Clauses, and all the other trappings which have crowded out the true meaning of the day.

FIRST READER: If we but look beyond ... Yes, I do see what you mean. There is more to Christmas than just the color and gaiety ... more even than the birth of the baby Jesus. I think you're saying that Christmas is the celebration of the beginning of new life—the life of Jesus, the Christ.

SECOND READER: Yes, the Christ—a Savior for you and for me.

FIRST READER: And if a Savior for you and me ... then He must be a Savior for our world.

SECOND READER: Are you ready to receive him?

FIRST READER: Me? Ready to receive him?

SECOND READER: We must prepare our hearts now to receive Him. We must make ready for the wonder and the glory of his coming. We must prepare ourselves for the whole new way of life he offers to each of us—a life of freedom, of peace. We, too, are the children of God and eternal life can be ours.

FIRST READER: Oh, I am grateful—grateful for this deepened understanding of Christmas. The glow of the candles is mellowed. The music will be sweeter now. The holy birth shall be more than just a lovely picture ... if only others could see it as I do now!

SECOND READER: Yes, if only the whole world could see God's love shining forth from the manger cradle! If only all people would reach out toward it and open their hearts to receive him!

FIRST READER: There must be some way. . . .

SECOND READER: There is a way. Let us kneel here in the quiet at the altar. Let us open our hearts and prepare to receive him. As we, and all the others who truly believe let his light shine through us, others cannot but see the radiance. Then they, too, will come searching and will be born anew as they receive him. This is the Christmas hope—this is the Christian hope for our world today.

FIRST READER: Let us not delay! Let us kneel quickly!

Readers kneel center altar, as choir sings first four stanzas of "O Come to My Heart, Lord Jesus." As they reach first refrain, the following begin coming from all entrances. They seem to come eagerly, searchingly, to kneel at manger and altar.

Mother and father with group of children, varying ages

Chinese coolie with water buckets on shoulder yoke
Indian mother, papoose on back
Army officer
South American girl
War veteran in wheel chair, pushed by nurse
Statesman, with tall hat and brief case
Musician carrying instrument
Naval officer
Farmer

VOICE 2 (when all are at altar): "I am the way, the truth, and the life. No man cometh unto the father but by me."
(Those at altar remain until after the benediction.)

HYMN: "Light of the World, We Hail Thee" (by entire congregation and choir).

BENEDICTION.

When You Go Caroling

Does your group go caroling at Christmas time? Do you make a special effort to sing for persons who are ill, aged, homebound, or in hospitals and homes?

A few moments of worship as you start your rounds will make this a more meaningful experience for everyone. Perhaps a brief Scripture reading and a prayer, or a poem and a prayer, or a combination of all three will be suitable. Here are some materials for use in planning for such worship moments. You can choose and combine those that seem best for your group.

SCRIPTURE READING:
>   For to us a child is born,
>   to us a son is given;
>   and the government will be upon his shoulder,
>   and his name will be called
>   "Wonderful Counselor, Mighty God,
>   Everlasting Father, Prince of Peace."
>   —ISA. 9:6 R.S.V.

O come, let us sing to the Lord;
　Let us make a joyful noise to the
　　rock of our salvation!
　Let us come into his presence with
　　thanksgiving!
　let us make a joyful noise to him
　　with songs of praise!
　For the Lord is a great God,
　　and a great King above all gods.
　　　　　　　　　　—Ps. 95:1-3 R.S.V.

POEM:

Sing in a big voice.
Sing in a cheerful voice . . .
Happy words and joyful music
The Lord has come to banish forever the fear
So long the oppressor of men
That there is no Lord of Life!

Sing in a big voice
The glorious words to exultant music.
Today is the Natal Day.
We celebrate the glorious news,
The Gospel news,
Worthy of soaring and gladsome singing.
"God has not forgotten!
God has remembered!
In his beloved Son
He has come to set men free!" [7]

PRAYER:

Our Father, we go out into the night with songs in our hearts and on our lips. May our carols bring something of the joy, the peace, and the beauty of this holy time of year to those who hear our singing. We pray in the name of Jesus, the Christ. Amen.

After the Christmas Party

The Christmas party is usually one of the high lights of the year. Decorations, food, presents, the gaiety of the season—everything about it is special. But when it's time to go home, we feel a need for something more. Here are some suggestions for these moments.

253

Sing. Turn out the lights, leaving only the candles burning. Or, turn off all the lights except those on the Christmas tree. In the glow of candles and lights sing two or three favorite carols. If you have been singing carols earlier in the evening, sing only one at this time. "O Little Town of Bethlehem" would be especially appropriate. (Sing from memory—only first stanzas unless the carol is well known. Don't break the spell of the moment by passing out songbooks and struggling to read words in the dark.)

Read from the Bible. A reader seated near the tree or candles might read the following story of the first Christmas from the Gospel of Luke as translated by J. B. Phillips:

There were some shepherds living in the same part of the country, keeping guard throughout the night over their flock in the open fields. Suddenly an angel of the Lord stood by their side, the splendor of the Lord blazed around them, and they were terror-stricken. But the angel said to them:

"Do not be afraid! Listen, I bring you glorious news of great joy which is for all the people. This very day, in David's town, a Savior has been born for you. He is Christ, the Lord. Let this prove it to you: you will find a baby, wrapped up and lying in a manger."

And in a flash there appeared with the angel a vast host of the armies of Heaven, praising God, saying,

"Glory to God in the highest Heaven! Peace upon earth among men of goodwill!"

When the angels left them and went back into Heaven, the shepherds said to each other,

"Now let us go straight to Bethlehem and see this thing which the Lord has made known to us."

So they came as fast as they could and they found Mary and Joseph—and the baby lying in the manger. And when they had seen this sight, they told everybody what had been said to them about the little child. And those who heard them were amazed at what the shepherds said. But Mary treasured all these things and turned them over in her mind. The shepherds went back to work, glorifying and praising God for everything that they had heard and seen, which had happened just as they had been told.

Pray. Close these moments with a brief prayer—your own or one similar to this:

254

Our Father, we rejoice and give thanks for thy great love declared in the birth of Jesus on that night in Bethlehem so long ago. As we celebrate his birth again this year, bring us to a deeper understanding of what love really means. Following his example, we would express love, deep and sincere, in all our relationships—not just at Christmas time, but every day. We pray in Jesus' name. Amen.

(If it is late and everyone is tired, you might prefer to use only a prayer, or a carol and a prayer for these worship moments.)

SOME ADDITIONAL RESOURCES

Scripture Selections

THE WISE MEN CAME

Jesus was born in Bethlehem, in Judea, in the days when Herod was king of the province. Not long after his birth there arrived from the east a party of astrologers making for Jerusalem and inquiring as they went: "Where is the child born to be king of the Jews? For we saw his star in the east and we have come here to pay homage to him."

When King Herod heard about this he was deeply perturbed, as indeed were all the other people living in Jerusalem. So he summoned all the Jewish scribes and chief priests together and asked them where "Christ" should be born. Their reply was "In Bethlehem, in Judea, for this is what the prophet wrote about the matter—

"And thou Bethlehem, land of Judah,
Art in no wise least among the princes of Judah:
For out of thee shall come forth a governor,
Which shall be shepherd of my people Israel."

Then Herod invited the wise men to meet him privately and found out from them the exact time when the star appeared. Then he sent them off to Bethlehem, saying: "When you get there, search for this little child with the utmost care. And when you have found him, come back and tell me—so that I may go and worship him too."

255

The wise men listened to the king and then went on their way to Bethlehem. And now the star, which they had seen in the east, went in front of them as they traveled until at last it shone immediately above the place where the little child lay. The sight of the star filled them with indescribable joy.

So they went into the house and saw the little child with his mother, Mary. And they fell on their knees and worshiped him. Then they opened their treasures and presented him with gifts— gold, incense and myrrh.

Then, since they were warned in a dream not to return to Herod, they went back to their own country by a different route.

(MATT. 2:1-12 PHILLIPS)

THE WORD BECAME FLESH

So the Word became flesh; he came to dwell among us, and we saw his glory, such glory as befits the Father's only Son, full of grace and truth.

(JOHN 1:14 THE NEW ENGLISH BIBLE)

THE CHRISTMAS STORY IN THE GOSPELS

Matt. 1:18-24 The birth of Jesus
Matt. 2:1-12 The coming of the Wise Men
Luke 1:26-31 The angel comes to Mary
Luke 2:1-20 The birth of Jesus; the shepherds

Hymns

"O Come, O Come, Immanuel"
"Hail to the Lord's Anointed"
"Hark! the Herald Angels Sing"
"Angels, From the Realms of Glory"
"Joy to the World! the Lord Is Come"
"All My Heart This Night Rejoices"
"Light of the World, We Hail Thee"
"Come, Thou Long-Expected Jesus"

Prayers

THANKS FOR CHRISTMAS

God, we thank you for your love and for the gift of Jesus Christ. On this Christmas Day may the gifts we receive and give make us

256

and others happy and remind us of the happiness which Jesus brought to men. Help us to know him better so that we may love him more and become more like him. Give us better understanding of your desire for us and increase our trust of you so we will try to obey you as Jesus did. Amen.[8]

—ROBERT AND DOROTHY COX

A PRAYER OF THANKSGIVING

O God, many persons have been born in these two thousand years, but we give thanks today for one, thy Son whom we call Christ Jesus. There was only one born to be the Savior of the world. There was only one born to be the Lord whom we worship. Today we feel drawn to him, as the shepherds must have felt drawn to him those many years ago. We want to show our devotion to him because through him you first loved us and taught us how to live. We want to live happily with everyone, everywhere, for the glory of God. Amen.[9]

—ARDEN AND MARY ANN TILEY

CHRISTMAS PRAYER

To love my God continually,
To serve Him always cheerfully,

To ask Him all things, patiently,
To trust Him always, faithfully,

To thank Him daily, happily,
To praise Him always, lastingly,

To treat my neighbor honestly,
To help the needy, tenderly,

To live each hour His Son's way,
This is my prayer, this Christmas Day.[10]

—CAROL ELY HARPER

AS CHRISTMAS DRAWS TO A CLOSE

The Christmas candles are burned down . . . the evergreens have been taken away . . . the tones of the carols have merged into the air . . . the dawn has dimmed the light of the star . . . the radiant song-thrilled night is past.

257

Thou, O God, Holy One, Mighty Spirit of Love—thou alone remainest, thou alone. But thou art enough.

Be to us, through all the coming days, more beautiful, more blessed, and more real than songs or candle or star. Live on through our thoughts. Amen.[11]

—CLARICE M. BOWMAN

CHRISTMAS PRAYER

O Father, who hast declared thy love to men by the birth of the holy Child at Bethlehem; help us to welcome him with gladness and to make room for him in our common days, so that we may live at peace with one another and in good will with all thy family;

Help us, O God, in the light of the shining star, to realize the wastes and desolation of the world, to feel the weight of the world's sorrow and need, to be made aware of the power of evil, to see that spiritual loss is caused by man's hatred and sins.

Suffer us not to become creatures and nations of selfishness, of narrow, foolish pride; marred with hardness of heart, and weakened by fear and suspicion.

In the light of the shining star that giveth happiness to little children and cheer to all, help us to renew our zeal for that good time when none shall be far off or forgotten, but shall live within the circle of the blessed life. Amen.[12]

PRAYER FOR NEW LIFE AT CHRISTMAS

Our Father, we would see thee, but our eyes are dim; we would love thee, but our hearts are divided; we would follow thee, but our feet are slow. Arouse us at this Christmas season to dedicate ourselves anew to purity of heart and integrity of purpose, as followers of Jesus Christ our Lord. Amen.[13]

—RUTH M. AND WALTER N. VERNON

A CHRISTMAS PRAYER

O God of Love, we are stilled before thee;
As silently and as simply as the falling snow

Thou dost hallow the moments of our living
With the Gift of thyself.

In the laughter and tears of little children,
In the unvoiced longings of growing parents,
In the unshaken faith of maturing oneness of
Home, nation, and the world,
In the goodness of sunshine and shadow,
Thou art of and through them all.

Thank you, God, for Christmas—
Its wonder, brightness, joy, its rememberings;
The birthday of thy Son, the angel song,
Starlit faces of humble shepherd folk,
The kneeling Great, and Least—
The warm, the cold; the loved, the scorned;
The serving and the served.

Accept each fragment of our living, when it
honors thee;
Forgive each blemished, broken promise—
And from contrite hearts

Hallow us all anew for the beginning of another year
With thee and with thine. Amen.[14]

—THELMA M. GUSTAFSON

Litany

FOR CHRISTMAS MUSIC

LEADER: For the songs of joy which resound around the world
at Christmas,

GROUP: We give thee thanks, our Father.

LEADER: For the joy in the hearts of those who wrote the Christmas carols,

GROUP: We give thee praise, O God.

LEADER: For the joy that is ours as we sing of the birth of Christ,

GROUP: We give thee thanks, Our Father.

LEADER: That we may share this joy with others through deeds
of love and kindness,

GROUP: We earnestly pray, O God. Amen.[15]

—ESTELLE BLANTON BARBER

259

Poems

ADVENT

The year ebbs out.
The days are dark.
But Christmas comes 'round
Once again! A spark
Of love on wings of song
Sets all aglow, a candle bright
Within our hearts—
A miracle which well might
Change our world . . .
Come, let us prepare for Him the inn.
Let it not be as once before.
This time may our candles
Guide Him to our door.[16]

—HELEN F. COUCH

CHRISTMAS IS WAITING TO BE BORN

When refugees seek deliverance that never
comes,
And the heart consumes itself, if it would
live,
Where little children age before their
time,
And life wears down the edges of the
mind,
Where the old men sit with mind grown
cold,
While bones and sinew, blood and cell,
go slowly down to death,
Where fear companions each day's life,
And Perfect Love seems long delayed,
Christmas is waiting to be born:
In you, in me, in all mankind.[17]

—HOWARD THURMAN

WISE MEN

The Wise Men passed through Herod's town
And on to Bethlehem.
They found the Babe; then, homeward bound,
A new road beckoned them.

So true it is. No wise man walks
Again the same old way,
Who once has found the living Christ
And knelt beneath his sway.[18]

—CLEO KING

A CAROL FOR TO SING

What sweeter music can we bring
Than a carol for to sing
The birth of this our heavenly King?
Awake the voice! Awake the string!
Heart, ear, and eye, and every thing.

. . . .

—ROBERT HERRICK

WHAT MEANS THIS GLORY?

"What means this glory round our feet,"
    The magi mused, "more bright than morn?"
And voices chanted clear and sweet,
    "Today the Prince of Peace is born."

"What means that star," the Shepherds said,
    "That brightens through the rocky glen?"
And angels, answ'ring overhead,
    Sang, "Peace on earth, good-will to men."

. . . .

All round about our feet shall shine
    A light like that the wise men saw,
If we our loving wills incline
    To that sweet Life which is the Law.

So shall we learn to understand
    The simple faith of shepherds then,
And, clasping kindly hand in hand,
    Sing, "Peace on earth, good-will to men."

261

And they who to their childhood cling,
But keep at eve the faith of morn,
Shall daily hear the angel-song,
"Today the Prince of Peace is born."
—JAMES RUSSELL LOWELL

THE CHRISTMAS SPIRIT

The Christmas Spirit is difficult, if not impossible, to define or explain.

It cannot be written about, but
it is the spirit in the writing.
It is not a gift, but
it is in giving of self.
It is not only for children, but
it is the spirit of man's maturity.
It is not a party, but
it is the jolly fellowship of good fun.
It is not a program, but
it is the inspiration of planned activity.
It is not a trip, but
it is the expanding urge which seeks new things.
It is not a big dinner, but
it is a feast on the Bread of Life.
It is not a family gathering, but
it is the tie of love which makes a family.
It is not a greeting card, but
it is the expression of lasting good will.
It is not work to weariness, but
it is the spirit which makes burdens light.
It is not color and noise, but
it is the longing for beauty and harmony.
It is not man turned pagan, but
It is Christ in man.[19]
—JOHN DAVID ERB

WITH THE MAGI

We, too, have seen the Star,
Bright with truth, and beckoning.
O guide us, Father, as we journey on
In faith—not reckoning

The hazards, but serene, assured
That each of us, most surely, will
Find for ourselves a Savior.
Let that knowledge fill
Each hour with purpose
And each act with poise.
Then, as we offer up our gifts,
May we know anew the joys
In giving of our best to Him,
And as we rise to go—
"Each to his own country"—
Thy constant guidance may we know—
On and on, wherever truth's bright star may lead,
On and on, wherever in thy kingdom there is need.[20]
—HELEN F. COUCH

THE WONDER OF IT

If I live to be a hundred
I shall always pause
To wonder at the things
That happen at the Christmastide—
How for that brief season
The world forgets its ugliness,
Its bickerings, its atoms—
And pauses long enough to stand beside
A lowly manger . . . dreaming . . .
Dreaming the great dream. . .
And how for a little while
Time seems suspended—
The present, past, future
So strangely and so beautifully blended
In the birth of love eternal . . .
And there beyond the candlelight
Where friends and enemies this night
Join voices, more than a carol rings—
You can hear a mighty chorus
And the beat of angel wings! [21]
—HELEN F. COUCH

263

THE SILENT STARS GO BY

O Little Child of Bethlehem,
   Why do your young eyes grieve?
What do your outstretched arms implore
   On this Christmas Eve?

"Look—in the dark streets shineth
   No Everlasting Light,
Hearts crucified by daily fears,
   Watch through the silent night.

"Their arms hold tight to little ones,
   Tear-blinded eyes turn East,
Too tired to ask for more than crumbs,
   Dropped from My Christmas Feast."

O Little Child of Bethlehem,
   Descend to us, we pray,
And show our hearts how best to share
   With these, on Christmas Day.[22]
      —HARRIET HARTRIDGE TOMPKINS

CHRISTMAS EVE PRAYER

Dear God,
I, too, would be a shepherd
On this Christmas Eve.
O lead me to a starlit hill
Where I can stand alone—
Serene and still—
Apart from all the rush!
In that holy hush
Let me, as they did long ago,
Hear the angel voices.

Dear God,
I, too, would go to Bethlehem
On this Christmas Eve
To seek the child newborn.
I, too, would kneel and worship;

Then rise to greet the morn,
Blessed by His peace—
Renewed, redeemed, and in release
Go forth to tend my sheep
As my heart rejoices! [23]
—HELEN F. COUCH

CAROL OF ADORATION

Infant Jesus, Child most holy,
Born within a stable lowly;
Friendly beasts stood 'round adoring
On that early Christmas morning.

Shepherds 'roused by radiant glory
Wake to hear the angel's story;
Leaving flocks and onward pressing,
Seek they for the promised blessing.

In the sky a star is guiding
Wise men from the east are riding;
They bear gifts to lay before him,
Reverently on knee adore him.

As of old the vision's splendour
Led all men their hearts to render,
We, too, honor Thee and praise Thee,
Consecrate our hearts to serve Thee.[24]
—LAURA COPES

WE WHO HAVE KNELT

We who have knelt at Bethlehem
Return to deepened days,
Eyes are alight with kindliness,
A Star has changed our ways.

O may we keep the whole year through
This loveliness aglow,
And share the radiance we have found
With all we come to know.[25]
—RUTH R. STARKEY

265

THE SINGING SHEPHERDS

Can you hear the Singing Shepherds
As they journey through the night,
Coming homeward from the stable
Where they saw the wondrous sight?
Hark! their song is full of gladness.
Loud and clear their voices rise,
As they thrill to all the meaning
In the starry Christmas skies.
Come! We'll join these Singing Shepherds
And go with them through the night;
For we too have heard the angels
And have seen the Christmas light.[26]

—LUCIUS H. BUGBEE

JESOUS AHATONHIA*

'Twas in the moon of winter-time
When all the birds had fled,
That mighty Gitchi-Manitou
Sent angel choirs instead;
Before their light the stars grew dim,
And wond'ring hunters heard the hymn,
"Jesus your king is born,
Jesus is born,
In excelsis gloria."

Within a lodge of broken bark
The tender Babe was found,
A ragged robe of rabbit skin
Enwrapp'd his beauty 'round;
But as the hunter braves drew nigh,
The angel song rang loud and high.
"Jesus your king is born,
Jesus is born.
In excelsis gloria."

* Jean de Brebeauf was a missionary to the Huron Indians of Canada, in the seventeenth century. This carol is his interpretation of the Incarnation in terms his Indian friends could grasp. This translation is by J. E. Middleton.

The earliest moon of winter-time
  Is not so round and fair,
As was the ring of glory on
The helpless Infant there.
The chiefs from far before him knelt
With gifts of fox and beaver-pelt.
  "Jesus your king is born.
Jesus is born.
In excelsis gloria."

O children of the forest free,
  O sons of Manitou,
The Holy Child of earth and Heaven
  Is born today for you.
Come kneel before the radiant Boy
Who brings you beauty, peace and joy.
  "Jesus your king is born.
Jesus is born.
In excelsis gloria." [27]

          —JEAN DE BREBEAUF

GIFTS

However swathed in tissue and tied
With scarlet ribbon, or glorified
With holly sprigs, or richly done
In blue and silver, never one
In all its glory upon the tree
Can be so lovely a gift as He
Who, that Star-ushered Christmas, lay
In swaddling clothes, in manger hay.[28]

          —ELAINE V. EMANS

FOR CHRISTMAS

A star that is shining,
A candle that's bright—
Now who would be greeting
The Christ Child tonight?

267

"I would," said the shepherd,
"I've come with my lamb;
I'm greeting the Small One,
Most surely I am."

"I would," said Sweet Mary
Holding her son;
"I greet Him and love Him,
My own precious One."

"I would," said kind Joseph,
"I'll guard Him well, too;
God gave me the work
I like best to do."

"We would," said the Wise Men,
"We've come very far
With our gifts for the Christ Child,
Following the star."

And so would we greet Him
On this Christmas night,
While candles are shining
And stars are so bright.[29]

—JOYCE COVERT

WANTED: ROOM

In busy, crowded Bethlehem,
There was no fitting rest for them,
But ass and oxen stepped aside
So Mother Mary might abide,
That still remembered Christmas night
When men were dull, but skies were bright.

I try to see that holy place,
Long back in time and far in space,
When heaven opening on earth
Gave men a token of the birth

Each heart, however poor, may share
If so God's love be tenant there.[30]
—ELINOR LENNEN

SOME GREATER GIFT

Not complete this giving time
With tree and gifts and cards and rhyme—
Not complete this midnight earth
Of winter white; nor feast, nor mirth.
Though carols sing of men's good will,
Something more is needed still,
Some greater gift—the peace that heals
The unsure heart, the faith that kneels
To worship here before the Star
Welcoming Him who came from far,
Evidence of oracle . . .
Be still—accept the miracle! [31]
—MAUDE RUBIN

SONG OF THE SMALLEST SHEPHERD BOY

Jesu, asleep in the straw, see me.
Never a carved ivory chest have I
for holding fine incense and gems.
Child Jesu, I kneel before Thee.

Jesu, so warm in the straw, hear me.
Only a sycamore crook have I
for keeping new lambs in the flock.
Child Jesu, I give it to Thee.

Jesu, awaken from sleep. Let me
ever your staff and your shepherd be
for seeking lost lambs on the hills.
Child Jesu, I love Thee, love me.[32]
—MARGARET SECRIST

THE DAY AND OUR DAYS

Store the bells and tinsel for a year;
Let hearts keep the music and the light

For those times when we shall need to hear
Singing, and have guidance in the night.

Christmas is both memory and hope;
Past its margins on the calendar,
Let all days unfold within the scope
Of the healing Song, the radiant Star! [33]
—ELINOR LENNEN

A CHRISTMAS CHALLENGE

Come rest you merry, O my friends,
When dawns the Christmas Day!
Our storm-tossed world needs joy and cheer!
Let us, in glad array,
Proclaim our faith that in the Child
Who lay on Mary's knee
Rests all the hope for this our age
And ages yet to be! [34]
—JANE CROWE MAXFIELD

Meditations

FOR ADVENT

He will be great, and will be called the Son of the Most High;
and the Lord God will give to him the throne of his father David,
and he will reign over the house of Jacob forever;
and of his kingdom there will be no end. (Luke 1:32-33 R.S.V.)

Gerald Heard talks about discerning the fruit in the seed. This, indeed, is true insight, the remarkable ability of a few truly great souls. For insight is the capacity to see in insignificance, greatness; to see in the incrusted little seed, the fruit. It is the same insight that sees in a little idea a revolution in men's thinking, and in a little child a prophet and a leader of mankind. This insight is due to faith, to experience, to the forward thrust of help at the right moment. Even a little seed of great potentialities can die if no one has the faith to plant it and tend it, to keep it free from the cutting worm and the blighting drought. Insight is an active quality of faith. We must all of us learn more and more to discern the fruit in the seed.

O God, whose advent in the person of Jesus was heralded by

270

the prophets at great peril, and was sung by the psalmists even in times of utter desolation, grant unto us in these dark days that we may discern the fruit of thy spirit in the acts of faith and love that are often small and unnoticed. We pray that this Advent season may be a time of increasing insight into what is worth living for and what is worth dying for. Amen.[35]

—HAROLD EHRENSPERGER

WE THE PEOPLE

"The people who walked in darkness . . ."
    We, the people who walked in darkness—
    Who stood alone—
    Who sought in vain, and sought again—
    We who chose glamorous goals, stoked our
        engines, pulled our bootstraps, and
        built our kingdoms in one generation—
"The people who walked in darkness
have seen a great light . . ."
    Far above and beyond us, a light seeking—
    Deep within us searing, but not us—
    The light the darkness cannot put out—
    "The light of the knowledge of the glory of
        God in the face of Jesus Christ"—
"Those who dwelt in a land of deep darkness,
on them has light shined."
    And no amount of darkness, no threatening glory,
    No scheme of man or man's adversary,
    No fumbling, not even the sincerest sin, can put it out.
    We shut our eyes against it, and say we do
        not see it—
    While on our self-made blindness it still shines.
    We seek earth's dark coziness, and
        claim we see no light—
    But still it enfolds us.
    We shade it with our hands and
        close it up in our logic,
    And all the time it shines
    And burns its way into our lives.

271

Enlighten us in this season of Advent, O God. May the light that lights all the world seek out our darkness and open our eyes to the light that always shines, even Jesus Christ. Amen.[36]

WE WAIT

On this second Sunday in Advent—the season in which we celebrate and anticipate the coming of Christ—we have no trouble with these familiar words:

For to us a child is born,
*   to us a son is given . . .*
And his name will be called
"Wonderful Counselor, Mighty God,
Everlasting Father, Prince of Peace."

Here is the promise of the Advent, and we know it is true, for Christ, the Redeemer, has come—and we have gladly named him all the approved names.

But the words that follow—what about them?

Of the increase of his government and of peace
there will be no end . . . .

If we shake our Handel-rhythms long enough to hear the words, and through them the Word, we are caught short and ask, "Indeed, now, and when was the *beginning?*" Two thousand bloody years of "Christian civilization" since Mary bore him whose advent we celebrate. Has his government increased, his peace never ended?

And then we are reminded that even in *this* Advent, Christ is yet to come. He has already truly come to us, yes. But he is also yet to come. The powers of darkness still play at the game of king-and-queen, not knowing they have been outplayed by the King of Kings. But we know, and we await the final Advent of him who comes in the name of the Lord . . .

To us a son is given . . .
Of the increase of his government and of peace
there will be no end.[37]

"POWER TO BECOME . . ."

The Word was with God from the beginning, and we would not hear it. Its light shone in all creation, as well as in the hearts of the men of God's love, and we would not see it. But the darkness

272

of our souls did not overcome it. And in God's own time, it sought to find us in our own terms.

"The true light that enlightens every man was coming into the world. He was in the world, and the world was made through him, yet the world knew him not. He came to his own home, and his own people knew him not."

He came with baby cries and woman's labor; with a worker's hands and a brother's care; with dreams and high purpose; with redeeming love for us.

And we knew him not.

We offered him a cow's stall, a carpenter's shop, a pair of sandals—and a cross.

But he transformed them all into trappings for a king, and gave us new life in his Kingdom.

"But to all who received him, who believed in his name, he gave power to become children of God . . . ."

Open the gates to thy Kingdom, O God, and let us enter. Amen.[38]

CHRISTMAS IN OPERA

Gian-Carlo Menotti has captured the tender, haunting beauty of Christmas in his contemporary opera "Amahl and the Night Visitors." Written for and produced annually on television, Amahl has become as traditional as Dickens *Christmas Carol* in many homes. The opera was inspired by the painting, "The Adoration of the Magi," by Hieronymus Bosch.

The story concerns Amahl, a crippled boy who lives in poverty with his widowed mother. Amahl has a vivid imagination, and his mother is continually annoyed by his flights of fancy. One evening he reports a king in gorgeous apparel approaching their cottage. She is ready to whip him, until he finally succeeds in persuading her to come to the door. There she sees not one but three kings, and a page laden with rich, exotic gifts. The kings have been following a star, they are weary and ask for a night's shelter. Fearful, yet hospitable, the widow and her son invite them in to share their humble cottage.

The kings describe the child they seek, and the mother sees her

273

own crippled son in their words; but no kings come to give him gifts nor to heal his twisted foot. Later, while her guests rest, she cannot resist the temptation to steal some of the gold to aid her in seeking a cure for her son's lameness. She is seized by the page, but Amahl fights for her. When peace is restored, Amahl learns that the king's treasure is for the child of Bethlehem, for whom the whole world is waiting.

"Keep the gold," says one of the kings. "The child we seek doesn't need it. On love alone he will build his kingdom. . . . He will bring us new light . . . and the keys to his city belong to the poor."

Ashamed of her act and moved by their description of the child born to be King, the widow says, "For such a king have I waited all my life."

Then Amahl, filled with the wonder of the Christ child, exclaims, "Let me send my crutch." And in his act of generous love, he walks without limping for the first time. Before their awe-struck eyes he walks, and the kings kneel before the miracle.

Amahl begs permission to accompany the kings on their way to the Christ child, and the opera closes as his mother waves him farewell.

The beauty, simplicity, and deeply moving quality of the story speak to us of the amazing healing quality of unselfish love. And we, like the kings, bow before its transforming power whenever we see it.[39]

—C. Clyde Dodder

MIRACLES IN CONTRAST

Christians are accustomed to miracles in contrast, especially at yuletide.

Sometimes the earth seems dark, as on that night when shepherds in the fields were keeping watch over their flocks. Then suddenly the heavens are bright, as they were when the angelic host sang of glory to God and peace in earth.

In our own times, as far back as even the oldest of us can remember, earth often has seemed dark. Dark with fear and suspicion. Dark with oppression and bondage. Dark with the failure of Christians to live up to their ideals. Dark with the clash of arms and the flight of refugees. Dark with ignorance of God's Word.

274

In such a setting everyone yearns for peace.

Many serious-minded people work for peace. They study and plan and strive. All too often their efforts fail.

The Christian knows that man, without divine guidance, can never find peace, let alone make it. He looks upward trustingly. There he sees the star and rejoices.

Earth may be dark, but God still leads . . . still speaks to men. God's promise of peace and the power of His love are the source of our confidence and hope. They give us incentive to work. Bright heavens! Bright with His Word and His truth! Bright with hope! [40]

A CHRISTMAS MEDITATION

Let us think of the first Christmas, and all it meant:
Hastening and crowding for Mary and Joseph . . .
Loneliness and longing for Mary, as her boy was born in a stable . . .
Hope and peace for all those who heard the angels and believed . . .
Joy and satisfaction for those who saw his Star and followed it.
Let us think of the life that followed the humble birth:
Of Jesus' growing in wisdom and stature and in favor with God and man—even as we seek to do . . .
Of Jesus' dread visit to the wilderness where all the evil of human living tempted him with its power—even as it does us . . .
Of Jesus' high victory over the voices of selfishness and greedy power, and of his ministry of simple teaching and preaching and healing—so different from the tinseled, tarnished lives we so often live . . .
Of Jesus' dedication to the will of his Father that all men must receive his love—even as we have received it . . .
Of Jesus' willingness to lay down the happiness of his earthly life in order to witness ultimately to God's love for us.
Let us think of Jesus, who was born and who lived his days in Galilee and its environs, but whom we own today to be Christ and Lord of all men:
Of Christ, God's Son, going about in the form of man, proclaiming the good news that there is salvation for man, even for us. . . .
Of Christ, who being the Son of God, yet thought equality with

275

God not a thing to be grasped, and was nailed upon the cross for our redemption . . .

Of Christ, who being crucified, dead, and buried, yet defeated death and granted to us all the hope of life eternal.

Let us thank God for the gift of his Son:

Whose life stands shining above and beyond us, beckoning us to live in faith the way he has shown . . .

Whose forgiveness measures us when we stumble or resist, and whose love enables us to continue to seek his way . . .

Whose death enables us to face death with faith and serenity, trusting in the limitless heart of God . . .

Let us offer God:

Our fullest dedication . . .

Our freest devotion . . .

Our hearty love, gone out to him, and to all those in his world. *In the name of Christ, Amen.*[41]

A MEDITATION ON GOD'S LOVE

In the beginning men trembled before manifestations of God's power. They worshiped him in fear and sought to win his favor with material offerings and meaningless ritual.

Always men hungered for God's love but were blinded by their own selfishness and cruelty. They didn't see that:

> "There's a wideness in God's mercy,
> Like the wideness of the sea;
> There's a kindness in his justice,
> Which is more than liberty.
>
> For the love of God is broader
> Than the measure of man's mind,
> And the heart of the Eternal
> Is most wonderfully kind."

So great was God's love for mankind, whom he created in his own image, he tried through long centuries to make men understand his loving care for them. Through the prophets, he urged men to love justice and mercy. He revealed his holiness and for-

276

giving love. Still men's minds were unable to comprehend the goodness of God.

But his love found a way. He sent his beloved Son to live among men. "In this was manifested the love of God toward us, . . ."

Today as we come to rejoice in God's love and to sing his praises, let us try to realize what the incarnation of God's love in Jesus has meant in our lives.

He taught us the sacredness of human personality—this has brought to each of us freedom and opportunities for life at its best.

He taught us that God is a loving Father and that we are co-laborers with God. This has given us assurance of our worth and added to our happiness and sense of security.

He taught us that all men are brothers and that the strong must help the weak. He has given meaning to our lives by showing us the way of the Good Samaritan.

Above all, he has taught us the meaning of unselfish love.

As we think of a Divine Creator of the Universe, full of majesty and power reaching out to draw us to him in loving obedience, do we not feel an urge to show our love and gratitude? Let us think of how this may be done. . . .[42]

MANY GO TO BETHLEHEM, BUT—

Do you not suppose that on that holy night long ago, there may have been other shepherds keeping sheep on hillsides who saw no star, heard no voices, took no journey, found no Babe? One can imagine them: here is a group arguing angrily about the political situation; here is another discussing the price of wool; here is another so busy amusing themselves with a game that they have no time to look up.

These did not see. The focus of eyes, thoughts, and whole selves was downward, not up and out into the vast reaches of God's eternal skies. One must needs busy himself with the nearby, the immediate, the everyday problems at times; but to every life there should come times for looking up, letting thoughts reach hopefully toward One greater than he, letting his mind stretch forth in wonder.

To certain shepherds, and to certain Wise Men as we are told in the other story, came a new meaning. These saw more than a star. They caught a message. Perhaps other shepherds saw sky-brightness but, not seeking to know its purpose, turned back to

277

their flocks or to sleep. Perhaps other Wise Men saw a light, but uncaring turned back to their books.

"Many people went to Bethlehem that Day so long ago," says Dr. Harry Emerson Fosdick, "but did not see the Babe nor guess that all the centuries after would be dated from his coming. It requires open eyes to see Christmas and true hearts to make its meaning real; and every year as at the first, many miss it though they ride to Bethlehem." [43]

—CLARICE M. BOWMAN

FOR A PERFECT CHRISTMAS

What makes a perfect Christmas?

A perfect Christmas day is a day of joy. The Wise Men were very happy when they saw the star over Bethlehem. Other signs, tokens and symbols are sources of joy.

A perfect Christmas needs more. Too many try to have a fine Christmas with Christ left out. Some let the star lead them to the door of the house and then never enter to see the Christ child. The Magi entered the house, saw the child, and worshiped. To make the day perfect, add worship to joy.

The Wise Men presented gifts of gold, frankincense and myrrh, as tokens of loving service. For Christmas, give service. Dedicate a life for Christmas.

The Wise Men went home by a different road. Who can go back to Herod after Christmas with Christ? Instead of returning to answer evil's temptations, go a new road. Discover new life. Give obedience to the king of life.

A perfect Christmas—joy, worship, service, obedience.

Make tomorrow the day for beginning. And let the spirit of Christmas stay with you forever.

O God, give us in this season a generous heart, a humble spirit, a concern for the welfare of our fellow men, and a new sense of thy presence. Help us to observe Christmas as Christians should. Amen. [44]

—JAMESON JONES

CHRISTMAS, WHERE I LIVE

"O little town of Bethlehem
How still we see thee lie—

. . . .

The hopes and fears of all the years
Are met in thee tonight."

My town is not little—it sprawls mile upon mile—
    from the filth of West Dallas to the cool green lawns
    of the Park Cities.
My town does not lie still, and there is no deep and
    dreamless sleep,
For the trolleys clang and long trains roll
    out to the plains
Through its back alleys.

But all the hopes and fears are here.
Every anxiety, every insecurity, every desperate human
    need,
Lies beneath the clear-bright air, the neon and tinsel
    of Christmas.

I am as beautiful and as filthy as my city,
Beautiful because I was created with such a capacity
    for love;
Filthy because selfishness has used love for its own
    purposes.
I harbor all the hopes and fears—
And I live behind a mask of neon and tinsel.

My city and I cry out together
"O God, my God, how have I sinned against thee!"
"Create in me a clean heart. . ."
But he does not hear.
How could he—
Perfect and holy—
Hear us the tainted ones?
And so we perish.

It's a lie.

And this is the glory of Christmas—
That we do not perish,
That an infinitely tender God
Wraps himself up in the flesh of man
And comes into a filthy, desperate world,
Making his answer once and for always
To all the dirty cities and all the dirty anxious people.

*Come unto me all ye that labor and are heavy laden,—
And I will give you rest.*[45]

THE CHRISTMAS CHURCH

"Glory to God in the highest, and on earth peace among men with whom he is pleased!" (Luke 2:14.)

On a small tropic island in the South Pacific an American airstrip was built. The chaplain and his crew tried to tell the natives about religion, but somehow they responded slowly. Christmas of 1943 came with orders to move on. The Americans gave a big farewell Christmas party with makeshift presents, and several tried to explain the origin of the Christmas spirit.

A few years later the same chaplain stopped at the island on his way to India as a missionary. He was greeted with excitement and taken to see something beautiful, a church. Over the doorway was written this crude inscription: "This is our church built on the faith and brotherly love which we know is." The chaplain stayed for a service. There were no seats in this church; everyone stood in the presence of God. The songs were all Christmas carols, for these were the only ones they knew. One explained, "After you leave we build church to worship Jesus. We worship him with the only service we know, Christmas, the day he was born. Every day is Christmas here. Every day Christ child born anew. Our gift to give is love. Our church we call her Christmas church."

What better way to worship than to sing Christmas carols all through the years? What better way to serve than to give gifts of love? What better way than to rule out all cruel wars forevermore, to show the faith of brotherly love which we know is? [46]

TRANSFORMING LOVE

In writing *A Child Is Born*, Stephen Benét said,
"The loves we had were not enough.

280

Something is loosed to change the shaken world,
And with it we must change!"

Our little loves have not been enough. On this Christmas day we think of a great love that gave a man to this world who has changed the shaken world. Because of His coming we dare not remain unchanged and call ourselves Christians.

Whoever understands the meaning of Christmas will be compelled to understand Jesus. And understanding Jesus will transform our love. Then our little loves will take on new perspective. We shall see the people around us in the new light of knowledge, for we shall know that we cannot fully and intimately know anything that we do not love.

Let's keep Christmas by realizing that "knowing" and "loving" are inseparably bound together, that one is dependent on the other. Then in the increasing of our love we shall get understanding, and in a more thorough understanding we shall get love.

This we need to know in our families, in our communities and in our sense of a world held together by these two greatest qualities of man.

Father, we join the shepherds and wise men this Christmas in a prayer for increased love and understanding. In darkness we wait for the new birth of the Christ-spirit in thy world.[47]

CHRIST MAKES CHRISTMAS

The coming of Christ made Christmas. Continually, every day and hour, Christ comes to some person for the first time, and Christmas is created again. Christmas says that Christ has come and is still coming.

There cannot be a Christmas world made up of un-Christmasy people. It is Christmas in the heart that puts Christmas in the air.

Resolution for today: I shall keep Christmas in my heart and spread its message through my life in all the days ahead.

O God, our loving Father, help us rightly to remember the birth of Jesus. Close the door to hate and open the door of love all over the world. Let kindness come with every gift, and good desires with every greeting.

We thank Thee for the gift of Thy Son. In the light of His star may we find eternal and abundant life, and in the song of angels

281

may we praise Thee for Thy love. Dwell in us, O God, as Thou dost dwell in Him.

Teach us deeper discipleship, greater courage, and clearer vision, that we may help speed the day when Thy kingdom shall be everywhere, and the way of Jesus known and followed by everyone. Amen.[48]

—JAMESON JONES

FIRST TO COMMON PEOPLE

The cool night air was expectant and breathless. The small group of men watching sheep on the hillside must have sensed something unusual in the atmosphere.

Suddenly, out of the vast diamond-strewn sky came a message of God. "Be not afraid; for behold, I bring you good news of a great joy which will come to all the people," the angel said. Thus it was, as far as we know, that the glorious news of Christ's birth was told first of all to a group of humble, probably unlearned men. After they had journeyed to Bethlehem to convince themselves of Jesus' existence, these men of the fields told everyone they saw of the miraculous visit and the miraculous child.

The world today is expectant and restless. People move about with less motive than sheep. The whole world is waiting for something miraculous to save it from impending destruction. God's visitor has told it of the way to salvation, but the world refuses to accept it. Teachers, pastors, Christian friends remind us of the good news that Jesus invites us to come to him as the shepherds came —with joy. When we have worshiped him as the shepherds did, we, too, will want to tell everyone we see of the peace that comes from God's Son.

Shepherds were Christ's first witnesses. They spread the word of the beautiful, forceful life begun so simply in a Bethlehem stable.

Lord, let me—also an ordinary person like the shepherds—tell of Christ's coming to my life. Amen.[49]

Choral Readings

WHEN THE ANGELS SANG

LEADER:

Calm were the thoughts of the shepherd men,
Still was the night. Quiet were the sheep.

282

Asleep were the lambs and asleep were the flowers,
Asleep were the leaves on the silent trees,
And the waters in the stream flowed quietly,
Silence . . . silence . . . stillness and quiet. . . .
The breezes were gentle and very, very mild—
When—

CHORUS:

> Glory!
> Glory!
> Glory to God! Glory to God!
> Glory to God in the highest!
> Glory! Glory! Glory! Glory!
> Glory to God in the highest!

LEADER:

The shepherds were quieter than quiet men,
The night was light and the sheep arose,
The lambs stirred happily,
The flowers woke with a dew-bright joy,
Leaves swayed joyously,
Trees bowed low,
Waters in the streams danced merrily and sang and sang,
Breezes gaily whirled themselves in wide, triumphant swirling whirls,
While—

CHORUS:

> On earth peace,
> Peace on the earth!
> On earth peace, good will!
> Good will toward men upon the earth,
> On earth peace, good will!
> Good will! . . .

LEADER:

Silent, once more, were the swaying trees,
Still were the flowers and the soft, gay breeze,
Silent the waters in the clear, cool stream,
And the lambs lay quiet, quiet;
Quiet were the thoughts of the shepherd men,
For the song was a song they had never heard before,

Peace was a dream, such a far-off dream,
They scarcely breathed with the wonder!

And then, like an echo from skies that had sung,
It pulsed alive in the shepherd men's blood!
Part of them, part of them, it leaped and it danced,
Never again could it be unsung!
Always would it sing through all kinds of skies,
Through long nights of shepherding . . .
Through days of praise . . .
Always would the hills resound with joy,
Joyfully re-echoing the Dream of dreams,
Until—

Until, one day, the world will sing,
Once they have sung it, it can never be unsung.

CHORUS:

> Glory!
> Glory!
> Glory to God in the highest!
> Peace!
> Peace!
> Peace on the earth, good will to men!
> Glory to God!
> Good will to man!
> Peace on the earth!
> God! . . .[50]

—MARY DICKERSON BANGHAM

Audio-Visuals

The Story of the Nativity. This strikingly beautiful and reverent filmstrip—in color—presents the stories of the birth of Jesus as found in Matthew and Luke, combining the two narratives into one tale, told as one of the wise men might have recounted it. This is one of the titles in the series, Great Stories of the New Testament. It is produced by Encyclopaedia Britannica Films, 1114 Wilmette Avenue, Wilmette, Illinois, and is available through most denominational film distributors. The reading script that comes with this resource makes it easy to adapt for purposes of worship.

Each With His Own Brush. See the audio-visual listing in the chapter on camping, Chapter 3.

Christmas Again. This color filmstrip consists of dramatic art photography of a hand-carved creche, with the Christmas story and traditional music providing a simple re-telling of the age-old tale of Jesus' birth. It is approximately fifteen minutes in length. One 33 1/3 rpm record, with the reverse side of the record including an excellent choral presentation of popular carols and hymns. Available for sale from denominational bookstores and from TRAFCO, 1525 McGavock Street, Nashville 3, Tennessee.

The Candlemaker. This delightful animated cartoon carries such a sincere note of devotion that it will lend itself to worship. It is the story of a candlemaker's son who falls down on his job of providing candles for the Christmas service at his church—and of how he and his father solve the problem. Produced by the United Lutheran Church, 2900 Queen Lane, Philadelphia, Pennsylvania, it is available for rent from most denominational film distributors or bookstores. It is fourteen minutes long, and is in color.

The Nativity. One of the outstanding films for Christmas use, this resource blends selected paintings from the fifteenth century into a tapestry that gives brilliance to the nativity stories of Matthew and Luke. Medieval choral themes make a perfect background. Available through United World Films, 542 South Dearborn Street, Chicago, Illinois, and from some denominational and university film libraries.

Notes

Chapter 1. Business and Committee Meetings

1. Adapted from a service prepared by Helen F. Couch for *Workers with Youth*, February, 1959. Used by permission of The Methodist Publishing House.
2. By Helen F. Couch. From *The Church School*. Copyrighted.
3. Korean Methodist Church.
4. Based on Ps. 51.
5. From *The American Rhythm*, by Mary Austin. Used by permission of the publisher, Houghton Mifflin Company.
6. Used by permission. Copyright. The Methodist Publishing House.
7. From *The School Hymnal*.
8. From *Come Spring*, by Frances G. Tower. Used by permission of Howard E. Tower.
9. From *Living Joyously*, by Kirby Page. Copyright 1950 by Kirby Page. Reprinted by permission of Holt, Rinehart and Winston, Inc.
10. *Ibid.*
11. From *Workers with Youth*, January, 1959. Used by permission of The Methodist Publishing House.
12. Used by permission of *Power*.

Chapter 2. Choir

1. "A Litany for Those Entering Upon Creative Work" from *Book of Services for Group Worship*. Used by permission of the National Board, Young Women's Christian Association of the U.S.A.
2. "The Footprints" by Eleanor B. Stock, from the series "Persons Are Part of the Answer," in *Classmate*. Used by permission of the author.
3. From *Work and Sing*, copyright 1948. Used by permission of Lynn Rohrbough.
4. By Carl R. Stockton in *Power*, May 9, 1959. Used by permission.
5. From *Acts of Worship* by W. B. J. Martin. Copyright © 1960 by Abingdon Press.
6. From *Etude*. Used by permission of the Theodore Presser Company.
7. Used with permission from the June, 1958, issue of the *International Journal of Religious Education*.
8. By Arthur Morris Hughes in *The Minister's Handbook of Dedications* edited by William H. Leach. Copyright © 1961 by Abingdon Press.
9. Used by permission of *The Church School*. Copyright The Methodist Publishing House.
10. Copyright 1961 Christian Century Foundation. Reprinted by permission from *The Christian Century* for February 8, 1961.
11. Used by permission of *Adult Teacher*. Copyright The Methodist Publishing House.
12. From *O Come, Let Us Worship* by Elizabeth Stinson. Copyright 1938 by Whitmore and Smith. By permission of Abingdon Press.

13. From *The Girl's Every Day Book*. Used by permission of the National Board, Young Women's Christian Association of the U.S.A.
14. From *Training for the Devotional Life* by L. A. Weigle and H. H. Tweedy. Used by permission of Harper and Brothers.

Chapter 3. Camping

1. Christina Rossetti.
2. From *Camping Together as Christians*, by Ensign and Ensign. John Knox Press. Used by permission.
3. From *Worship Ways for Camp*, by Clarice Bowman. Used by permission of Association Press.
4. From *Services for the Open*, by Mattoon and Bragdon. Used by permission of Association Press.
5. From *The Church Woman*. Used by permission.
6. From *The New Hymnal for American Youth*, H. Augustine Smith. By permission of Fleming H. Revell Co.
7. From *Services for the Open*, by Mattoon and Bragdon. Used by permission of Association Press.
8. From *Morning Worship and Other Poems*, © 1957, by Mark Van Doren. Reprinted by permission of Harcourt, Brace, and World, Inc.
9. From *Church School Worker*, copyright 1961. Used by permission.
10. Used by permission of H. W. Gray Company.
11. From *The Christian Home*. Used by permission of the author.
12. From *The Te Deums and Sacraments*, by John Oxenham. The Pilgrim Press. Used by permission.
13. From *Trails for Juniors*, June 5, 1960. Used by permission of The Methodist Publishing House.
14. Used by permission of the author.
15. From *Blue Smoke*, by Karle Wilson Baker. Yale University Press. Used by permission.
16. Used by permission of the author.
17. "Living with Others" from *Thoughts of God for Boys and Girls*, July, 1952. Adapted from A. F. S. C. Bulletin.
18. Copyright 1934 by William L. Stidger in "I Saw God Wash the World." Used by permission.
19. Quoted in *Poems for Life*, edited by Thomas Curtis Clark.
20. Used by permission. Copyright, The Methodist Publishing House.
21. Used by permission of the author.
22. From the book *God's Drum*, by Hartley Alexander. Copyright, 1927, by E. P. Dutton and Company, Inc. Renewal, 1955, by Hartley Alexander. Reprinted by permission of the publishers.
23. By permission of Miss Theo. Oxenham.
24. Quoted by permission of Camp Fire Girls, Inc., from the *Book of the Camp Fire Girls*.
25. From *Camping Magazine*. Used by permission.
26. From *Collected Poems* by Sara Teasdale. Copyright 1920 by The Macmillan Company, renewed 1948 by Mamie T. Wheless. Used with permission of The Macmillan Co.
27. From *The Christian Home*. Used by permission of the author.
28. *Ibid.*
29. Used by permission of Houghton Mifflin Company.
30. Used by permission of Bishop Palmer.
31. From *Life Together*, by Dietrich Bonhoeffer. Harper and Brothers. Used by permission.

287

32. From *Let's Go Camping*, by Lynn and Campbell Loughmiller. Copyright 1953 by Pierce and Washabaugh. By permission of Abingdon Press.

33. From *Our Dwelling Place*, by Clarence L. Seidenspinner. Used by permission of the author.

34. From *Children's Praises*, by N. Simpson and L. E. Cox. Student Christian Movement Press. Used by permission.

35. From *Power*, November 24, 1960. Used by permission.

36. From *Power*, April 7, 1960. Used by permission.

37. From: *Peace in the Heart*, by Archibald Rutledge. Copyright 1927, 1928, 1929, 1930 by Archibald Rutledge. Reprinted by permission of Doubleday and Company, Inc.

38. From the United States Department of Agriculture.

39. From *Trails for Worship*, by Mae Sigler. Copyright 1951 by Pierce and Smith. By permission of Abingdon Press.

40. Used by permission of Bishop Palmer.

Chapter 4. Out-of-doors

1. Adapted from a worship service "Like a Tree" by V. Helen Fox. Used by permission of *The Church School*. Copyright The Methodist Publishing House.

2. By Sabine Baring-Gould.

3. From *How to Plan Informal Worship* by Winifred Wygal. Used by permission of Association Press.

4. By Ruth Love. Used by permission of *Workshop*. Copyright The Methodist Publishing House.

5. From the Sanskrit.

6. "In the Morning" from *Young People's Prayers*, by Percy R. Hayward. Used by permission of Association Press.

7. "Beyond a Star" by Jane Merchant. Used by permission of *The Church School*. Copyright The Methodist Publishing House.

8. Used with permission, from the January, 1961, issue of the *International Journal of Religious Education*.

9. By Francis of Assisi.

10. From *Thanksgiving Worship in the Home*. Used by permission of the Department of the Christian Family, Board of Education, The Methodist Church.

11. Reprinted from *The Bethany Guide*, June, 1959, Christian Board of Publication, St. Louis 66, Missouri. Used by permission.

12. Used by permission of *The Church School*. Copyright The Methodist Publishing House.

13. *Ibid.*

14. From *Jesus Way—Our Way, A Worship Anthology*. Used by permission of the author.

15. Copyright © 1960 by The Methodist Publishing House. Reprinted by permission of Abingdon Press from the book *Blessed Are You* by Jane Merchant.

16. Reprinted from *The Bethany Guide*, February, 1961. Christian Board of Publication, St. Louis 66, Missouri.

17. From "A Forest Hymn."

18. From *Song of the Earth*, by Fred D. Wentzel. The Christian Education Press, 1946. Used by permission.

19. From *The Hand of God*, by Oswald McCall. Used by permission of Harper and Brothers.

20. From *Song of the Earth*, by Fred D. Wentzel. The Christian Education Press, 1946. Used by permission.

Chapter 5. Dinners and Banquets

1. By James L. Wiggins. Used by permission of *Roundtable*. Copyright The Methodist Publishing House.
2. By Washington Gladden.
3. From "Help Youth Have a Second Birthday" by George Harper. Used by permission of *The Church School*. Copyright The Methodist Publishing House.
4. By George Croly.
5. From *Devotions for Junior Highs* by Helen F. Couch and Sam S. Barefield. Copyright © 1960 by Abingdon Press. Used by permission.
6. By Frances Frost. Used by permission.
7. By Charles Wesley.
8. An adaptation of "Some of God's Plans" written by pupils of the Trinity Episcopal Church, Hartford, Conn. Used by permission of the rector.
9. Used by permission of *The Church School*. Copyright The Methodist Publishing House.
10. From *Worship Services for Special Days*. The Christian Education Press. Used by permission.
11. From *Roundtable*. Used by permission of the author.
12. Reprinted by permission of Dodd, Mead and Company from *The Hour Has Struck*, by Angela Morgan.
13. Used by permission of *The Church School*. Copyright The Methodist Publishing House.
14. From *Classmate*. Used by permission of the author.
15. By Dorothy Clyce Smith in *Classmate*. Used by permission of the author.
16. From *Devotions for Junior Highs* by Helen F. Couch and Sam S. Barefield. Copyright © 1960 by Abingdon Press. Used by permission.

Chapter 6. Parties

1. Ascribed to Dorothy A. Thrupp.
2. By Marion Brown Shelton. Copyright, The Pilgrim Press. Used by permission.
3. From *Power*, November 1, 1948. Used by permission.
4. From *Power*, January 19, 1948. Used by permission.
5. From *Masterpieces of Religious Verse*. By permission of Harper & Brothers.
6. From *Devotions for Junior Highs*, by Helen F. Couch and Sam S. Barefield. Copyright © 1960 by Abingdon Press. By permission.
7. From *Power*, January 11, 1947. Used by permission.
8. From *Classmate*. Used by permission of the author.
9. From *Power*, May 30, 1959. Used by permission.

Chapter 7. The New Year

1. Adapted from "Better Than Light" by Helen F. Couch. Used by permission of *Workers with Youth*. Copyright The Methodist Publishing House.
2. From *The Gate of the Year* by M. Louise Haskins. Used by permission of Christy and Moore, Limited.
3. From *Let Us Pray*, by Robert French Leavens. Used by permission.
4. Adapted from Charles E. Jefferson in an early edition of *The Fellowship of Prayer*, a publication of the Commission on Evangelism and Devotional Life of the Congregational Christian Churches. Used by permission.
5. Reprinted with the permission of Charles Scribner's Sons and Oxford University Press from *A Diary of Private Prayer* by John Baillie. Copyright 1949 Charles Scribner's Sons.
6. From *Be Still and Know* by Georgia Harkness. Copyright 1953 by Pierce and Washabaugh. By permission of Abingdon Press.

7. "Rehabilitation" by Helen F. Couch in *The Christian Advocate*. Copyrighted. Used by permission of *The Christian Advocate*.

8. From Frances R. Havergal.

9. By Robert A. Knowles. Used with permission from the November, 1956, issue of the *International Journal of Religious Education*.

10. Adapted from a worship service by Helen F. Couch in *Christian Action*. Copyright The Methodist Publishing House. Used by permission.

11. From the *Book of Services for Group Worship*. Used by permission of the National Board, YWCA of the U.S.A.

12. From *Sing to the Lord*. The Christian Education Press, 1959.

13. Used by permission of the author.

14. From *Children's Work Bulletin*, a publication of the Department of Christian Education of Children, Board of Education, The Methodist Church. Used by permission.

15. From *Classmate*. Used by permission of Margot Stanton Wisner.

16. Used by permission of *The Church School*. Copyright The Methodist Publishing House.

17. *Ibid.*

18. Reprinted by permission of *The Christian Advocate*.

19. Used by permission of *The Church School*. Copyright The Methodist Publishing House.

20. From *Acts of Worship* by W. B. J. Martin. Copyright © 1960 by Abingdon Press.

21. From *Devotions for Junior Highs* by Helen F. Couch and Sam S. Barefield. Copyright © 1960 by Abingdon Press. Used by permission.

22. From *Power*, December 31, 1950. Used by permission.

23. From *Power*, January 1, 1950. Used by permission.

Chapter 8. National Holidays and Celebrations

1. From *A Book of Services for Group Worship*. By permission of the National Board, YWCA of the U.S.A.

2. From the *Classmate* series, "Persons Are a Part of the Answer," by Eleanor B. Stock. By permission of the author.

3. By John Oxenham. Copyright 1938 by Abingdon Press.

4. From *When We Share* by Frances Maeda. Used by permission of Friendship Press, Inc.

5. From *Stories for Junior Worship* by Alice Geer Kelsey. Copyright 1941 by Whitmore and Stone. By permission of Abingdon Press.

6. From *Prayers for All Occasions*. Forward Movement Publications.

7. From *Worship Ways for Camp* by Clarice Bowman. Association Press. Used by permission.

8. From *Union Prayer Book*. Published by the Central Conference of American Rabbis.

9. From *The Church School*. Copyrighted.

10. Copyright 1934 by The Modern Library, Inc. Reprinted from *Collected Poems, 1928-1953*, by Stephen Spender. By permission of Random House, Inc. and Faber and Faber, Ltd.

11. By permission of Miss Dorothy Tarrant. Based on Eccles. 44:1-9, 15.

12. Used by permission of Stanwood K. Bolton.

13. By permission of Rabbi Silver.

14. From *Parts of His Ways* by Rita F. Snowden. Published in Great Britain by Epworth Press and in the United States by Muhlenberg Press. By permission of Epworth Press, London.

15. From *Complete Poems of Robert Frost*. Copyright 1935 by Holt, Rinehart and Winston, Inc. Reprinted by permission of Holt, Rinehart and Winston, Inc.
16. From *The Church School*. Copyrighted.
17. From *Come Spring*, by Frances G. Tower. Used by permission of Howard E. Tower.
18. Reprinted by permission of Dodd, Mead and Company from *Silver Saturday* by Nancy Byrd Turner. Copyright 1937 by Dodd, Mead and Company.
19. Used by permission of *McCall's*.
20. By permission of the *International Journal of Religious Education*.
21. From the Introduction to *Chronicles of the Pilgrim Fathers*, by permission of E. P. Dutton and Company and J. M. Dent and Sons, publishers of Everyman's Library.
22. From *Power*, April 16, 1955. Used by permission.
23. From the *Classmate* series, "Persons Are a Part of the Answer," by Eleanor B. Stock. Used by permission of the author.

Chapter 9. Lent and Easter

1. By Mrs. Walter Ferguson. Used by permission of *The Pittsburgh Press*.
2. By Leslie Savage Clark. Copyright 1954, Christian Century Foundation. Reprinted by permission from *The Christian Century*.
3. Final prayer is from the *Book of Common Prayer*.
4. Meditation by Sam Clark, from *Power*, March 27-31, 1961. Used by permission.
5. *Ibid.*
6. *Ibid.*
7. *Ibid.*
8. *Ibid.*
9. From *Acts of Worship*, by W. B. J. Martin. Copyright © 1960 by Abingdon Press.
10. Copyright 1961, Christian Century Foundation. Reprinted by permission from *The Christian Century*.
11. By Sam S. Barefield. Used by permission of *Twelve/Fifteen*. Copyright The Methodist Publishing House.
12. From *A Book of Invocations for Use Throughout the Year* by Herman Paul Guhse. By permission of Fleming H. Revell Co., publishers.
13. From *Power*, February 15, 1961, adapted. Used by permission.
14. Based on Isa. 52:14–53:7.
15. By Helen F. Couch. From *The Church School*. Copyrighted.
16. Copyright 1957, Christian Century Foundation. Reprinted by permission from *The Christian Century*.
17. From *Trails for Juniors*. Used by permission.
18. Copyright 1961 by Christian Century Foundation. Reprinted by permission of *The Christian Century* and the author.
19. From *Mentor Book of Religious Verse*, edited by Horace Gregory and Marya Zaturenska.
20. By permission of *International Journal of Religious Education*.
21. From *Christendom*. By permission of *Ecumenical Review*.
22. From *The Cross Is Lifted* by Chandran Devanesen. Friendship Press, Inc., publisher. By permission.
23. From *The Child on His Knees*, by Mary Dixon Thayer. Copyright 1926 by The Macmillan Company and used with their permission.
24. From *The Cross Is Lifted* by Chandran Devanesen. Friendship Press, Inc., publisher. By permission.
25. By permission of the author.
26. From *The Christian Home*. By permission of the author.

27. Used by permission of Martha Rutan.
28. Used by permission of Miss Ora Searle.
29. By permission of the author.
30. By permission.
31. By permission of Burns and Oates, Ltd.
32. From *Trails for Juniors*. Used by permission.
33. From *Power*, March 25, 1961. Used by permission.
34. By Paul Scherer in *The Interpreter's Bible*. By permission of Abingdon Press.
35. From *Power* March 26, 1961. Used by permission.
36. From *The New Being*, by Paul Tillich. Charles Scribner's Sons, publishers. By permission.
37. By Roy L. Smith. By permission of The Methodist Weekly Bulletin Service, Abingdon Press.
38. From the *Classmate* series, "Persons Are a Part of the Answer," by Eleanor B. Stock. Used by permission of the author.
39. Used by permission of *Twelve/Fifteen*. Copyright, The Methodist Publishing House.
40. Reprinted from *The Bethany Guide*, March 1960, Christian Board of Publication, St. Louis, Missouri.
41. Used by permission of *Twelve/Fifteen*. Copyright, The Methodist Publishing House.
42. Used by permission of *Foundations of Christian Teaching in Methodist Churches*.

Chapter 10. Advent and Christmas

1. Adapted from "A Litany for Christmas" from the *Book of Worship for Church and Home*. Used by permission.
2. By Christina G. Rossetti.
3. By William C. Dix.
4. An adaptation of a worship service for intermediates by Jeanne D. Birrell. Used by permission of *Workers With Youth*. Copyright The Methodist Publishing House.
5. By Clarice M. Bowman. Used with permission from the November, 1936, issue of the *International Journal of Religious Education*.
6. Adapted from "O Come . . ." a worship service by Helen F. Couch. Used by permission of *The Church School*. Copyright The Methodist Publishing House.
7. By Edward C. Peterson in *The Christian Home*. Used by permission of the author.
8. From *Christmas Worship in the Home, 1959*. Used by permission of the Department of the Christian Family, Board of Education, The Methodist Church.
9. From *Christmas Worship in the Home, 1960*. Used by permission of the Department of the Christian Family, Board of Education, The Methodist Church.
10. From *Trails for Juniors*. Copyright 1959 by The Methodist Publishing House. Used by permission.
11. Used with permission, from the November, 1960, issue of the *International Journal of Religious Education*.
12. Adapted from *Modern Worship* by Von Ogden Vogt. Used by permission of Yale University Press.
13. From *The Christian Home*. Used by permission of the authors.
14. From *The Christian Home*. Used by permission of Dr. Lloyd A. Gustafson.
15. Used by permission of *The Church School*. Copyright The Methodist Publishing House.
16. *Ibid.*
17. Used by permission of the author.
292

18. Used by permission of *The Church School*. Copyright The Methodist Publishing House.
19. From *Zion's Herald*, December, 1956. Used by permission.
20. From *The Christian Home*. Used by permission of the author.
21. *Ibid.*
22. Used by permission of *World Call*.
23. From *Presbyterian Survey*, December, 1956. Used by permission.
24. From *The Christian Home*. Used by permission of the author.
25. Used by permission of *The Church School*. Copyright The Methodist Publishing House.
26. *Ibid.*
27. Printed by permission of the copyright owner, The Frederick Harris Music Company, Limited; Oakville, Ontario, Canada.
28. From *The Christian Home*. Used by permission of the author.
29. *Ibid.*
30. *Ibid.*
31. *Ibid.*
32. *Ibid.*
33. *Ibid.*
34. *Ibid.*
35. From *Power*, December 23, 1951. Used by permission.
36. By Sam S. Barefield, from *Power*, December 3, 1961. Used by permission.
37. By Sam S. Barefield, from *Power*, December 10, 1961. Used by permission.
38. By Sam S. Barefield, from *Power*, December 24, 1961. Used by permission.
39. Used with permission from the November, 1959, issue of the *International Journal of Religious Education*.
40. Used by permission of The Commission on Promotion and Cultivation of The Methodist Church.
41. By Sam S. Barefield. Used by permission of *The Church School*. Copyright The Methodist Publishing House.
42. Used by permission of *The Church School*. Copyright The Methodist Publishing House.
43. Used with permission, from the November, 1960, issue of the *International Journal of Religious Education*.
44. From *Power*, December 24, 1951. Used by permission.
45. From *Power*, December 25, 1954. Used by permission.
46. From *Power*, December 26, 1950. Used by permission.
47. From *Power*, December 24, 1950. Used by permission.
48. From *Power*, December 24, 1960. Used by permission.
49. From *Power*, December 23, 1954. Used by permission.
50. Used by permission of *The Church School*. Copyright The Methodist Publishing House.

Index of Authors

Index of Titles

296

Index of Topics

302